Cities Leading Climate Action

T0299933

This book provides local governments and interested stakeholders with insights into the challenges and opportunities inherent in addressing climate change.

Drawing on in-depth case study research on Vancouver, Portland, Glasgow and Dublin, Dekker examines the policy development processes employed by urban policy makers to respond to climate change, looking specifically at the utilisation of collaborative planning. Emerging from the case studies are lessons for local governments in relation to the role of organisational structure in supporting climate leadership; the importance of leadership, trust, relationship building and narratives for supporting ownership of the responses to climate change by stakeholders; and the need for creative and innovative public engagement to expand the reach of traditional methods such as social media and other technology-based solutions. Finally, Dekker reflects on her experience in the development of climate change action plans for the Dublin Local Authorities.

This book will be of great relevance to students, scholars and policy makers with an interest in climate change resilience, environmental policy and urban planning.

Sabrina Dekker is a climate change researcher, and holds a DPhil from the UCD School of Architecture, Planning and Environmental Policy, Ireland.

Routledge Advances in Climate Change Research

For more information about this series, please visit: www.routledge.com/
Routledge-Advances-in-Climate-Change-Research/book-series/RACCR

Cities Leading Climate Action

Urban Policy and Planning

Sabrina Dekker

LONDON AND NEW YORK

First published 2019
by Routledge

2 Park Square, Milton Park, Abingdon, Oxfordshire OX14 4RN
52 Vanderbilt Avenue, New York, NY 10017

Routledge is an imprint of the Taylor & Francis Group, an informa business

First issued in paperback 2020

British Library Cataloguing-in-Publication Data
A catalogue record for this book is available from the British Library

Library of Congress Cataloging-in-Publication Data
Names: Dekker, Sabrina, author.
Title: Cities leading climate action : urban policy and planning /
Sabrina Dekker.
Description: 1 Edition. | New York : Routledge, 2019. | Series: Routledge
advances in climate change research
Identifiers: LCCN 2018019541| ISBN 9781138485907 (hardback) | ISBN
9781351047807 (ebook)
Subjects: LCSH: City planning–Environmental aspects–Case studies. |
Urban policy–Case studies. | Climatic changes–Environmental aspects–
Case studies.
Classification: LCC HT166 .D376 2019 | DDC 307.1/16–dc23
LC record available at https://lccn.loc.gov/2018019541

ISBN: 978-1-138-48590-7 (hbk)
ISBN: 978-0-367-51886-8 (pbk)

Typeset in Times New Roman
by Wearset Ltd, Boldon, Tyne and Wear

Contents

Illustrations

Figures

Table

Boxes

1 Cities leading on climate action

Introduction

Cities are home to over half of the world's population (Castán Broto, *et al.*, 2013; United Nations Human Settlements Programme (UN-Habitat), 2016): as hubs of economic and social life they continue to draw people with the promise of better opportunities. In recent times though, the flow of populations to urban centres is also being driven by climate change (Campbell-Lendrum and Corvalàn, 2007; Crawford *et al.*, 2010; IPCC, 2014; Gouldson *et al.*, 2016; United Nations Human Settlements Programme (UN-Habitat), 2016; Siders, 2017), the impacts of which have created challenges for rural populations; for example droughts, extreme weather events, and extreme temperatures have had adverse impacts on food and water supplies. Extreme weather events, such as Hurricane Katrina, Hurricane Sandy, Hurricane Irma and more recently Storm Emma, flooding, and the growing frequency and intensity of heat waves globally, have seen cities grapple with human casualty and the high economic and social costs of climate change.

Climate change's impacts are not limited to rural and urban areas, or developing and developed countries; they are global, which consequently has seen responses of a global nature be developed and implemented through international agreements and national commitments. Increasingly though, it has become evident that global level policies are too far removed from the everyday anthropogenic causes of climate change (United Nations Human Settlements Programme (UN-Habitat), 2016). Global targets can be set, but the reality is that achieving targets is not fully within the capacity of international bodies. In short, it is people in their daily lives who can engage in tangible actions that enable adaptation to the impacts of climate change. How people's behaviours are influenced and changed and who leads, guides, and promotes these pressing changes is a question for which one answer is the level of government responsible for living environments. As such there has been an emerging recognition that the potential for achieving gains in the realm of climate change adaptation lies in the capacity of local government and their ability to respond. Cities acknowledge their role in addressing climate change and the challenges they face in creating tangible responses (Doherty *et al.*, 2016; Eckersley, 2016; Huang-Lachmann and

Lovett, 2016; Mees, 2017). This is demonstrated by movements and partnerships led by cities namely: the EU Covenant of Mayors, C40 Cities for Climate Change, ICLEI's Green Growth Cities, the World Mayor's Council on Climate Change and Rockefeller's 100 Resilient Cities. These movements are aimed at developing the capacities of cities to respond to urban challenges, namely climate change, by creating an environment where knowledge can be exchanged and cities can 'compete' with each other.

Often though, the demand to respond to climate change comes to the fore in the aftermath of a natural disaster that has resulted in a high number of casualties, e.g. Hurricanes Irma, Katrina and Sandy, heat waves, floods and droughts. However, climate change must be understood in the context of day-to-day life, as it is not a sudden shift, but a gradual one whose cumulative effects have far-reaching consequences. This is significant for developing policies and plans; it is in this context that the research, that is the basis for this book, set out to explore how cities, particularly the local governments that are responsible for them, are responding to anticipated climate change risks through the development and implementation of policies that adapt and build resilience to climate change. In other words, the research investigates how cities are taking the lead on climate action, in the face of constraints.

At the global level, through the work of the International Panel for Climate Change (IPCC) (IPCC, 2014), there has been an acknowledgement that responses to climate change need to be multifaceted (Rodin, 2014; Carter *et al.*, 2015; Gouldson *et al.*, 2016) and include measures that cut across the environment, economy, and society. As such, responses need to engage a range of stakeholders (Betsill and Bulkeley, 2007; Dodman, 2009; Rosenzweig *et al.*, 2010; Carter *et al.*, 2015). Therefore, this book explores the role of adaptive governance in building urban resilience and the role of interactive, stakeholder-based policy making in developing pathways to a more resilient future, through the lens of collaborative planning. Critically, the book aims to understand how local governments develop policies to respond to climate change to achieve urban resilience, specifically to:

1   Understand how local governments perceive their role in addressing climate change.
2   Examine the processes of building institutional capacity for adaptive governance through the lens of collaborative planning.
3   Understand how collaborative processes with multiple stakeholders can inform the policy development process. In doing so examine how collaborative governance informs climate change planning and how climate change re-shapes planning, both practice and theory.
4   Identify the barriers/challenges to successful collaboration as experienced by urban policy-makers through 'stories of practice'.
5   Identify the narratives employed by urban policy makers to engage stakeholders, from citizens to higher levels of government in policy development and implementation process.

6   Connect theory with practice and vice versa through lessons from the development process of climate change action plans based on the research findings emerging from stories of practice.

To develop an understanding of how cities are responding a three-part methodology was employed. The first phase was a content analysis of plans globally of cities with populations over 500,000 and that were members of a climate initiative. Second was a survey of these cities, to assess their perceptions of their role in responding to climate change, and finally four case studies of the challenges and opportunities that responding to climate change have provided and how the cities have taken a lead, which are the subject of this book.

Through investigating the processes of policy development via case studies (Vancouver, Canada; Portland, USA; Glasgow, UK and Dublin, Ireland), the book aims to contribute to theoretical and practical understandings of resilience and collaborative planning, particularly the importance of: policy ownership by local government and stakeholders, the role of the planner, leadership, technology, and narratives. Further, as the author was involved in the development of the climate change action plans for the four local authorities of County Dublin in Ireland: Dublin City Council, Fingal County Council, South Dublin County Council and Dún Laoghaire-Rathdown County Council, findings of the initial research were applied to the development of the climate change action plans and the process is discussed in the final chapter of this book.

This chapter discusses the key climate change issues facing cities and the role that cities have in responding to climate change based on the recognition that climate change, while a global issue, calls for action at the local level. The challenges faced by cities in transposing global policy recommendations into policy suited to local contexts are also examined. The chapter also discusses the theoretical framework that guided the research and was used to understand the processes of developing climate change adaptation policy, specifically the concept of resilience and the practice of collaborative planning as they pertain to cities and climate change response in cities aimed at achieving climate resilience. Lastly an outline of the remaining chapters is provided.

Cities and climate change

The scientific research investigating the impacts of climate change indicates that it is happening now, and that action needs to be taken now (Betsill and Bulkeley, 2007; Le Treut, 2007; Dodman, 2009; IPCC, 2014; Carter *et al.*, 2015; Doherty *et al.*, 2016; Huang-Lachmann and Lovett, 2016; United Nations Human Settlements Programme (UN-Habitat), 2016; Mees, 2017; Siders, 2017). In the dialogue and debates around how to respond to climate change, cities are increasingly viewed as being the level of government best able to respond and to form policy that will build climate resilience (Betsill and Bulkeley, 2007; Dodman, 2009; Rosenzweig *et al.*, 2010; Carter *et al.*, 2015). Moreover, with the knowledge that at present, 50 per cent of the world's population lives in cities and by 2050 this number will rise to 70 per cent, the need for cities to have the capacity to respond is pressing and challenging (Castán Broto *et al.*, 2013; Foss, 2016; Huang-Lachmann and Lovett, 2016; United Nations Human Settlements Programme (UN-Habitat), 2016; Mees, 2017). Cities acknowledge their unique position and capacity to engage with people and lead people in the process of adapting to climate change and to address the anthropogenic causes of climate change. However, whilst cities may increasingly present themselves as leaders in responding to climate change, there are possible limitations to their capacity to respond stemming from institutional structures, legislation, and financial capacity, to name a few. How cities and the local governments that run them respond to these barriers and challenges to achieve climate resilience is valuable to building capacity of cities globally.

The literature discussing resilience in relation to climate change calls for adaptive governance, which in this research is understood through the framework of collaborative planning. It is implied that addressing climate change globally and locally calls for the cooperation of multiple stakeholders, all of whom may have varying objectives and agendas. Building consensus on actions to respond to climate change is not a simple agreement that something must be done. It is much more nuanced and requires that stakeholders work together to address the complexities of climate change, which is not solely an environmental issue, but an economic and social issue. As such, it is no longer enough to agree that climate change is happening, and action should be taken. Recognising this, global agreements have called for national governments to address climate change by setting targets for emissions. However, setting targets for emissions is a challenge, as in the absence of tangible actions to achieve targets, reaching the target is an aspirational goal. It is in the development of actions to achieve those targets that cities (local governments) play a role. However, as discussed developing actions requires cooperation and an understanding of climate change.

To understand how cities, specifically urban policy makers, are responding to climate change through collaboration with stakeholders, from citizens to higher levels of government; the author interviewed policy makers in four cities. The cities were Glasgow, Vancouver, Portland and Dublin. Due to the author residing in Ireland, Dublin is a significantly more detailed case study. Further, the author's role in the development of the climate change action plans for Dublin City Council and its neighbouring local authorities has provided the opportunity to apply the lessons from Vancouver, Portland, and Glasgow.

Finally, the case studies are of cities that, while similar in population and geographic size, operate within different institutional structures that shape the policy development process; thus, it is recognised that the capacity of the cities to develop policy will be different. However, given the global demand for cities to respond and the evidence of cities enacting policy to respond to climate change, this research endeavours to understand the policy development lessons that enable cities to take action irrespective of institutional challenges. Critically, demonstrating that through identifying narratives from which to engage diverse stakeholders in a dialogue around climate change adaptation, local governments can collaborate with stakeholders and lead on actions to achieve resilience to climate change.

Climate change: causes and impacts

While many factors continue to influence climate, scientists have determined that human activities have become a dominant force, and are responsible for most of the warming observed over the past 50 years. Human-caused climate change has resulted primarily from changes in the amounts of greenhouse gases in the atmosphere, but also from changes in small particles, as well as, changes in land use.

(Le Treut, 2007), p. 105

Climate change is the result of complex interactions between humans and the environment (Betsill and Bulkeley, 2007; Le Treut, 2007; Dodman, 2011; Carter *et al.*, 2015). There are three means by which to change the earth's climate (Le Treut, 2007):

1 Changing the incoming solar radiation by altering the earth's orbit or the sun's.
2 Changing the fraction of the solar radiation that is reflected back into space (albedo) via cloud cover, particulate matter in the air, and terrestrial vegetation.
3 Changing the long-wave radiation from earth towards space through concentration changes of greenhouse gases (GHGs).

Human activities influence two of the three means for altering the earth's climate: the fraction of solar radiation that is reflected and the concentration of GHGs. Research has determined that human activities during which GHGs and aerosols are released and land-use change are the key contributors to climate change. GHGs enter the atmosphere through dust from agriculture, smoke from the burning of biomass and other industrial waste, and exhaust fumes from vehicles. GHGs consist of water vapour, carbon dioxide, methane, ozone, and nitrous oxide. Once in the atmosphere, GHGs alter the absorption and scattering of solar radiation, consequently impacting on the earth's natural greenhouse effect. As the gases are suspended in the atmosphere they act as barriers to radiation coming in and leaving the earth (Le Treut, 2007; Dodman, 2009; IPCC, 2014). Radiation bounces off the gas particles in a range of directions, thus heating the air and transferring energy through the atmosphere. Increasing the concentration of GHGs decreases the ability of excess heat to leave the atmosphere. Land use change, for example, forestry, agriculture, industry and urban development in addition to releasing particles in to the atmosphere alter the natural environment. Research has shown that land use change has impacted on surface albedo; this is the reflection of solar radiation back into the atmosphere by the earth. (Dark surfaces absorb light and heat while light surfaces reflect light and heat.) The 'snow/ice-albedo feedback' is amplifying the impacts of climate change, as increased concentrations of GHGs that warm the atmosphere result in snow and ice melting leading to an increase in exposed dark surfaces that absorb the sun's heat, leading to rising temperatures which perpetuate the cycle (Le Treut, 2007; Dodman, 2009; IPCC, 2014). These changes to climate manifest themselves in the forms of rising temperatures, increasing frequency and intensity of rainfall, extreme temperatures, rising sea levels, flooding and extreme weather events, all of which impact upon urban environments.

Air pollution and air quality

The connections between air pollutants and air quality is an on-going field of study; it is acknowledged that the greenhouse gases (GHGs) discussed earlier degrade air quality, which is a measure of the pollutants in the air (IPCC, 2014; Slovic *et al.*, 2016; United Nations Human Settlements Programme (UN-Habitat), 2016). However, as discussed it is known that human activity contributes to climate change, specifically the increased concentration of greenhouse gases (GHGs) and aerosols in the air (IPCC, 2014; Slovic *et al.*, 2016). Air quality then is a measurement of the concentration of specific pollutants harmful to human health. In urban environments, air quality is dependent on numerous factors such as wind, temperature, and other atmospheric and anthropogenic factors (Campbell-Lendrum and Corvalàn, 2007; Le Treut, 2007; IPCC, 2014; Slovic *et al.*, 2016; United Nations Human Settlements Programme (UN-Habitat), 2016).

The connections between air pollutants and climate change are also an ongoing field of study, as the relationship is complex. When air pollution is considered, anthropogenic GHGs and aerosols need to be differentiated. GHGs absorb the infrared radiation emitted by the earth's surface, which results in an increase in temperature around the GHG molecules. This is specific to GHG molecules. The effect of aerosols is more complex, as they interact with solar and infrared radiation, and with clouds.

The impact of aerosols is dependent on their size: large particles can reflect solar radiation towards or away from earth or trap radiation in the lower atmosphere. Aerosols also play a role in cloud formation depending on their size and chemical make-up (Le Treut, 2007; IPCC, 2014). If the radius is too small, clouds will not form, or if injected into a cloud it will dissipate. The complexity of these two processes provides insight into why feedback effects related to aerosols are an ongoing field of study even within current understandings of the climate system. One feedback effect that is well understood is the positive feedback loop around heating, meaning that heating causes a further heating due to the increased amount of water vapour in the atmosphere and a loss of ice-covered surfaces. This in turn is resulting in climate change impacts of sea level rise, flooding, increased frequency of extreme weather events, and extreme temperatures.

Policy addressing air quality has therefore focused on the reduction of pollutants and particulate matter in the air (Slovic *et al.*, 2016). Humans contribute to air pollution, namely the concentration of GHGs and aerosols in the atmosphere, through the use of motor vehicles and industry. The consumption of goods and services and the subsequent production of waste are the leading factors in the increasing concentration of GHGs and aerosols in the atmosphere (Le Treut, 2007; Barton, 2009). Reducing the concentration of GHGs has revolved around shifting from the use of carbon-based fuels (used for power, transport, cooking, heating, building, etc.), to alternative energy sources: wind, solar, and hydro-electric (Vários, 2005; IPCC, 2014; United Nations Human Settlements Programme (UN-Habitat), 2016). Transportation and land-use policies are also a means of mitigating the impacts of climate change on air pollution and air quality, at the city, regional and national levels.

Specifically, in urban contexts cities are moving towards strengthening public transportation networks, to discourage people from using cars (van de Ven *et al.*, 2016; Mees, 2017; Younger *et al.*, 2018). Land-use plans are working towards reducing sprawl by focusing on density and mixed use development, and developing green spaces such that people can live, work and play in complete compact communities, reducing their dependency on private transport and energy needs (Heller and Adams, 2009; Hunt and Watkiss, 2011; Rydin *et al.*, 2012; Younger *et al.*, 2018). While these policies primarily address the 'health' of the urban environment in terms of climate change and air quality, they also have secondary benefits that address human health and well-being (Barton, 2009).

Research on air quality and pollution has demonstrated that there are links with human health. Air pollution has been shown to contribute to the following: chronic obstructive pulmonary disease (COPD), cardiovascular disease, acute asthma, lung cancer, birth defects, fatigue, headaches, and eye irritations. Additional effects are low productivity and concentration stemming from poor health, which have economic and social impacts. The solutions for improving air quality in cities also have environmental, social, economic and health benefits. Green spaces, such as parks, and green belts, and improved access to nature also improve health. These spaces provide opportunities for physical activity, improve mental well-being by reducing stress, and foster a sense of community; while sequestering carbon and reducing the concentration of GHGs in the atmosphere and providing sustainable urban drainage systems that serve as water attenuation, mitigating flood risk. Studies have also shown that green space reduces violent and aggressive behaviour, reduces the amount of pain experienced by some chronically ill patients, and enables children with ADD to concentrate.

Extreme temperatures

Extreme temperatures, particularly heat, have received significant attention in the context of cities due to their high human costs. For example, in Europe, the heat wave experienced in 2003 is believed to have played a role in between 22,000 and 35,000 deaths and resulted in affected cities developing heat plans (Baccini *et al.*, 2008; Corburn, 2009; Hajat *et al.*, 2010). Plans related to heat in the urban context focus on the built environment and land use to mitigate urban heat island (UHI) effects. UHIs occur as a result of the high thermal capacity of buildings. Research has shown that built-up urban areas retain heat for longer periods of time than rural areas; consequently, urban areas are often five to ten degrees warmer than rural areas (Campbell-Lendrum and Corvalàn, 2007; Hajat *et al.*, 2010; Haque *et al.*, 2010). Adaptation responses for UHI has focused on treating the urban environment by looking at options that facilitate the cooling of the built environment, for example through green infrastructure and tree planting. An example of this comes from Corburn (2009), who investigated the policy and programming challenges of addressing UHI in the context of the New York City Regional Heat Island Initiative (NYCRHII). His study highlighted a challenge with climate change adaptation responses – the scaling down of global models of climate change to the local level (Corburn, 2009). He also addressed the challenges of translating science into policy, an essential component in successfully responding to climate change. The research observed the process of cooperation between scientists and policy makers (and various other stakeholders) as they decided between three options of UHI mitigation: tree planting, surface lightening, and green roofs (Barton *et al.*, 2003; Barton, 2009; Corburn, 2009). Trees cool the urban environment and provide shade; moreover, trees provide a safe environment for individuals to become acclimatised to heat, and rest. Green roofs have supplementary benefits; as they reduce energy demands of buildings, thus reducing the demand for cooling systems (Corburn, 2009). Research has also shown that during heat waves air quality is degraded and the concentration of pollutants increases.

Rising sea levels and flooding

Significant attention concerning climate change and cities has revolved around the issue of rising sea levels and its impacts on coastal cities and communities. The key issues here are the salination of freshwater, increased pressure on water and sanitation systems, displacement of populations, and damage to critical infrastructure caused by coastal erosion, sea level rise and storm surges. Inland cities built around rivers on floodplains or other bodies of water that have the propensity to flood face similar risks. There are several types of flooding that can be experienced by cities: pluvial flooding from increased rainfall and storm surges, fluvial flooding also caused by rainfall (extended periods or extreme high intensity) resulting in rivers exceeding their capacity, and network flooding resulting from drainage systems being inundated with water (Kovats and Akhtar, 2008; IPCC, 2014; United Nations Human Settlements Programme (UN-Habitat), 2016). Rising sea levels and floods can be attributed to the positive feedback loop that is responsible for melting ice, the 'snow/ice-albedo feedback' which amplifies temperature and subsequently the rate at which ice melts (Le Treut, 2007; IPCC, 2014). Snow or ice that has melted does not immediately enter the sea or ocean; it passes through tributaries, rivers, lakes, etc. before reaching the ocean (Le Treut, 2007; IPCC, 2014). Consequently, for cities located on flood plains and rivers there is a high risk of flooding especially when there is the 'perfect storm' of contributing factors. For example, the City of Calgary, built on the flood plains of the Bow and Elbow Rivers, experienced floods in 2013 that caused widespread disruption in the city. Scientists attributed the devastation to heavy rainfall for an extended period of time, frozen ground that was unable to absorb excess water and the city's physical characteristics. In short, the perfect storm of contributing factors that maximised the damage to the city.

Extreme weather events/ natural disasters

The World Meteorological Organisation (WMO) has shown that the last decade (2001–2010) has been the worst on record for extreme climate events. Hurricanes, typhoons and cyclones have wreaked havoc around the globe. The increased frequency of these extreme storms can be attributed to climate change, particularly the increases in temperature that facilitate accumulation of moisture in the atmosphere. Coastal cities bear the brunt of these storms and consequently face immense recovery costs. However, super storms are not the only form of extreme weather; droughts and heat waves are also part of extreme weather events (Campbell-Lendrum and Corvalàn, 2007; Zanobetti *et al.*, 2013). Droughts present risks to urban ecosystems, by creating water shortages and food shortages. Water and food shortages pose significant health risks for urban populations, particularly in a Global South context. Other health risks include the spread of airborne diseases, such as meningitis and others that thrive in dry conditions. Violence resulting in physical injury and death, from conflict over scarce resources is increasingly a public health issue in the context of water and food scarcity (Barnett, 2003; Barnett and Adger, 2007). Finally, as with flooding and rising sea levels, extreme weather events have the ability to displace populations. As discussed above displacement is a complex issue not just with regards to urban planning but in terms of public health. Cities are faced with an influx of people whose health and safety needs they may not have sufficient resources to guarantee. Consequently, these populations are at increased risk of disease and poor mental health.

Given the breadth and depth of the complexity of the interactions between the various climate change impacts, cities face an immense challenge in responding that is complicated by their unique nature.

Responding: the role of cities

City planners need to link climate-change issues to broader agendas. Discussions about whether to invest in a more efficient fossil fuel power plant or renewable energy sources, for example, need to be connected to discussions about the cost of energy and localised pollution impacts on power plant operations. Issues such as sustainable water supplies and sewage treatment strategies must be evaluated for their links to climate concerns.

(Rosenzweig *et al.*, 2010, p. 909)

Cities have evolved from places where people's basic needs of shelter, food and water are met; into a complex social ecological system comprised of various interdependent systems: the economy, transportation networks, education, society, and health, that provide people with the opportunity to live, work and play (Mumford, 1961; Rees and Wackernagel, 1996; Botkin and Beveridge, 1997; Rees, 1997; Barton, 2009). The complexity of the social ecological system has implications for responding to climate change, one of which is the governance systems in which urban policy makers operate. Governance of cities is not the same around the world; many local governments are still dependent upon regulations and legislations determined by regional and national governments, which influences the financial capacity of cities (Friedmann, 2005; Betsill and Bulkeley, 2007; Rosenzweig *et al.*, 2010; Dodman, 2011). This however, has not limited local government action on climate change. Since 1997, there have been an increasing number of partnerships and alliances formed by cities, sub-national governments, and philanthropic and community groups to respond to climate change such as Climate Alliance, Cities for Climate Protection, and the C40 Cities Climate Leadership Group (Betsill and Bulkeley, 2007). While initially comprised of North American and European cities, the reach of these movements has expanded to include cities in Asia, Africa, Australia and South America, demonstrating the increasing importance of cities in responding to climate change (Betsill and Bulkeley, 2007; Rosenzweig *et al.*, 2010; Geddes *et al.*, 2012; Castán Broto, *et al.*, 2013). These initiatives also demonstrate an important role of the city and local government in responding to climate change, namely their ability to bridge the divide between national governments and citizens (Betsill and Bulkeley, 2007).

The 'gap' between policies at the national level and the realities of daily life has been a barrier to implementing national policies on climate change (Kalkstein and Greene, 1997; Betsill and Bulkeley, 2007; Rosenzweig *et al.*, 2010; Geddes *et al.*, 2012; Carter *et al.*, 2015; Campbell, 2016). Cities through local government, have the benefit of being able to respond quickly and proactively to the demands of local climate protection groups and advocates, as well as local businesses and individuals whose livelihoods are impacted by climate change (Betsill and Bulkeley, 2007; Rosenzweig *et al.*, 2010; Romero Lankao and Qin, 2011). This capability is important, as climate change can impact the ability of cities to grow economically, socially and physically by placing numerous pressures on cities ranging from rural to urban migration, which creates challenges for housing and the economy, to physical vulnerabilities stemming from flood risk, sea level rise, and heat waves (Carter *et al.*, 2015; United Nations Human Settlements Programme (UN-Habitat), 2016). The complex causal pathways that contribute to the vulnerabilities created by climate change are demonstrated in Figure 1.1. There is no one-size-fits-all strategy for cities to address climate change. Planners and urban policy makers need to engage with a range of stakeholders from scientists and engineers to community groups and citizens, to gain in-depth understanding of the impacts of climate change, in order to develop responses that make the urban environment resilient to climate change.

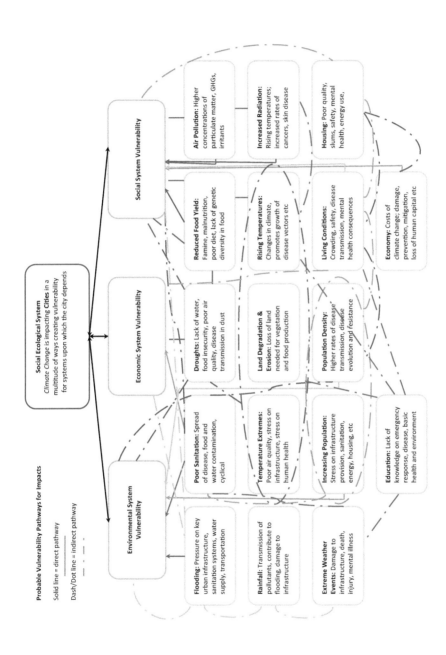

Probable Vulnerability Pathways for Impacts

Solid line = direct pathway

Dash/Dot line = indirect pathway

Social Ecological System
Climate Change is impacting **Cities** in a multitude of ways creating vulnerability for systems upon which the city depends

Social System Vulnerability

Economic System Vulnerability

Environmental System Vulnerability

Air Pollution: Higher concentrations of particulate matter, GHGs, irritants

Increased Radiation: Rising temperatures; increased rates of cancers, skin disease

Housing: Poor quality, slums, safety, mental health, energy use,

Reduced Food Yield: Famine, malnutrition, poor diet, lack of genetic diversity in food

Rising Temperatures: Changes in climate, promotes growth of disease vectors etc

Living Conditions: Crowding, safety, disease transmission, mental health consequences

Economy: Costs of climate change; damage, prevention, mitigation, loss of human capital etc

Droughts: Lack of water, food insecurity, poor air quality, disease transmission in dust

Land Degradation & Erosion: Loss of land needed for vegetation and food production

Population Density: Higher rates of disease transmission, disease evolution and resistance

Poor Sanitation: Spread of disease, food and water contamination, cyclical

Temperature Extremes: Poor air quality, stress on infrastructure, stress on human health

Increasing Population: Stress on infrastructure provision, sanitation, energy, housing, etc

Education: Lack of knowledge on emergency response, disease, basic health and environment

Flooding: Pressure on key urban infrastructure, sanitation systems, water supply, transportation

Rainfall: Transmission of pollutants, contribute to flooding, damage to infrastructure

Extreme Weather Events: Damage to infrastructure, death, injury, mental illness

Figure 1.1 Pathways – vulnerability and climate change.

Resilience to climate change: a long-term collaborative effort

Determining how cities can become resilient to climate change by addressing the vulnerabilities it creates via adaptation, while continuing to develop economically and socially, requires consideration of policy success being demarcated by achieving targets or engaging in a long-term process (Cutter *et al.*, 2008; Miller *et al.*, 2010; Masson *et al.*, 2014). Before determining this, it is essential to acknowledge the 'faults' with resilience, one being its broad all-encompassing, omnipotent nature, that stems from its efforts to fully understand a system's resilience 'to what and from what'; in other words, all the potential vulnerabilities stemming from a threat or threats to the system. Critics of resilience have argued that due to this ambiguity, resilience is merely an evolved form of sustainability, which supports policies that restrict and limit the abilities of communities to be resilient (Brenner and Schmid, 2013; Satterthwaite, 2013; Kythreotis and Bristow, 2017). Further, resilience is argued to homogenise cities and therefore, do more harm to the vulnerable segments of society whom it purports to support and improve their resilience (Brenner and Schmid, 2013; Satterthwaite, 2013). Some would argue that if people are perceived to be resilient they can face further difficulty. In other words, resilience is a policy objective for those who can afford it, as opposed to those who need policies that support their individual resilience (Brenner and Schmid, 2013; Satterthwaite, 2013). Critiques of resilience highlight its weaknesses and risks of becoming a buzzword that contributes to uneven growth by calling for market-driven solutions to make cities resilient as opposed to reducing inequity; the critiques, though, are arguably focused on the economic and physical dimensions of resilience in the urban context (Kythreotis and Bristow, 2017). In practice, resilience calls for policy makers to give consideration to how threats create vulnerability across all dimensions of urban life, including social and environmental dimensions, and with this understanding develop responses that enable the city and its citizens to adapt. Further, becoming resilient is not a matter of linking a threat to a solution, but about creating a 'net' of solutions, such that should one policy fail others compensate due to the inherent redundancies built into the process of being resilient (Rodin, 2014).

At a broader level resilience is an active concept: resilience centres on the idea of *response* to shocks, where the response is either an action accomplished by a whole system or an individual within a system: critical to this is the survival of the 'shock' (Teigão dos Santos and Partidário, 2011; Barr and Devine-Wright, 2012). Dependent on the field in which resilience is being used the act of responding is connected to pre-conditions, namely that there is something to respond to, something that threatens or can weaken a system or individual. This is a challenge for resilience that lies in consensus in the existence of a threat and what that threat is (Carver, 1998; Norris *et al.*, 2008; Gotham and Campanella, 2010; Miller *et al.*, 2010; Pendall *et al.*, 2010). If there is agreement that a threat exists then the next step is to acknowledge the mechanisms of the threat (Carver, 1998; Norris *et al.*, 2008; Gotham and Campanella, 2010; Miller *et al.*, 2010;

Pendall *et al.*, 2010), which leads into further challenges related to agreement and consensus around perceptions of the threat, its relative impact, and outcomes if not addressed (Bowen *et al.*, 2012; Davoudi *et al.*, 2012). Debates regarding the impacts and outcomes could vary extensively based on perceptions and the value of the impact. It is nuanced. The scale of the threat also needs to be debated both in spatial and temporal contexts, in other words the extent of a threat and what are the costs of acting versus not acting (Carver, 1998; Norris *et al.*, 2008; Gotham and Campanella, 2010; Miller *et al.*, 2010; Pendall *et al.*, 2010). This debate occurs before consideration can be given to using resilience as an objective for action and formulating responses. Confirmation of a threat is dependent on the body of research and evidence showing that something is a threat to a system or individual. The research itself can also be subject to scepticism and disbelief (Norris *et al.*, 2008). The scientific evidence undeniably states that climate change is a global threat, which permits the assumption that it is also a threat at national, regional, state/provincial, and city levels (Middleton, 2008; Cote and Nightingale, 2011). How the threat manifests itself in each city though is contested. With numerous and various causal pathways it is difficult to clearly indicate how climate change will impact a city.

Even once the threat has been recognised, and the pathways investigated, there is still a barrier to responding and to implementing actions to become resilient. The desire to act and respond is needed; this aspect is inherent to non-biological ecosystems where the process of resilience is innate, as discussed below (Holling, 1973; Walker *et al.*, 2004; Folke, 2006; Davoudi *et al.*, 2012). These preconditions as such are primarily in the realm of human-based systems and as such it is only human action that can effectively move in the direction of resilience.

With the acknowledgement of a threat that creates a vulnerability to which a system must become resilient, the question arises as to whether resilience is an end state demarcated by something, or if it is a process of continually evolving states of resilience to something (Carver, 1998; Adger *et al.*, 2003; Adger, 2006; Norris *et al.*, 2008). In simple ecosystems, that natural progression towards achieving resilience is biologically inherent to the system and its species; it essentially follows a process where a threat is introduced into a system, to which species and the system then respond via behavioural changes and/or natural selection processes. Finally, the system and species either survive and return to their previous state, evolve into a new state, or the system and species perish (Carver, 1998; Sandler, 2001; Cutter *et al.*, 2008; Norris *et al.*, 2008; Gotham and Campanella, 2010). Admittedly the natural environment can face multiple threats and over varying time spans which will ultimately shape this process (Norris *et al.*, 2008). However, the non-biological ecosystems into which the concept of resilience has been introduced are complex by virtue of their man-made nature, which allows for a multitude of options for alterations to the system to achieve resilience. Moreover, the response process of resilience involves the following described in Table 1.1 (Norris *et al.*, 2008; Gotham and Campanella, 2010):

Success is ultimately being a resilient system with resilient species/individuals and identifying when and how that happens (Norris *et al.*, 2008): as mentioned

Table 1.1 Resilience process – complex system

Resilience Process	
Pre-conditions	Recognition of a threat
	Perceptions of:
	• Vulnerability created by threat • Risks stemming from threat
	Knowledge of:
	• Threat • Causal pathways • Mechanisms
	Desire to DO SOMETHING
Agreement of Threat	Action to become RESILIENT
Resilience Process	Analysis of Threats:
	• Risks • Assessment of impacts • Knowledge exchange (i.e. information about threat outcomes) • Collaboration/ Collective action • Integrated action
	Debate on Action:
	• Assessment of possible actions • Assessment of risk associated with actions • Role clarification (stakeholders and their agendas) • Options: short and long term
	Visioning of state of being resilient
	Implementation
	Monitoring and evaluation
	• Resilience achieved as an endpoint or an ongoing process

above, there are two options. A resilient system can be demarcated by an end-point defined by indicators and targets for achieving success (Cutter *et al.*, 2008; Norris *et al.*, 2008; Pendall *et al.*, 2010; Davoudi *et al.*, 2012). Alternatively, resilience can be seen as an ongoing process where targets provide a road map for the direction of the city's actions. Depending on the context in which resilience is used, this will determine whether or not it is an end-point or a process of continual response. In this research the context is the city and its capacity to adapt to climate change; as such, resilience is an ongoing process. Consequently, developing resilience-based policy to address climate change is dependent on the collaboration of stakeholders, such as individuals and communities with policy makers, to engage in dialogue around the impacts of climate change and the responses needed in order to create a resilient city (Betsill and Bulkeley, 2007; Norris *et al.*, 2008; Pizzo, 2015).

Defining a resilient city

The city is the nexus where the systems discussed and their interpretations of resilience meet. As such, defining a resilient city is a complex challenge. Moreover, is resilience an accepted concept in the context of cities? The language of planning and planners has been focused on the concept of sustainability (Miller *et al.*, 2010; Davoudi *et al.*, 2012), a term that has evolved and acquired complexity due to its use in numerous fields, but what has emerged is uncertainty about what sustainability is. Resilience presents the same dilemma. Given the complex number of systems that comprise the city, what does a resilient city look like? These two questions are challenging to answer. If one considers how resilience is applied in each system and its meanings, there is the potential for resilience, a term that has a concrete definition and pathway in the sciences, to lose its value in urban planning due to the complexity of the urban system (Miller *et al.*, 2010; Cote and Nightingale, 2011; Romero Lankao and Qin, 2011; Davoudi *et al.*, 2012). Resilience, though, is argued to be a valid concept and a tangible objective for cities. As Rodin states, resilience is a 'net of policies' (Rodin, 2014). Cities can extend this to be a net of policies and programs that function together to ensure that cities continue to provide for citizens the basics of quality iving environments in the face of climate change (Miller *et al.*, 2010; Davoudi *et al.*, 2012; Rodin, 2014). The assumption underlying this though is that for cities to construct their net of policies they will need to broaden their 'networks'. Urban policy makers will need to engage with stakeholders possessing a range of knowledge, expertise and lived experiences to create policies; in short, they need to collaborate.

Planners engaging and collaborating with a range of stakeholders brings to the fore the question of how policy makers and planners address what is likely to lead to the failure of collaboration – power struggles and co-opting (Allmendinger *et al.*, 2003; Innes, 2004; Innes and Booher, 2004). The promotion of dialogue whereby all actors can equitably put forth their ideas ensures the achievement of collaboration, and therefore the development of comprehensive policy and plans (Innes and Booher, 2004). Whilst, resilience-based policy making in the urban environment faces challenges similar to comprehensive planning, due to perceptions of the complexity surrounding resilience nature, it is similarly achievable (Folke, 2007; Norris *et al.*, 2008; Gotham and Campanella, 2010; Davoudi *et al.*, 2012). When thinking of constructing or enabling resilience, the city highlights both the positives and negatives of resilience. One negative is the debates that will arise and prolong the process, yet debates are an asset in creating policy. Further, local governments are faced with balancing the power dynamics that will emerge in a collaborative process and the costs of engaging in the process (Healey, 1998a). Consensus will not be achieved without disagreement on what is a threat, what knowledge is important and how to respond (Healey, 1998a, 1998b; Innes, 2004; Innes and Booher, 2004). Resilience places cities on the path to achieving a meaningful 'how' that requires a deepened understanding of mitigating the threat of climate change and the recognition that it adversely affects people at the core of their being, their health (Cutter *et al.*, 2008; Norris *et al.*, 2008; Davoudi *et al.*, 2012). Thus, the debate becomes a matter of how resilience is achieved.

Considering resilience from a positivist approach, resilience operates under the assumption that everyone agrees that something is a threat to the city and is consequently committed to taking action. Further, that action needs to be taken in a collaborative manner, as the recognition exists that the threat has multiple causal pathways and will impact systems within the city in varying means and degrees. There is also the keen recognition that solutions do not solely come from the top down, but that it is critical to have bottom-up approaches and buy-in (Sandler, 2001; Cutter *et al.*, 2008; Norris *et al.*, 2008; Davoudi *et al.*, 2012). The resilience of cities is a responsibility taken on by all individuals, as their cooperation is inherent to being resilient.

Based on this knowledge, it is evident that there are challenges to achieving resilience. The most significant challenge for resilience will be attaining consensus amongst stakeholders. Further, with urban environments evolving and facing growing challenges with provision of services (i.e. housing, water, education and healthcare) for which various regulatory agencies, movements and stakeholders are striving and competing to influence and shape, as argued by Brenner and Schmid (2015), it is evident that achieving resilience to climate change is not without challenges. Simultaneously, building resilience to a common threat, climate change, presents an opportunity to align diverse stakeholders and foster collaboration amongst stakeholders to shape the city. Further, resilience will not work without consensus through all stages from threat identification through to response action (Norris *et al.*, 2008; Pendall *et al.*, 2010; Davoudi *et al.*, 2012), a process that requires resources from a range of sources, followed by the collective shaping of the ideas into a plan and action (Innes, 1996, 2004). Moreover, this process as discussed in the literature on comprehensive planning is one that requires long-term commitment to the process; stakeholders cannot expect to only be involved for a specified amount of time (Innes, 2004). This is not to say that the process will not produce a result, as the process is measured by achieving agreed upon goals (Healey, 2003). There can be short-term results, however, short-term results if used effectively can feed into the long-term/ lifelong-process of being resilient (Norris *et al.*, 2008; Gotham and Campanella, 2010; Davoudi *et al.*, 2012). In addition to this issue of time is the complexity of resilience stemming from its efforts to understand all possible outcomes of a threat and to take action accordingly and respond if initial actions do not work, or if new threats emerge (Norris *et al.*, 2008). Efforts then to simplify resilience become encumbered by agreement and consensus on scales related to: geography, spatial and temporal dimensions (Carver, 1998; Cutter *et al.*, 2008; Norris *et al.*, 2008; Gotham and Campanella, 2010). Thus, this research proposes that in developing resilience-based climate change policy, policy makers need to identify narratives that unify stakeholders and enable collaboration.

Outline of book

Chapter 2 discusses the governance of climate change responses through adaptive governance and collaborative planning in the context of resilience. Chapter 3 discusses the institutional structures of the case study cities and the challenges each faces in responding to climate change. Following from this, Chapter 4 presents the informal approaches used by the cities; specifically, how the processes undertaken by these cities contribute to theory and subsequent practice. Chapter 5 provides additional background on Dublin, concentrating on its experience with collaborative planning in developing responses to the demands by citizens to address cycling and flooding that were considered in the development of the climate change action plans. Finally, Chapter 6 presents the experience of developing the Climate Change Action Plans for the four Dublin Local authorities. This chapter is a reflection on the process and the learning and presents the challenges ahead for Dublin, perhaps providing insights for other cities.

References

Adger, W. N., Huq, S., Brown, K., Conway, D., Hulme, M. and Hulme, M.(2003) 'Adaptation to climate change in the developing world developing world'. *Progress in Development Studies*, 3(3) pp. 358–366. doi: 10.1191/1464993403ps060oa.

Adger, W. N. (2006) 'Vulnerability', *Global Environmental Change*. Pergamon, 16(3), pp. 268–281. doi: 10.1016/J.GLOENVCHA.2006.02.006.

Allmendinger, P., Tewdwr-Jones, M. and Morphet, J. (2003) 'Public Scrutiny, Standards and the Planning System: Assessing Professional Values within a Modernized Local Government', *Public Administration*, 81(4), pp. 761–780. doi: 10.1111/j.0033–3298.2003.00370.x.

Baccini, M., Biggeri, A., Accetta, G., Kosatsky, T., Katsouyanni, K., Analitis, A., Anderson, H., Bisanti, L., Ippoliti, D., Danova, J., Forsberg, B., Medina, S., Paldy, A., Rabczenko, D. and Schindler C (2008) 'Heat Effects on Mortality in 15 European Cities', *Epidemiology*, 19(5), pp. 711–719. doi: 10.1097/EDE.0b013e318176bfcd.

Barnett, J. (2003) 'Security and climate change', *Global Environmental Change*. Pergamon, 13(1), pp. 7–17. doi: 10.1016/S0959–3780(02)00080–8.

Barnett, J. and Adger, W. N. (2007) 'Climate change, human security and violent conflict', *Political Geography*. Pergamon, 26(6), pp. 639–655. doi: 10.1016/J.POLGEO.2007.03.003.

Barr, S. and Devine-Wright, P. (2012) 'Resilient communities: sustainabilities in transition', *Local Environment*. Routledge, 17(5), pp. 525–532. doi: 10.1080/13549839.2012.676637.

Barton, H. (2009) 'Land use planning and health and well-being', *Land Use Policy*. Pergamon, 26, pp. S115–S123. doi: 10.1016/J.LANDUSEPOL.2009.09.008.

Barton, H., Mitcham, C. and Tsourou, C. (2003) 'Healthy urban planning in practice: experience of European cities', *Report of the WHO City Action Group on Healthy Urban Planning, WHO*, p. 59. doi: 10.1093/heapro/dap059.

Betsill, M. and Bulkeley, H. (2007) 'Looking Back and Thinking Ahead: A Decade of Cities and Climate Change Research', *Local Environment*. Routledge, 12(5), pp. 447–456. doi: 10.1080/13549830701659683.

Botkin, D. B. and Beveridge, C. E. (1997) 'Cities as environments', *Urban Ecosystems*, 1(1), pp. 3–19. doi: 10.1023/A:1014354923367.

Bowen, K. J., Friel, S., Ebi, K., Butler, C. D., Miller, F. and McMichael, A. J. (2012) 'Governing for a Healthy Population: Towards an Understanding of How Decision-Making Will Determine Our Global Health in a Changing Climate', *International Journal of Environmental Research and Public Health*, 9(1), pp. 55–72. doi: 10.3390/ijerph9010055.

Brenner, N. and Schmid, C. (2013) 'The "Urban Age" in Question', *International Journal of Urban and Regional Research*, 38(3), pp. 731–755. doi: 10.1111/1468-2427.12115.

Campbell-Lendrum, D. and Corvalàn, C. (2007) 'Climate Change and Developing-Country Cities: Implications For Environmental Health and Equity', 84(1), pp. 109–117. doi: 10.1007/s11524-007-9170-x.

Campbell, S. (2016) 'Green Cities, Growing Cities, Just Cities?: Urban Planning and the Contradictions of Sustainable Development', *Readings in Planning Theory: Fourth Edition*, (November 2013), pp. 214–240. doi: 10.1002/9781119084679.ch11.

Carter, J. G., Cavan, G., Connelly, A., Guy, S., Handley, J. and Kazmierczak, A. (2015) 'Climate change and the city: Building capacity for urban adaptation', *Progress in Planning*, 95, pp. 1–66. doi: 10.1016/j.progress.2013.08.001.

Carver, C. S. (1998) 'Resilience and Thriving: Issues, Models, and Linkages', *Journal of Social Issues*, 54(2), pp. 245–266. doi: 10.1111/j.1540-4560.1998.tb01217.x.

Castán Broto, V., Oballa, B. and Junior, P. (2013) 'Governing climate change for a just city: challenges and lessons from Maputo, Mozambique', *Local Environment*, 18(January 2015), pp. 678–704. doi: 10.1080/13549839.2013.801573.

Corburn, J. (2009) 'Cities, Climate Change and Urban Heat Island Mitigation: Localising Global Environmental Science', *Urban Studies*, 46(2), pp. 413–427. doi: 10.1177/0042098008099361.

Cote, M. and Nightingale, A. J. (2011) 'Resilience thinking meets social theory: Situating social change in socio-ecological systems (SES) research', *Progress in Human Geography*. SAGE Publications Ltd, 36(4), pp. 475–489. doi: 10.1177/0309132511425708.

Crawford, J., Barton, H., Chapman, T., Higins, M., Capon, A. and Thompson, S. (2010) 'Health at the Heart of Spatial Planning Strengthening the Roots of Planning Health and the Urban Planner Health Inequalities and Place Planning for the Health of People and Planet: An Australian Perspective', *Planning Theory & Practice*. Routledge, 11(1), pp. 91–113. doi: 10.1080/14649350903537956.

Cutter, S. L., Barnes, L., Berry, M., Burton, C., Evans, E., Tate, E. and Webb, J. (2008) 'A place-based model for understanding community resilience to natural disasters', *Global Environmental Change*. Pergamon, 18(4), pp. 598–606. doi: 10.1016/J.GLOENVCHA.2008.07.013.

Davoudi, S., Shaw, K., Haider, L., Quinlan, A., Peterson, G., Wilkinson, C., Fünfgeld, H., McEvoy, D. and Porter, L. (2012) 'Resilience: A Bridging Concept or a Dead End? "Reframing" Resilience: Challenges for Planning Theory and Practice Interacting Traps: Resilience Assessment of a Pasture Management System in Northern Afghanistan Urban Resilience: What Does it Mean in Planning Practice?', *Planning Theory and Practice*, 13(2), pp. 299–333. doi: 10.1080/14649357.2012.677124.

Dodman, D. (2009) 'Blaming cities for climate change? An analysis of urban greenhouse gas emissions inventories', *Environment and Urbanization*, 21(1), pp. 185–201. doi: 10.1177/0956247809103016.

Dodman, D. (2011) 'Forces driving urban greenhouse gas emissions', *Current Opinion in Environmental Sustainability*. Elsevier, 3(3), pp. 121–125. doi: 10.1016/J.COSUST. 2010.12.013.

Doherty, M., Klima, K. and Hellmann, J. J. (2016) 'Environmental Science & Policy Climate change in the urban environment: Advancing, measuring and achieving resiliency', *Environmental Science and Policy*. Elsevier Ltd, 66, pp. 310–313. doi: 10.1016/j.envsci.2016.09.001.

Eckersley, P. (2016) 'Cities and climate change: How historical legacies shape policy-making in English and German municipalities', *Politics*. SAGE Publications Ltd, 37(2), pp. 151–166. doi: 10.1177/0263395716670412.

Folke, C. (2006) 'Resilience: The emergence of a perspective for social–ecological systems analyses', *Global Environmental Change*. Pergamon, 16(3), pp. 253–267. doi: 10.1016/J.GLOENVCHA.2006.04.002.

Folke, C. (2007) 'Social-ecological systems and adaptive governance of the commons', *Ecological Research*, 22(1), pp. 14–15. doi: 10.1007/s11284-006-0074-0.

Foss, A. (2016) 'Divergent responses to sustainability and climate change planning: The role of politics, cultural frames and public participation', *Urban Studies*. SAGE Publications Ltd, 55(2), pp. 332–348. doi: 10.1177/0042098016651554.

Friedmann, J. (2005) 'Globalization and the emerging culture of planning', *Progress in Planning*. Pergamon, 64(3), pp. 183–234. doi: 10.1016/J.PROGRESS.2005.05.001.

Geddes, A., Adger, W., Arnell, N., Black, R. and Thomas, D. (2012) 'Migration, Environmental Change, and the "Challenges of Governance"', *Environment and Planning C: Government and Policy*. SAGE Publications Ltd STM, 30(6), pp. 951–967. doi: 10.1068/c3006ed.

Gotham, K. F. and Campanella, R. (2010) 'Toward a Research Agenda on Transformative Resilience: Challenges and Opportunities for Post-Trauma Urban Ecosystems', *Critical Planning*, Summer (December), pp. 9–23.

Gouldson, A., Colenbrander, S., Sudmant, A., Papagyropoulou, E., Kerr, N., McAnulla, F. and Hall, S. (2016) 'Cities and climate change mitigation: Economic opportunities and governance challenges in Asia', *Cities*, 54, pp. 11–19. doi: 10.1016/j.cities.2015. 10.010.

Hajat, S., O'Connor, M. and Kosatsky, T. (2010) 'Health effects of hot weather: from awareness of risk factors to effective health protection', *The Lancet*. Elsevier, 375(9717), pp. 856–863. doi: 10.1016/S0140-6736(09)61711-6.

Haque, M. A., Yamamoto, S., Malik, A. and Sauerborn, R. (2012) 'Households' perception of climate change and human health risks: A community perspective', *Environmental Health*. BioMed Central Ltd, 11(1), p. 1. doi: 10.1186/1476-069X-11-1.

Healey, P. (1998a) 'Building Institutional Capacity through Collaborative Approaches to Urban Planning', *Environment and Planning A: Economy and Space*. SAGE Publications Ltd, 30(9), pp. 1531–1546. doi: 10.1068/a301531.

Healey, P. (1998b) 'Collaborative planning in a stakeholder society', *Town Planning Review*, 69(1), p. 1. doi: 10.3828/tpr.69.1.h651u2327m86326p.

Healey, P. (2003) 'Collaborative Planning in Perspective', *Planning Theory*, 2(2), pp. 101–123. doi: 10.1177/14730952030022002.

Heller, A. and Adams, T. (2009) 'Creating healthy cities through socially sustainable placemaking', *Australian Planner*, 46(2), pp. 18–21. doi: 10.1080/07293682.2009. 9995305.

Holling, C. S. (1973) 'Resilience and Stability of Ecological Systems', *Annual Review of Ecology and Systematics*, 4(1), pp. 1–23. doi: 10.1146/annurev.es.04.110173.000245.

Huang-Lachmann, J. T. and Lovett, J. C. (2016) 'How cities prepare for climate change: Comparing Hamburg and Rotterdam', *Cities*. Elsevier B.V., 54, pp. 36–44. doi: 10. 1016/j.cities.2015.11.001.

Hunt, A. and Watkiss, P. (2011) 'Climate change impacts and adaptation in cities: a review of the literature', *Climatic Change*, 104(1), pp. 13–49. doi: 10.1007/s10584-010-9975-6.

Innes, J. E. (1996) 'Planning Through Consensus Building: A New View of the Comprehensive Planning Ideal', *Journal of the American Planning Association*. Routledge, 62(4), pp. 460–472. doi: 10.1080/01944369608975712.

Innes, J. E. (2004) 'Consensus Building: Clarifications for the Critics', *Planning Theory*. SAGE Publications, 3(1), pp. 5–20. doi: 10.1177/1473095204042315.

Innes, J. E. and Booher, D. E. (2004) 'Reframing public participation: strategies for the 21st century', *Planning Theory & Practice*. Routledge, 5(4), pp. 419–436. doi: 10. 1080/1464935042000293170.

IPCC (2014) *Climate Change 2014: Mitigation of Climate Change. Summary for Policymakers and Technical Summary, Climate Change 2014: Mitigation of Climate Change. Part of the Working Group III Contribution to the Fifth Assessment Report of the Intergovernmental Panel on Climate Change*. doi: 10.1017/CBO9781107415416.005.

Kalkstein, L. S. and Greene, J. S. (1997) 'An evaluation of climate/mortality relationships in large U.S. cities and the possible impacts of a climate change.', *Environmental Health Perspectives*, 105(1), pp. 84–93. Available at: www.ncbi.nlm.nih.gov/pmc/articles/PMC1469832/.

Kovats, S. and Akhtar, R. (2008) 'Environment and Urbanization'. doi: 10.1177/09562 47808089154.

Kythreotis, A. P. and Bristow, G. I. (2017) 'The "resilience trap": exploring the practical utility of resilience for climate change adaptation in UK city-regions', *Regional Studies*. Routledge, 51(10), pp. 1530–1541. doi: 10.1080/00343404.2016.1200719.

Masson, V., Marchadier, C., Adolphe, L., Aguejdad, R., Avner, P., Bonhomme, M., Bretagne, G., Briottet, X., Bueno, B. and Munck, C. (2014) 'Urban Climate Adapting cities to climate change: A systemic modelling approach', *Urban Climate*. Elsevier B.V., 10, pp. 407–429. doi: 10.1016/j.uclim.2014.03.004.

Mees, H. (2017) 'Local governments in the driving seat? A comparative analysis of public and private responsibilities for adaptation to climate change in European and North-American cities', *Journal of Environmental Policy & Planning*. Routledge, 19(4), pp. 374–390. doi: 10.1080/1523908X.2016.1223540.

Middleton, J. (2008) 'Environmental health, climate chaos and resilience', *Medicine, Conflict and Survival*. Routledge, 24(sup1), pp. S62–S79. doi: 10.1080/13623690801 957406.

Miller, F., Osbahr, H., Boyd, E., Thomalla, F., Bharwani, S., Ziervogel, G., Walker, B., Birkmann, J., Van der Leeuw, S., Rockström, J., Hinkel, J., Downing, T., Folke, C. and Nelson, D. (2010) 'Resilience and vulnerability: Complementary or conflicting concepts?', *Ecology and Society*, 15(3), p. 11. doi: 10.5751/ES-03378-150311.

Mumford, L. (1961) *The City in History. Its Origins, Its Transformations, and Its Prospects*, New York (Harcourt, Brace & World).

Norris, F. H., Stevens, S., Pfefferbaum, B., Wyche, K. and Pfefferbaum, R. (2008) 'Community Resilience as a Metaphor, Theory, Set of Capacities, and Strategy for Disaster Readiness', *American Journal of Community Psychology*, 41(1–2), pp. 127–150. doi: 10.1007/s10464-007-9156-6.

Pendall, R., Foster, K. A. and Cowell, M. (2010) 'Resilience and regions: building understanding of the metaphor', *Cambridge Journal of Regions, Economy and Society*, 3(1), pp. 71–84. doi: 10.1093/cjres/rsp028.

Pizzo, B. (2015) 'Problematizing resilience: Implications for planning theory and practice', *Cities*, 43, pp. 133–140. doi: https://doi.org/10.1016/j.cities.2014.11.015.

Rees, W.E (1997). 'Urban Ecosystems the human dimension. *Urban Ecosystems*, 1 pp. 63–75. https://doi.org/10.1023/A:1014380105620

Rees, W. and Wackernagel, M. (1996) 'Urban Ecological Footprints: Why Cities Cannot Be Sustainable – and Why They Are a Key To Sustainability', *Environmental Impact Assessment Review*, 16(96), pp. 223–248.

Rodin, J. (2014) *The Resilience Dividend: Being Strong in a World Where Things Go Wrong*. PublicAffairs. Available at: https://books.google.ie/books?id=E7GMAw AAQBAJ.

Romero Lankao, P. and Qin, H. (2011) 'Conceptualizing urban vulnerability to global climate and environmental change', *Current Opinion in Environmental Sustainability*. Elsevier, 3(3), pp. 142–149. doi: 10.1016/J.COSUST.2010.12.016.

Rosenzweig, C., Solecki, W., Hammer, S. and Mehrotra, S. (2010) 'Cities lead the way in climate-change action', *Nature*, 467(7318), pp. 909–911. doi: 10.1038/467909a.

Rydin, Y., Davies, M., Davila, J., Hallal, P., Hamilton, I., Lai, K. and Wilkinson, P. (2012) 'Healthy communities', *Local Environment*, 17(5), pp. 553–560. doi: 10. 1080/13549839.2012.681465.

Sandler, I. (2001) 'Quality and Ecology of Adversity as Common Mechanisms of Risk and Resilience', *American Journal of Community Psychology*, 29(1), pp. 19–61. doi: 10.1023/A:1005237110505.

Satterthwaite, D. (2013) 'The political underpinnings of cities' accumulated resilience to climate change', *Environment and Urbanization*, 25(2), pp. 381–391. doi: 10.1177/ 0956247813500902.

Siders, A. R. (2017) 'A role for strategies in urban climate change adaptation planning: Lessons from London'. Regional Environmental Change, pp. 1801–1810. doi: 10.1007/ s10113-017-1153-1.

Slovic, A. D., de Oliveira, M., Biehl, J. and Ribeiro, H. (2016) 'How Can Urban Policies Improve Air Quality and Help Mitigate Global Climate Change: a Systematic Mapping Review', *Journal of Urban Health*, 93(1), pp. 73–95. doi: 10.1007/s11524-015-0007-8.

Teigão dos Santos, F. and Partidário, M. R. (2011) 'SPARK: Strategic Planning Approach for Resilience Keeping', *European Planning Studies*. Routledge, 19(8), pp. 1517–1536. doi: 10.1080/09654313.2011.533515.

Le Treut, H. (2007) 'Historical Overview of Climate Change', *Climate Change 2007: The Physical Science Basis. Contribution of Working Group 1 to the Fourth Assessment Report of the Intergovernmental Panel on Climate Change*. Cambridge University Press. Available at: http://ci.nii.ac.jp/naid/10024874143/en/ (Accessed: 25 March 2018).

United Nations Human Settlements Programme (UN-Habitat) (2016) *World Cities Report 2016 – Urbanization and Development: Emerging Futures*, *International Journal*. doi: 10.1016/S0264-2751(03)00010-6.

Vários (2005) 'Ecosystems and Human well-being: Health Synthesis', *World Health*, p. 63. doi: 10.1196/annals.1439.003.

van de Ven, F., Snep, R., Koole, S., Brolsma, R., van der Brugge, R., Spijker, J. and Vergroesen T. (2016) 'Adaptation Planning Support Toolbox: Measurable performance information based tools for co-creation of resilient, ecosystem-based urban plans with urban designers, decision-makers and stakeholders', *Environmental Science & Policy*, 66, pp. 427–436. doi: 10.1016/j.envsci.2016.06.010.

Walker, B., Holling, C., Carpenter, S. and Kinzig, A. (2004) 'Resilience, Adaptability and Transformability in Social – ecological Systems', *Ecology and Society*, 9(2), p. 5. doi: 10.1103/PhysRevLett.95.258101.

Younger, M., Morrow-Almeida, H., Vindigni, S. and Dannenberg, A. (2018) 'The Built Environment, Climate Change, and Health', *American Journal of Preventive Medicine*. Elsevier, 35(5), pp. 517–526. doi: 10.1016/j.amepre.2008.08.017.

Zanobetti, A., O'Neill, M., Gronlund, C. and Schwartz, J. (2013) 'Susceptibility to Mortality in Weather Extremes: Effect Modification by Personal and Small Area Characteristics In a Multi-City Case-Only Analysis', *Epidemiology* (Cambridge, Mass.), 24(6), pp. 809–819. doi: 10.1097/01.ede.0000434432.06765.91.

2 Governance structures for adaptive and collaborative climate change action

Adaptation, responding to climate change

Building from the discussion in Chapter 1, this chapter discusses adaptive governance and collaborative planning. Due to the recognition that responding to climate change calls for integrated and comprehensive responses, collaborative planning lends itself to developing effective policy. As such, it was employed as a framework for understanding and analysing the policy development process in each city, which was the focus of interviews held with key stakeholders. First it is important to understand the theory behind the practice, to truly gain insights into how cities can or cannot take action on climate change and become resilient.

Having recognised that a threat creates vulnerability and therefore a reason to make a system resilient, the next step is choosing a path: mitigation of the threat or adaptation to the threat (Miller *et al.*, 2010). In the earlier discussion of resilience and its definitions, a case was made for 'change' as a means for achieving resilience. While a viable means of attaining resilience, mitigation policy is focused on preventative measures for addressing climate change (Miller *et al.*, 2010). In the context of climate change and the vulnerability it creates for cities, prevention is an important aspect of policy; however, mitigation does not prepare systems for shocks that may force change in the urban system. Therefore, adaptation policies are increasingly viewed as the approach to take in addressing climate change (Smit and Wandel, 2006; Heltberg, *et al.*, 2009; Pizzo, 2015). More importantly, adaptation actions are often also mitigation. As such, the development of adaptation policy responses to the threats presented by climate change is the focus of this book. Further, climate change is increasingly recognised to be something that is here now, in the present, not in the future. Therefore, this section discusses adaptation, and adaptive governance as a framework for responding to climate change with multiple stakeholders.

Adaptation

Adaptation is a characteristic associated with resilience, which has its roots in the life sciences (Adger, 2006; Smit and Wandel, 2006). To begin a discussion on adaptation it is logical to present its definition in the sciences by returning to Holling's work. Adaptation looks specifically at the ability of an organism to adopt new or use certain inherent characteristics to respond to changes in its environment. Species vary in their genetic make-up, thus some members of species may be at an advantage when their environment changes (Holling, 1973). Their specific genetic expressions and behavioural characteristics may enable them to adapt and survive when their environment changes (Smit and Wandel, 2006). Consequently, their genes that are adapted for survival are passed onto the next generation, while members with the genes not suited to the new environment die off (Smit and Wandel, 2006). The process of adaptation is visible over time in the natural ecosystem. In the context of cities, climate change and social ecosystems, adaptation maintains the principles of survival and response, however, the process is not as 'simple' and straightforward as it is with species in natural environments (Holling, 1973; Walker *et al.*, 2004; Smit and Wandel, 2006; Miller *et al.*, 2010; Cote and Nightingale, 2011).

It is important to consider adaptation by discussing a shift in resilience thinking, the move from 'bounce back' to 'bounce forward' (Davoudi *et al.*, 2012). A state of equilibrium underlies the concept of resilience in ecological systems, thus when faced with shocks the systems 'bounce-back' to their original state (Holling, 1973; Walker *et al.*, 2004; Smit and Wandel, 2006; Miller *et al.*, 2010; Davoudi *et al.*, 2012; Kythreotis and Bristow, 2017). Translating this aspect of resilience to social ecological systems does not account for the system's complexity and ability to change over time. However, even in natural systems there is change, and this evolution to new states is not accounted for in ecological resilience's equilibrium state (Pendall *et al.*, 2010; Davoudi *et al.*, 2012). Evolutionary resilience emerged in response, bringing forth the argument that over time natural ecosystems change in the absence of shocks (Davoudi *et al.*, 2012; Mark, 2013). Therefore, systems can be resilient to threats that are both sudden and progressive (Norris *et al.*, 2008; Miller *et al.*, 2010; Pendall *et al.*, 2010; Davoudi *et al.*, 2012; Mark, 2013; Younger *et al.*, 2018). By broadening the definition of resilience to include aspects of time and change, consideration is given to the ability of systems to 'bounce forward' and evolve into 'better' systems (Pendall *et al.*, 2010; Davoudi *et al.*, 2012).

Where people are concerned, adaptation is focused not on biological changes but rather on the environment around people (Miller *et al.*, 2010; Younger *et al.*, 2018). Adaptation involves the changes people make to the system such that the system is optimised to meet their needs. Adaptation is expressed through the action of adjustment in response to external pressures on the social ecosystem (Adger, 2006; Smit and Wandel, 2006). The changes that occur depend on the type of threat, thus threats may be economic, social, political or scientific in their nature. Ultimately, the change results in a response that enables the system to continue to support humans. For a change to happen there needs to be something to make adaptation necessary.

The issue with adaptation in the context of resilience is its high subjectivity in terms of threat identification: resilience from what and to what (Folke *et al.*,

2002; Walker *et al.*, 2004; Adger, 2006; Miller *et al.*, 2010). Simplification of threats runs the risk of missing information and implementing an inappropriate response; conversely, overstating the complexity of a threat may also impede the response. Uncertainty also affects the response to threats, as it is not clear what the outcomes of a threat will be (Folke *et al.*, 2002; Walker *et al.*, 2004; Adger, 2006; Miller *et al.*, 2010). Predicting such outcomes is far from easy, yet as has been highlighted in the literature it is certain that the outcomes of climate change will be adverse, and as such inaction is not an option (Adger, 2006; Barnett and Adger, 2007; Wilkinson and Wilkinson, 2012). In cities, the threats of climate change and its impacts will vary according to the geographical characteristics and location of each city (Campbell-Lendrum and Corvalàn, 2007; Corburn, 2009; Galvão *et al.*, 2009). The outcomes of the various impacts of climate change are broad and diverse, and the implications of not responding are being demonstrated with the rising frequency and intensity of extreme weather events. Cities are challenged by these events, and by the slower onset impacts of climate change.

Cities must not only be physically resilient but must also promote the physical and psychosocial resilience of people (Turner *et al.*, 2003; Cote and Nightingale, 2011; Pickett *et al.*, 2011; Wilkinson and Wilkinson, 2012). The physical adaptation of the social ecological system may not be sufficient (Miller *et al.*, 2010; Cote and Nightingale, 2011; Rutter, 2012). In other systems, where resilience is also dependent on the species that support that system, all species must be resilient, a characteristic that is determined by their genetics and biology. In other words, resilience embodying adaptation requires that people alter their behaviour to adapt to the changes occurring in their environment to ensure their individual survival and quality of life (Betsill and Bulkeley, 2007; Pickett *et al.*, 2011; Proust *et al.*, 2012). However, the city is a collective effort (Healey, 1998b), and as such its resilience is dependent on the ability of stakeholders to collaborate on actions to respond to the vulnerabilities created by climate change. Therefore, the role of urban policy makers is dual: 1. To create a system that is resilient to climate change and 2. To create a system that fosters behavioural adaptation by people (Turner *et al.*, 2003; Cote and Nightingale, 2011; Pickett *et al.*, 2011; Wilkinson and Wilkinson, 2012). Research has focused on the former, not the latter (Yohe and Tol, 2002). Consequently, cities must work towards addressing means of achieving behavioural adaptation in meaningful ways. This is where identifying a narrative for resilience to climate change can provide insight into effective policy actions, and guide collaborative process led by local governments. The mode of governance in which cities operate is an important and vital aspect of how cities can become resilient. A mode that is rigid can inhibit the uptake of valuable policy and one that is laissez-faire could perpetuate the negative impacts. Finding a mode that is balanced and allows for collaboration is essential.

Adaptive governance

Achieving resilience will require strong policy leadership, the responsibility of which lies in all levels of government (Helm, 2008; Carter, 2011; Geddes *et al.*, 2012; Carter *et al.*, 2015; Duit, 2016; United Nations Human Settlements Programme (UN-Habitat), 2016). However, this is dependent upon determining a mode of governance through which all levels of government can achieve cohesion and consensus on policy actions (Geddes *et al.*, 2012; Proust *et al.*, 2012). Termeer *et al.*, 2010 provided a comparison of models of governance in operation: mono-centric governance, multi-level governance and adaptive governance. Each type of governance has its strengths and weakness. Mono-centric governance places responsibility of policy in the hands of one level of government, resulting in policy being heavily top down (Termeer *et al.*, 2010). The assumption is that one level of government knows the best course of action and therefore should determine how and what policies should be implemented (Helm, 2008). A hierarchy of power divides levels of governments and compartmentalises roles. Connecting levels is achieved via constitutional agreements and laws. Ultimately, the objective is control of society under the assumption that government knows best, beginning with the highest level of government (Helm, 2008; Termeer *et al.*, 2010; Bowen *et al.*, 2012). It is evident that this is not the case in the context of climate change, where various levels of government possess diverse knowledge and expertise and local governments have the knowledge and capacity to respond to climate change due to their proximity to the place-based impacts (Kenzer, 1999; Schulz and Northridge, 2004; Galvão *et al.*, 2009; Rydin *et al.*, 2012).

Multi-level governance emerged in response to mono-centric governance. In the context of multi-level governance policy formation involves building consensus amongst various levels of government and across scales; ultimately sharing responsibility for policy development and taking account of the knowledge and capacities of different levels of government (Bulkeley and Betsill, 2005; Termeer *et al.*, 2010; Bowen *et al.*, 2012). This form of governance is a structural reform, in that it removes the hierarchical nature of mono-centric governance. Yet, it is still encumbered by its focus on equal sharing of power, and its narrow focus on jurisdiction and spatial scales. Policy actions cannot move forward without the consensus of all stakeholders (Bulkeley and Betsill, 2005; Bowen *et al.*, 2012; Watts *et al.*, 2018). Therefore, while multilevel governance is focused on distributing power, and improving the exchange of information and knowledge used to construct policy, there is an absence of flexibility (Bulkeley and Betsill, 2005; Termeer *et al.*, 2010).

Adaptive governance works to address the challenges of multilevel governance by moving towards a model whereby multiple dimensions of policy problems can be acknowledged and encompassed in policy through a dynamic process (Folke, 2007; Termeer *et al.*, 2010; Geddes *et al.*, 2012). Adaptive governance takes a balanced approach that complements the fluctuating nature of the social ecosystem (Folke, 2007; Termeer *et al.*, 2010; Pisano, 2012). Calling for active and dynamic responses, adaptive governance affords responses to threats and vulnerability to climate change to fit immediate and long-term needs. Critically, adaptive governance, as highlighted by Folke (2007), shifts focus away from a unilateral one-dimensional solution to problems that achieve a single state of equilibrium, to a multidimensional focus that regards the multi equilibrium states of social ecosystems (Geddes *et al.*, 2012; Pisano, 2012). Further, adaptive governance approaches give attention to the cross-system influences that can alter equilibriums, thereby emphasising the necessity for dynamic solutions. Policy formation consequently is not a stagnant process, it is responsive and aims for an outcome that is all encompassing and can address multiple problems and achieve stability in multiple states (Folke, 2007; Termeer *et al.*, 2010; Geddes *et al.*, 2012; Pisano, 2012). As such adaptive governance plays a role in the collaborative development and implementation of policy. Further it permits cities to take leadership and responsibility for climate change resilience in an institutional structure that supports knowledge exchange (Rodin, 2014).

Adaptive governance: planning cities collaboratively

> Adaptive Governance assumes a world that is characterized by both continuous and abrupt changes, often with largely unpredictable consequences.
>
> (Termeer *et al.*, 2010)

Planning for resilience in the context of cities involves adaptation. Cities are constantly evolving, developing and growing to better their capacity to provide environments that support life (Rees and Wackernagel, 1996; Ernstson *et al.*, 2010). Adaptation is an integral part of this process of maintaining cities' capacity to sustain human life (Rees and Wackernagel, 1996; Folke, 2006; Rees, 1997; Ernstson *et al.*, 2010; Spirn, 2014). Striving for a resilient city without adaptation fails to take into consideration the function of the city as a promoter and an agent for sustaining human life (Rees and Wackernagel, 1996; Folke, 2006; Ernstson *et al.*, 2010; Spirn, 2014). Lastly, cities bond and connect people together through neighbourhoods, networks, and infrastructure, causing people from different backgrounds to interact each day in ever-changing ways (Zolli and Healy, 2013). As such, planning for a city that is resilient to climate change is about preparing people and preparing the systems that support people in their every day activities (Rees and Wackernagel, 1996; Ernstson *et al.*, 2010).

> Humanity is a major force in global change and shape ecosystem dynamics from local environments to the biosphere.
>
> (Folke, 2006, p. 253)

Climate change is one of the most pressing threats to humans and the environment. Cities and the people that inhabit them are vulnerable to the various effects that climate change has on their daily lives, such as their health (Rydin, 2012; Rydin *et al*, 2012). Occupying a unique space for a body with governing power, a city government has the capacity to connect with individuals on a personal level (Mumford, 1961; Rees and Wackernagel, 1996; Botkin and Beveridge, 1997; Betsill and Bulkeley, 2007; Tol, 2009). Where the challenge and the benefit exist for cities is in moving beyond the physical aspects of adaptation as the sole means of becoming resilient, to investigating and researching the social means for resilience; such as how climate change impacts health and well-being, which in turn has effects on broader aspects of society, namely the economy. This is challenging, yet appealing to ethical and moral motivations for adapting and may provide support for utilising resilience in the social context of climate change (Adger, 2006).

While resilience is an active and innate response to threats by ecosystems in the natural environment, cities as the social ecological system of humans, by contrast, are tasked with creating the responses and adaptations necessary for maintaining all aspects of human life through policies and plans (Botkin and Beveridge, 1997; Turner *et al.*, 2003; Geddes *et al.*, 2012; Poortinga, 2012). To achieve this, cities must first consider their core function, which is to provide high quality living environments that are safe, where people can live, work and be active (Barton, 2009). This core function is achieved through multiple actions via supportive sub-systems: the health system, the economic system, the education system, and the transportation system. Second, cities must consider how the social ecosystem works as a whole in relation to the systems it is comprised of. Adding to this complexity is that cities are tasked with predicting the outcomes of climate change's impacts on these systems and communicating those impacts to a wider audience of stakeholders (Rosenzweig *et al.*, 2010; Castán Broto *et al.*, 2013; Mees, 2017).

Cities can create a reserve of alternative adaptation plans and actions based on possible climate change scenarios (Smit and Wandel, 2006). However, devising plans will involve more than scenario planning based on two probable outcomes, as there are a multitude of variables that interact, leading to multiple outcomes (Carter, 2011; Zimmerman and Faris, 2011; Bowen *et al.*, 2012). Notably, plans and actions for addressing climate change must give consideration to both the positive and negative effects, and the long-term outcomes (Smit and Wandel 2006; Zimmerman and Faris, 2011). *The objective of resilience is to promote the development of policies that cope with, respond to, and adapt to change as opposed to striving for control over change* (Miller *et al.*, 2010). Planning for climate change is also about opportunity, using change for transformation, learning and innovation, as will be demonstrated by the case study cities (Heltberg, *et al.*, 2009; Miller *et al.*, 2010; Carter, 2011; Bowen *et al.*, 2012; Geddes *et al.*, 2012). This also needs to be balanced with practicality.

> Resilience forces us to take the possibility even necessity of failure seriously, and to accept the limits of human knowledge and foresight. It assumes we don't have all the answers, that we'll be surprised, and that we'll make mistakes.
>
> (Zolli and Healy, 2013, p. 16)

For non-man-made ecosystems, resilience and adaptation are continuous processes that happen over time. The process of adaptation in nature is cyclical 'beginning' with: a growth phase/exploitation to threat, a conservation phase, a release phase and a reorganisation phase (Holling, 1973; Folke, 2006). The cycle takes time to reach a stable state. In the ecosystem of the city, that process may not be linear or predictable (Corburn, 2009; Miller *et al.*, 2010; Geddes *et al.*, 2012). However, it still requires time to test the success of measures taken, which in the context of climate change is costly. As urban policy makers formulate their scenarios and accompanying plans and actions, they face the challenge and demand of addressing immediate needs and the unknown in the long term. Dynamic capacity, and re-configurability, can enable city planners and assist in the achievement of formulating policy that balances present and long-term demands (Folke, 2007; Geddes *et al.*, 2012; van de Ven *et al.*, 2016).

Responding to climate change, is a complex process with varying outcomes; as such, adaptation plans need to be dynamic (Rees and Wackernagel, 1996; Ernstson *et al.*, 2010; van de Ven *et al.*, 2016). Restricting a response to a single objective does not account for the nonlinear nature of social ecosystems (Rees and Wackernagel, 1996; Rees, 1997; Ernstson *et al.*, 2010; van de Ven *et al.*, 2016); a system that behaves and reacts to perturbations and threats in 'surprising, nonlinear ways' does not call for predictable linear responses (Zolli and Healy, 2013). Cities need to be open to adapting existing systems, as being restrictive and focused on fixing or creating an entirely new system may only work in the short term, (unless the system genuinely requires an overhaul) (Rees and Wackernagel, 1996; Ernstson *et al.*, 2010; Spirn, 2014). Again, resilience is about the long term, not short-term quick fixes. It is a dynamic process complicated by uncertainty. Yet, uncertainty may be a benefit for innovation and creative problem solving given that multiple causal pathways equates to multiple options. There is value in asking 'what if?'.

Cities in the process of balancing present and future climate change impacts on human vulnerability will be faced with understanding and defining their role in the short and long run (Norris *et al.*, 2008). Under an adaptive governance model there is recognition of the fluidity of the roles of stakeholders and that power is neither monopolised or equally shared but dynamic and dependent on need and expertise (Termeer *et al.,* 20 10; Pisano, 2012). As such, cities, specifically local governments will be challenged with determining their role in the development of policies to adapt to climate change (Folke, 2007; Norris *et al.*, 2008; Galvão *et al.*, 2009; Gotham and Campanella, 2010). It is likely that urban policy makers will need to operate in a range of capacities from mediators, knowledge disseminators, educators, innovators, and integration experts, an important aspect of linking the diverse knowledge on climate change adaptation (Forester, 1999, 2006; Alexander, 2001)

Cities can address climate change through multiple mechanisms. For example, plans and policies can focus on physical system-based approaches that are based on measurable targets, such as reductions in carbon emissions and increased use of sustainable transport options, (modal shift) (Heltberg *et al.*, 2009; Miller *et*

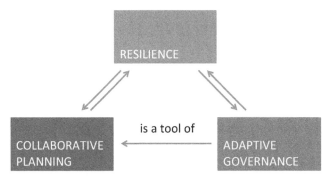

Figure 2.1 Relationships between resilience, collaborative planning and adaptive governance.

al., 2010; Carter, 2011; Zimmerman and Faris, 2011; Bowen *et al.*, 2012; Geddes *et al.*, 2012). The assumptions in this approach are that individual systems do not interact. In reality, systems are inherently intertwined; the effects that a plan or policy has on one system reaches into others (Rees and Wacker- nagel, 1996; Ernstson *et al.*, 2010; van de Ven *et al.*, 2016; Mees, 2017). There are benefits to addressing climate change holistically and at a sub-system level. Planning for climate change will require action from people, and shaping and influencing how people engage in climate change policy and recognise the bene- fits to action will be a challenge for cities and urban policy makers (Rees and Wackernagel, 1996; Ernstson *et al.*, 2010; Foss, 2016; Mees, 2017). Responding to climate change is a collaborative effort, as urban policy makers cannot be solely responsible for making the city resilient, nor can citizens be expected to act alone. Rather, resilience is achieved through collaborative processes, dependent on people working in concert to respond to the vulnerabilities created by climate change and actively contributing to the development and implementa- tion of policy. Identifying a narrative that empowers, enables and moves people to action is necessary for resilience to climate change (this is discussed in the following chapters as part of the discussion on the case study cities).

Defining collaborative planning

It is necessary to understand collaborative planning and its value in the urban context. The quality of urban environments is contingent upon planning prac- tices that maintain quality by responding to the changing demands placed on urban space not only by citizens, but by the environment, and economic and social forces (Healey, 1998a). Historically planning has followed the assumption that planners know what is best for a city (Forester, 1994, 1999; Allmendinger *et al.*, 2003; Friedmann, 2005; Whittemore, 2014). However, in recent decades there has been an increase in citizen-led action to ensure the built environment meets their needs (Goldstein and Butler, 2010; Hawkins and Wang, 2011;

Morton *et al.*, 2012). Conflict arising between citizens and developers is a potential consequence of this; the response to which by urban policy makers would be to engage in dispute resolution to quell discontent. In other words, citizens are placated and their participation in the process is tokenistic: as such their experiential knowledge is disregarded and public participation becomes a 'box ticking' exercise for urban policy makers (Arnstein, 1969; Healey, 1998a; Innes and Booher, 1999; Hawkins and Wang, 2011). Collaborative planning emerged from this as an alternative to legal action and as a response to the demand for 'real' public participation in policy-making processes (Arnstein, 1969; Healey, 1998a; Brand and Gaffikin, 2007; Goldstein and Butler, 2010; Morton *et al.*, 2012).

Collaborative planning has its roots in the work of Habermas, and his concept of ideal speech in the 60s. Habermas opened the door for public participation to become a focus of political process (Alexander, 2001). Communication is central to Habermas' work, specifically his concept of 'ideal speech', the idea that actors (stakeholders) should be able to voice their opinions and be included in the political (and planning) process (Habermas *et al.*, 1974; Alexander, 2001; Whittemore, 2014). Habermas viewed the public sphere as the point where society and state met; it was in this space that the public could interact with policies, by accepting or fighting the policies being put forth (Habermas, 1970; Habermas *et al.*, 1974). Public voice, in his eyes, is critical to policy formation and the accountability of politicians, particularly in the democratic capitalist system (Habermas, 1970; Habermas *et al.*, 1974; Healey, 2002; Whittemore, 2014). Specifically, and what would eventually become an influence on planning practice in the 1980s, is Habermas' attention to the communicative process (Habermas, 1970; Habermas, *et al.*, 1974; Healey, 2002; Whittemore, 2014). Communication is more than just the words that are used in a message; it encompasses aspects of delivery, transmission of the message, and reception of the message (Habermas *et al.*, 1974; Whittemore, 2014). There are rules that govern communication, and ultimately shape understandings of the message (Whittemore, 2014). Arguably, the beginnings of phenomenology influencing planning practice can be seen in Habermas' work and are relevant to today's iteration of communicative planning or rather, collaborative planning. Meaning is a key component in communication, especially shared meaning and understanding in the context of groups. Natural language, Habermas (1964) posits, possesses meaning and shared understandings amongst those who use it, as it has emerged as a means of creating a group identity, and exclusivity. The use of language to effectively disseminate a message and have it understood is termed communicative competence (Habermas, 1970). This ability to understand is central: without understanding the meaning of a message is lost, in turn the ability to act is lost, and communication has failed (Forester, 2012). Considering this, it becomes clear that how resilience is defined in the urban context needs to be debated and inclusive, otherwise the value of resilience is lost, particularly in terms of what the city is becoming resilient to, and how that resilience is maintained and nurtured (adaptation and evolution) (Romero Lankao and Qin, 2011; Davoudi *et al.*, 2012; Rodin, 2014; Kythreotis and Bristow, 2017). Furthermore, it risks becoming a buzzword and thus fails to achieve its purported goal of supporting inclusive growth.

Returning to the context of the public sphere and political debate, for Habermas language used in communication must be sincere, legitimate and truthful, in other words transparent and free of hidden meanings (Whittemore, 2014). However, the challenge with achieving transparent and clear communication is the linguistic histories that actors bring with them (Habermas, 1970; Forester, 2012). This creates a challenge for communication in that 'new' shared meanings need to be created, through clarification of the language being used and the meanings being developed. In the context of planning and public participation, planners need to 'interpret' planning terminology such that it is understood by those involved in the process of plan development (Allmendinger *et al.*, 2003; Forester, 2006, 2012). Without translation, the potential for conflict arises and ultimately leads to policy implementation barriers in processes where collective agreement and action is desired. Clear communication is therefore imperative and requires the development of shared meaning amongst stakeholders.

Emerging from the recognition that communication is a necessary tool in the facilitation of public participation in the planning process, phenomenology came to the fore in planning. While Habermas emphasised the importance of facilitating communication to give voice to stakeholders in the political process; this idea is furthered by Forester to empower planners to see their 'freedom' from political agendas. Forester furthers this idea by delving into the issue of the conflict that can emerge in the communicative process from interpretation of meanings and that can potentially result in misunderstandings (Forester, 1990; Whittemore, 2014). Phenomenology is highly subjective in its nature. It aims to acknowledge various perceptions, emotions and feelings that emerge in the process of learning, and to recognise that individuals learn through a variety of processes and mechanisms, resulting in different perceptions and therefore interpretations of the message being delivered (Whittemore, 2014). For Habermas, this represented a lack of focus, and served only to recognise that learning happens through various mechanisms (Whittemore, 2014). However, recognising that knowledge, when it is acquired and disseminated is highly subjective and at the will of the 'teacher' and 'student', presents an added value for the planning field (Forester, 2012). A key value of phenomenological thought to planning, especially in the context of climate change, is that it forces the consideration that policy solutions can be layered and interconnected, and not be singular in their focus. It offers alternative visual lenses from which to understand policy formation, delivery and evaluation.

Whilst Forester values phenomenology, he also recognises the weaknesses it poses in practice, namely that a phenomenological process cannot be devised for planners to follow as a prescription for engaging stakeholders; rather planners (and urban policy makers) should use the theory of phenomenology as an underlying tool in their practical interactions with stakeholders (Forester, 2012). In other words, planners work dynamically to create shared meanings with stakeholders, and to clarify the meanings behind their objectives and actions (Forester,

1990). This permits planners to reduce the potential for misunderstandings and conflicts, as the development of shared understandings is an ongoing process that is shaped by place-based characteristics. For example, in the context of this research, which is concerned with the development of policy responses to climate change, it is recognised that urban policy makers face a unique challenge. Responses to climate change impacts, as discussed, requires a shared understanding of what resilience to climate change means for all stakeholders (Goldstein *et al.*, 2013). Moreover, the experience of climate impacts will vary depending on the stakeholders, and as such perceptions of appropriate responses will differ. Thus, the challenge for urban policy makers lies in identifying a narrative that unifies and engages stakeholders in the short term and long term. This invariably will be a process that will find planners and urban policy makers encountering conflict and uncertainty, which can add value.

Uncertainty and conflict have the potential to arise, yet under a phenomenological mindset, where acknowledgement of different perspectives is valued, they can contribute positively to the process, rather than hindering it. Healey puts forth the idea that conflict is valuable in the sense that it brings forth different reference points allowing for more comprehensive planning (Healey, 2002, 2003). Conflict is an acknowledgement of difference (Whittemore, 2014). The potential for conflict, and conflict itself, acknowledge the reality that the city has different meanings and expressions for different people, and that the planner is not the sole proprietor of the city, but rather their role is to formulate a cohesive city from the array of imagined cities by citizens (Healey, 2002). Therefore, the city is a collective effort that is the responsibility of planners.

Planners as collaborators

The city is a representation of geographic, social and economic histories; it is constructed over time, with density and layers representing changes in attitudes about how the city should be constructed (Healey, 2002, 2003; Van Assche and Lo, 2011). Planners have at times seen themselves as the sole experts on making a city liveable and healthy, but as has been discussed, the role of the planner has evolved (Forester, 1994, 1999; Yiftachel and Huxley, 2002; Allmendinger, *et al.*; 2010; Whittemore, 2014). The planner does not limit their work to interpreting theory on planning cities and how cities should be built; rather, as Forester (1994 and 1999) argues in his work, the planner is an advocate for citizens and their interests, a step in the democratic process. Planners have the power to facilitate dialogue between citizens and politicians, and with the added value of their expertise, to inform all stakeholders of how a policy can impact a city, a community and a neighbourhood (Healey, 1992). They are interpreting their planning language such that it can be communicated effectively to all stakeholders, who have vested interests that are political or personal (Whittemore, 2014). Forester highlights the skills of planners that enable them to engage with the public: diplomacy, listening, negotiating, acknowledging, mediation, probing, inventing, and facilitating (Forester, 1994, 2006, 2012). In the absence of these skills, planners limit themselves and their work to bureaucratic processes, which may or may not be beneficial to the city and its citizens.

Conversely, a planning process that is heavily guided by bottom-up approaches can be as detrimental as top-down approaches (Allmendinger *et al.*, 2003). For Allmendinger and Tewdwr-Jones (2003), the emphasis on bottom-up engagement undermines the planning profession, as being a professional planner is defined by the acquisition of knowledge that permits their expertise. Collaborative planning's call for the inclusion of pluralistic voices devalues a planner's expertise (Allmendinger *et al.*, 2003). However, the inclusion of stakeholders is intended to strengthen decision-making (Alexander, 2001). The key for planners is to strike a balance between top-down and bottom-up, as well as horizontally, meaning that knowledge can come from experts in other fields, in similar positions (Healey, 1992, 2003). Therefore, finding the 'right' balance for inclusion to achieve successful policy goals and objectives requires that planners carefully consider how to incorporate the objectives and opinions of diverse stakeholders (Healey, 1992; Forester, 1994, 1999). This is invariably a challenge for planners, not only in incorporating the multitude of ideas and perceptions of what should be included in policy that constructs a community, but recognising what adds value and effectively informs the policy process. In other words, planners must discern what knowledge will contribute to policy and the future of the city (Healey, 1992).

Striving to include every stakeholders' 'expertise', planners and policy makers risk producing misinformed policy, just as they could in holding the assumption that their training places them in the position of knowledge-expert on all matters (Forester, 1990, 1999; Healey, 1998a; Alexander, 2001). As such, planners need to find a balance between their theoretical and practical knowledge, with the knowledge of stakeholders. This is a challenge for collaborative planning processes. Forester proposes that planners recognise the planning process as an ongoing opportunity for learning (Forester, 2006). However, learning in this context is not focused on producing a prescribed set of actions that can be repeated; rather the focus is on *how* actions were developed, and *how* problems were solved (Forester, 1994, 2006, 2012). As such, Forester (2006) put forth eight principles for planners to acquire this knowledge and incorporate it into the planning process (Box 2.1).

Forester's objective behind these principles is to change the way knowledge is perceived in the planning community (Forester, 2006). For him, it is not about scientific proofs but the realities of the everyday, where problems and solutions emerge simultaneously. Moreover, it is a means for giving a voice to stakeholders in the process in a constructive manner that effectively contributes to the planning process rather than hinders it. Knowledge is valuable and it does not come only from tried and tested theory, especially in a field that is dynamic and constantly facing new challenges; knowledge is dynamic and its sources are varied (Forester, 1994).

Acquisition of knowledge is achieved through communication between stakeholders, and communication can come in many forms, including conflict. Ideally

---

Box 2.1 Forester's guidelines

- Choose actors, not spectators, intimately engaged with a problem.
- Ask those actors to tell the stories of instructive cases revealing both challenges and opportunities.
- Do not ask the actors 'what did you think about X?' Ask, 'How did you handle X?'
- Get the actor's story with a trajectory.
- Help actors help us: ask for relevant details.
- Ask for practical implications.
- Allow time for reflections and 'lessons learned'.
- Give 'reflection'.

---

conflict is avoided, however, as has been previously discussed, stakeholders arrive at the collaborative process with their own 'language' and their own understandings of concepts and issues (Habermas, 1970; Forester, 1994). Therefore, misunderstandings, miscommunication and conflicts are likely to arise as stakeholders strive to have their voice and opinions heard over others and come to an agreement (Habermas *et al.*, 1974; Healey, 1998b; Forester, 2006).

This could be seen to adversely affect the collaborative process, or alternatively, it can be seen as an opportunity to learn and clarify the language being used to develop policy and communicate policy to the wider public, hence positively shape the collaborative process (Innes, 1996; Healey, 1998a). The differing language used by for example, health professionals and urban planners to describe a public health issue experienced in cities, can result in a proposed policy being written in neutral terminology that is less immersed in the theoretical language of the respective fields, thereby making the policy 'approachable'. Conflict can be an asset in collaborative efforts, as it forces engagement in the process of consensus building. In building consensus, planners acknowledge that stakeholders possess different goals, aims, and values that shape their perspectives on problems (Forester, 1994, 2006; Healey, 1998a; Alexander, 2001). Box 2.2 presents Healey's principles for collaborative planning, and it is evident that conflict and consensus building are tools for planners in the collaborative planning process. For Healey, collaboration is not about 'perfect agreement' as that does not permit the progression of planning debates and the evolution of responses to policy issues. Conflict, as such brings to the fore debates that positively contribute to the long-term process.

Building on the value of conflict, Alexander (2001) imparts a positive perspective on conflict by reframing it as interdependence; in other words, stakeholders need each other to achieve their goals. Therefore, planners work to identify the pragmatic reasons for stakeholders to collaborate through identifying their common interests and working to identify actions. Critically, planners with an objective lens can demonstrate to stakeholders their mutual interdependencies and the benefits of working together (Alexander, 2001). Lastly, and

---

Box 2.2   Healey's principles for collaborative planning (Healey, 1992)

- Planning is an interactive and interpretative process.
- Planning being undertaken among diverse and fluid discourse communities.
- A respectful interpersonal and intercultural discussion methodology.
- Focusing on the 'arenas of struggle' where public discussion occurs and where problems, strategies, tactics, and values are identified, discussed, evaluated and where conflicts are mediated.
- Advancing multifarious claims for different forms and types of policy development.
- Developing a reflective capacity that enables participants to evaluate and re-evaluate.
- Strategic discourses being opened up to be inclusionary of all interested parties, which, in turn, generate new planning discourses.
- Participants in the discourse gaining knowledge of other participants in addition to learning new relations, values and understandings.
- Participants being able to collaborate to change the existing conditions.
- Participants being encouraged to find ways of practically achieving their planning desires, not simply to agree and list their objectives.

---

perhaps most critical to the collaborative process, is addressing conflict between stakeholders through the acknowledgement of their interdependence, which simultaneously addresses the issue of power dynamics (Forester, 1999). Interdependence, unlike dependence, removes the aspect of power or the ability of one stakeholder to sway another stakeholder's opinion through their perceived possession of power in a relationship; interdependence equalises stakeholders through the acknowledgement that stakeholders need each other for their individual and collective success (Innes, 1996, 2004; Healey, 1998a; Alexander, 2001). In the context of resilience building in cities, a particularly critical point is the recognition of interdependence. The systems that make up the urban ecosystem are heavily intertwined and interdependent; one system's inability to adapt and therefore become resilient impacts all other systems adversely, something that has been observed in the wake of extreme weather events.

There is a challenge with conflict that can potentially undermine the collaborative process. Often those that voice their concerns, as in any process, may be the 'loudest' voices, and not necessarily the representative voices (Allmendinger *et al.*, 2003; Flyvbjerg, 2012). Planners need to take care to acknowledge this, as well as recognise that there is also value in the loudest voices in that whilst the opinions voiced may not be fully informed; they present an opportunity (Healey, 1998a; Innes, 2004). How planners achieve this, and if they do, plays a role in the capacity to collaborate. In recognising that those who may be participating in a collaborative process may bring forth what appear to be concerns stemming from a lack of information, they are nonetheless concerns that planners must acknowledge. Therefore, rather than dismissing these ideas, planners and policy makers can use these perspectives as a guide for further investigation of an issue, or as an opportunity to clarify their communication of policy and plans to the public. As Forester (2009) states, 'good processes cannot guarantee good results' meaning that even policies with the best intents, if developed in a vacuum by planners without public participation can fail. Collaborative planning is about learning and engaging in an on-going process of addressing problems and issues in the urban environment that do not have definitive solutions, as there are many factors that will contribute to the evolution of the problem and its perceived solution. Thus, it has evolved into a process whereby planners must effectively negotiate, incorporate, translate and disseminate knowledge, by carefully navigating the processes of identifying participants, and building consensus through the recognition of the interdependent relationships that exist between stakeholders; and finally, sustain the continued engagement of stakeholders, throughout the policy development, implementation, monitoring and evaluation process (Healey, 1998a; Foss, 2016; van de Ven *et al.*, 2016; Mees, 2017). In theory collaborative planning is an ideal form of adaptive governance for addressing climate change, however, in practice the challenge lies in identifying a narrative to engage stakeholders and enable the collaborative development of policy responses to climate change.

Collaborative planning in practice

Acknowledging that public acceptance of policy was dependent on more than informing the public of the policy, the value of citizen engagement and local knowledge came to the fore of planning as an asset for developing plans and policies (Arnstein, 1969; Healey, 1998a; Heywood, 2004; Brand and Gaffikin, 2007; Hawkins and Wang, 2011). This can be seen in the shift towards collaborative planning that has grown and evolved as a response to challenges with public engagement emerging from integrated approaches to planning.

In the North American context, particularly in Canada, integrated community planning has been viewed as a long-term planning process that emphasises public participation in the development of community sustainability plans that has dominated the planning dialogue in the last decade (Heywood, 2004; Goldstein and Butler, 2010; Morton *et al.*, 2012). Globally, this is referred to as comprehensive planning, where the emphasis is placed on considering all aspects of life in the urban environment and how they interact (Innes, 1996; Innes and Booher, 1999; Brand and Gaffikin, 2007; Goldstein and Butler, 2010). Both are focused on engaging the public through focus groups, public meetings, and public consultation to inform the public of the decisions being made by local government; with regards to planning these methods of engagement have been referred to as tokenistic (Arnstein, 1969), as opposed to actively engaging the public in a collaborative process whereby input from the public is sought after and included in policy development (Friedmann, 2005; Agger and Löfgren, 2008; Hawkins and Wang, 2011; Goldstein *et al.*, 2013; Foss, 2016). As such, in practice the transfer of knowledge is top down; and public opinion is taken into consideration once policy is developed and at the implementation stage

(Goldstein and Butler, 2010; Faehnle and Tyrväinen, 2013). Moreover, the assumption with integrated and comprehensive planning is that planners are the experts and therefore, are best suited to guide the policy process and assess the needs of citizens and ensure that they are met through the plan (Alexander, 2001; Heywood, 2004; Goldstein and Butler, 2010; Hawkins and Wang, 2011; Whittemore, 2014). Consequently, planning frameworks sought to engage citizens in theory, but in practice tokenised public involvement and relied on the achievement of targets to determine success; rather than engage in a debate with citizens about policy in a dynamic ongoing process (Arnstein, 1969; Friedmann, 2005; Hawkins and Wang, 2011; Pitt and Bassett, 2014; Foss, 2016; Castán Broto, 2017). Collaborative planning in theory moves to address this challenge with public participation in planning by actively engaging stakeholders in political processes via the creation of partnerships (Arnstein, 1969; Friedmann, 2005).

Historically, planning has based action on 'scientific proofs' as a reason for policy, and the assumption that the investigation of knowledge through the scientific process could predict futures (Krizek *et al.*, 2009; McKay *et al.*, 2011). In short, a one-size-fits-all attitude towards planning however, in practice urban policy makers are faced with addressing the unique traits of the city in which they work, specifically the needs of citizens. Public engagement is an important element of planning that contributes to planners' understandings of citizen needs, as these needs are varied and cannot be predicted by scientific reason (Arnstein, 1969; Tewdwr-Jones and Allmendinger, 1998; Allmendinger, *et al.*, 2003; Friedmann, 2005; Whittemore, 2014). For Allmendinger and Tewdwr-Jones (2003), public participation as it was initially put forth in collaborative planning theory is a challenge due to its attempts to include all voices and the nullification of the planner's expertise, in favour of an idealised form of planning where all participants have an equal say. Critics such as Yiftachel and Huxley (2000) view this as detrimental to the technical practice of planning, as the emphasis on including stakeholders in the planning process removes the credibility of the planning profession. However, their critique presents planning as a field that is solely concerned with the spatial dimensions of the urban environment. In practice, planning is not solely about designing cities that are rooted in theories of how place and spaces should be used, but how people use space to meet their needs. More broadly, planning has evolved to broaden its scope to include social, economic and environmental dimensions. Therefore, in responding to critiques, collaborative planning thinkers have emphasised that in practice collaborative planning calls for a keen awareness of the realities of the context in which it operates (Brand and Gaffikin, 2007; Huang-Lachmann and Lovett, 2016). Critically, it differs from its predecessors in its approach to public engagement and participation, by in practice seeking out opportunities for partnerships with stakeholders to address problems collectively (Healey, 2003, 2004, 2007b; Forester, 2006; Pitt and Bassett, 2014).

Collaborative planning differs from integrated community planning and comprehensive planning in that it is concerned with the process of developing plans (Healey, 1998a; Brand and Gaffikin, 2007; Agger and Löfgren, 2008). Whilst public participation and civic engagement are part of the process, it is specifically the inclusion of stakeholders who add value through expert and experiential knowledge to the planning process that differentiates collaborative planning from its predecessors. Participation is not solely about input, but meaningful and valuable contribution to the formation and implementation of policy and plans through the provision of expertise and knowledge (Arnstein, 1969; Innes, 2004; Agger and Löfgren, 2008; Goldstein and Butler, 2010; Hawkins and Wang, 2011). Additionally, engagement in the process is active not passive. The role of public participation evolves beyond input and feedback, to knowledge providers and active evaluators of the plan's outcomes (Healey, 1998a). Within the collaborative planning process, the role of local government, particularly urban policy makers, shifts from that of experts to facilitators and knowledge integrators (Healey, 1998a; Goldstein and Butler, 2010). Accountability for the outcomes and outputs of the plan lies with all participants in the plan development process. This is guaranteed through the evaluative nature of the collaborative planning process. There is a continuous assessment of the process to guarantee stakeholders are adding value and that this translates into successfully implemented policy that achieves its purported objectives (Healey, 1998a, 2003; Heywood, 2004). The success of a plan is demarcated by the ability to achieve consensus; how consensus is achieved is first understood by understanding the concepts of participation, and then how knowledge acquired from the participation process is exchanged and used.

Healey (1997) developed several key considerations for engaging in collaborative processes. In her 1997 book *Collaborative Planning*, Healey emphasises that the beginnings of collaboration lie in thoroughly exploring who has a stake in an issue, then determining when and where discussions on issues can occur. Next is the 'how': how do discussions occur, and what are the forums and styles used? Healey builds on the work of Habermas and Forester in this area by asking what is the verbal language being used to communicate, (a key focus of Habermas' work) and what is the non-verbal language being used to communicate; in other words, using Forester's focus on the place, location, set-up of a room, and the body language used by stakeholders (Habermas, 1970; Forester, 1994; Healey, 1997, 1998a). How these tools can be used to effectively influence collaboration and hence foster a process that is successful and achieves consensus, contribute to her recommendations for the promotion of policy discourse, which is also influenced by issues of when, where and how this discourse takes place. Planners and urban policy makers need to give careful thought to the stakeholders with whom they engage and how (Healey, 1997). Inevitably, there needs to be the recognition that conflict will arise and that it can serve the policy development process when effectively managed and ultimately clarify the policy objectives such that they are widely accepted, thereby achieving consensus (Innes and Booher, 2004). Agreement on the action to be taken should be documented, according to Healey, as a means of maintaining consensus in the present and future. Healey (1997) notes that agreement is not finality on policy, but rather a starting point for future collaborative processes; in other words, once

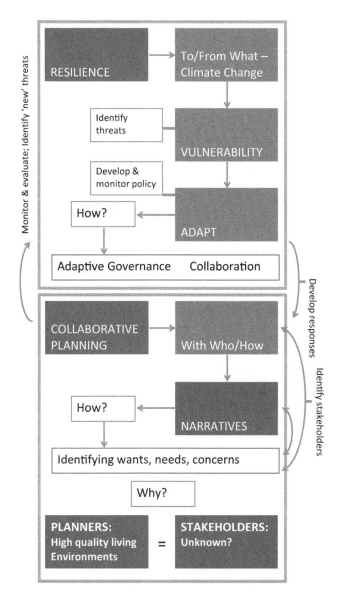

Figure 2.2 Linking resilience and collaborative planning.

consensus is achieved it is not the end of the process. In having documented the process and the outcomes, stakeholders effectively have acknowledged their understanding of the issues being addressed and the actions that they have agreed to, such that in future, if a need arises to re-address the issue, there is a starting point for future debates.

Consensus building

Consensus building is a vital aspect of collaborative planning, and therefore, calls for closer consideration. The term is used in the active voice, typically, not the passive voice, indicative of consensus building being an ongoing process (Innes and Booher, 2004). Innes and Booher (2004) highlight that consensus building is a boundary-less process. It is fluid, continuously adapting and evolving. One process may lead to an outcome, but that outcome may in turn lead into another process (Innes and Booher, 2004). Consensus building offers the opportunity to transform not only the issues that initiated the process, but the stakeholder's perceptions of the problem and their objectives to generate a collective response (Healey, 1998a; Innes and Booher, 1999, 2004; Innes, 2004). As a dynamic process it offers insights into how to facilitate planning and policymaking processes such that they become more inclusive and adaptive. However, achieving consensus building is a process that not unlike other processes faces challenges and conflict in its achievement.

The key difference is that in consensus building the management of the challenges and conflicts that arise is a continual and evolving process (Healey, 1996, 1997, 1998a, 2007a). In the predecessors to collaborative planning, namely comprehensive planning and integrated planning, public participation was an objective, and agreement on an objective to be achieved by policy was the focus (Allmendinger *et al.*, 2003; Burton, 2009; Whittemore, 2014). Stakeholders were engaged in the process but primarily for their opinions or thoughts on the process and outcomes, not their potential as experts, who are able to contribute to the process. Planners still maintained their expert position. In consensus building, there is a focus on dialogue around the issues that a city is facing with stakeholders (Innes, 2004; Forester, 2006; Burton, 2009). The objective is to acquire knowledge and an in depth understanding of the issues (Tewdwr-Jones and Allmendinger, 1998; Healey, 2009). Additionally, there is an emphasis on understanding the varying perspectives on an issue and approaches to addressing the problem, in order to arrive at a jointly devised response. This is where the process faces challenges in the form of conflict and power dynamics (Healey, 1997).

Conflict is often given a negative valuation; however, in the context of consensus building it can add value to the process. How conflict is managed though determines whether or not it is a benefit or a detriment to the process (Healey, 1998a; Innes, 2004). This is connected to the issue of power. Conflict emerges where there is a perception that an individual or a group of individuals possesses power over others, and uses their power to intimidate or sway others to take their position on an issue and subsequently their solution (Healey, 1997; Innes and Booher, 2007). Power in this context can have its origins in various sources from politics, and economics, to knowledge (Allmendinger, 2001). What matters is that there is a perception held by a stakeholder that they have power and that it is acknowledged, and this enables these stakeholders to push their agenda, which may or may not be beneficial to the wider community (Innes and Booher, 2007). Collaborative planning processes rely on consensus building to remove this perceived notion of power by placing the focus on equity thereby removing the perception that one stakeholder has power over the rest. However, Arnstein's (1969) work on public participation, in particular her ladder of citizen participation, draws attention to the issues and risks associated with power, by acknowledging differences between the powerless (those that public participation strives to give power to) and the powerful (those that public participation attempts to take power from). Arnstein (1969) warned planners that tokenistic engagement of citizens in the forms of: informing, consultation and placation, merely masks power, as decisions still lie with power-holders. In their criticism of collaborative planning, Allmendinger and Tewdwr-Jones (2003) echo Arnstein's warning and suggest that in practice stakeholders will still act strategically to assert their power and agendas to a wider audience. Further, Yiftachel and Huxley (2000) argue that the efforts to include stakeholders for the purposes of knowledge acquisition isolate planners from 'knowledge bases from which they should draw inspiration' (p. 338). Therefore, the proposed shift to deliberate and meaningful engagement is undermined by prevailing cultural norms where those with power continue to hold power, which is further assisted by the call for planners to listen and learn from the public (Yiftachel and Huxley, 2002; Allmendinger *et al.*, 2003). Collaborative planning theorists have responded by acknowledging the realities of practice by clarifying the role of conflict.

Inclusionary argumentation, as Healey (2002) terms it, is supported as a means of promoting positive conflict in the absence of power dynamics. The objective is to promote the development of relationships/partnership between stakeholders that enables collective action (Healey, 2002); this is reflective of the final three rungs of Arnstein's ladder: partnership, delegated power and citizen control (Arnstein, 1969). Moreover, it allows for debates and dialogue that lead to effective adaptation of knowledge from various sources to be formed into cohesive policy responses (Shin and Lee, 2017). This is a theoretical ideal that in practice may not be achieved, as there is the potential for power alliances to emerge in the collaborative process. Again, Healey (2002) acknowledges that alliances are likely outcomes in the collaborative planning process, and terms them as entrepreneurial consensus, whereby local alliances arise from shared development agendas. However, in the efforts of planners to build consensus, these alliances can be addressed with the recognition that they represent the soft aspects of policy: values, beliefs and ideals of how things should be (Healey, 2002). These aspects need to be combined with hard aspects of policy formation, which are laws, regulations and duties, how things are in practice (Healey, 2002). Therefore planners have the capacity to address power alliances that emerge in the process by returning the focus to the process as a collective effort, by acknowledging that these alliances have value in that they can inform planners and policy makers of opinions on issues, and therefore be used as knowledge that contributes to the development of policy (Healey, 2002). Critically, the emergence of alliances and struggles for power, present an opportunity for planners to actively build trust, an essential part of consensus building.

Establishing trust with stakeholders in the consensus-building process requires openness; confronting differences that may lead to conflict, and confronting conflict when it arises with honesty and openness allows trust to be developed (Healey, 1997). Openness also allows networks to grow and therefore include more stakeholders in the process and contribute knowledge to the process, leading to increased knowledge resources and intellectual capital from which debates and discussions on issues can emerge. Promoting valuable dialogue between stakeholders that permits new strategies and approaches to develop, an objective of planners in collaborative planning as collaborative processes are intended to increase the quantity and quality of responses available on an issue (Healey, 1997).

However, once initial consensus is achieved at the outset of a collaborative process there remains the challenge of maintaining consensus, as collaboration is an ongoing process so too is consensus building. Maintaining consensus is argued by Healey (1997) to be built on shared agreement to commit to a specific policy outcome. Second, there is the assumption in the initial process of building consensus, that stakeholders have developed a shared identity and culture that binds them and holds them accountable to action (Healey, 1998a; Innes, 2004). However, in spite of this, there is the chance that stakeholders will challenge the agreement. Therefore, maintaining consensus is a necessity. Within this lies the recognition, that stakeholders hold the right to challenge the agreed-upon action. Therefore, dialogue and debate on issues and responses remains open, which is in line with the objective of continuous learning and knowledge exchange in the collaborative process (Healey, 1998a; Innes, 2004). In short, maintaining consensus is dependent on the ability of stakeholders to continually critique and reflect upon issues and responses. While consensus building is one challenge of the collaborative planning process there are others that create challenges and opportunities for planners and urban policy makers.

Limits to collaborative planning

Collaborative planning calls for stakeholders to address problems emerging in the urban environment in meaningful and sustainable ways, this is contingent upon achieving consensus (Innes, 1996; Innes and Booher, 2004; Brand and Gaffikin, 2007; Goldstein and Butler, 2010). However, achieving consensus presents a challenge for collaborative planning and demonstrates the limits to collaborative planning in practice. In the context of participatory planning the assumption is held that all stakeholders have valuable input, in terms of expert and local knowledge of the urban environment, and therefore should be considered. Under the frameworks of integrated community planning and comprehensive planning, high value is placed on public opinion, yet planners still hold the position of experts. Public opinion becomes an assessment tool and a means of verifying that planners are considering all possible outcomes in *their* policy responses (Arnstein, 1969; Whittemore, 2014). Under collaborative planning the role of planners is still that of an expert, but with the added roles of facilitators, knowledge integrators and educators (Forester, 1990, 1994, 2012; Brand and Gaffikin, 2007; Morton *et al.*, 2012), the latter being a critical role in achieving meaningful public participation in the planning process, as educating the public can be a catalyst for dialogue around policy issues and is valuable in narratives for climate change policy (Burton, 2009; Laurian, 2009). Thus, while theory proposes that planners take on diverse roles, in practice the realities of local context may dictate the roles that planners are able to take on, due to institutional structures and histories (Mees, 2017).

In the local context, however, local governments being in tune with the challenges facing their populations are accountable for that knowledge and its value in identifying whom to engage in the collaborative planning process (Healey, 1998a; Innes, 2004; Goldstein and Butler, 2010; Morton *et al.*, 2012; Pitt and Bassett, 2014; Foss, 2016; Mees, 2017). If local governments attempt to follow the lead of other local governments and replicate their processes, there is a risk that the process becomes generic and prescriptive, as opposed to diagnostic and in tune with the local characteristics that create a city's unique identity (Friedmann, 2005). This is also a critique of collaborative planning raised by Yiftachel and Huxley (2000), for whom planning is a context-specific practice that manages the production of space in relation to its history and culture. Having stated this, there are general guidelines for collaboration that local governments can adapt to their contexts. Healey (2001) has put forth recommendations for initiating collaboration. The first priority is to identify an issue of common concern and focus, then to explore who has a stake in the issue, then to identify where discussion and dialogue can occur such that knowledge is exchanged. However, identifying a narrative can be a challenge, as priority is often placed on issues facing a local government, which may stem from institutional regulations. Further, identifying an issue that has a common thread to inspire stakeholders into a collaborative process may be challenging due to history and culture, and other unknown realities of the local context.

It is important to discuss public participation and public engagement; in particular, how they are understood and viewed in the context of this research. (Laurian and Shaw, 2008) in their discussion of public participation define 'participation as a mode of relationship between state and civil society that involves the public in decision making' (Laurian and Shaw, 2008: pp. 294). As has been discussed throughout this chapter, collaborative planning has emerged out of call for planning to move beyond tokenistic engagement. Participation by the public in the planning process is acknowledged to be a central tenet of the planning process, that has evolved as planning theories have called for greater consideration for the impacts of government decisions on citizens' livelihoods (Friedmann, 2005; Laurian, 2009; Davoudi *et al.*, 2012; Flyvbjerg, 2012). Moreover, participation in decision-making is viewed as a strengthening of democracy by giving citizens a voice (Arnstein, 1969; Habermas, 1970; Laurian, 2009). However, as has been shown, public participation and engagement in planning has involved planners seeking input from the public through public meetings, and public hearings. Yet, in the context of achieving resilience to climate change through adaptive governance as discussed, this engagement with the public is an ongoing process that involves collaboration; public participation in the policy development process calls for engagement with citizens such that there is a breadth and depth of understanding of the vulnerabilities that are barriers to resilience for individuals and communities. This will lead to collaboration between policy makers and citizens that results in the development and implementation of policy, and subsequently the evaluation, monitoring and adaptation of these policies. Therefore, public participation in collaborative planning goes beyond workshops and meetings to verify policies that have been developed, but needs to include the public in the process of identifying policy challenges and responses. The challenge, however, is that not every citizen can be included nor will every citizen choose to engage with urban policy makers.

Collaboration calls for the inclusion of stakeholders who add value to the process with their knowledge, expertise and lived experiences; which is then passed on to the public by local government to educate and attain feedback (Innes, 2004; Innes and Booher, 2004; Goldstein and Butler, 2010; Morton *et al.*, 2012). Critically, stakeholders add value to the process by providing a different perspective on an issue with their expertise. Herein lies a challenge for the collaborative planning process: the selection of stakeholders who possess the expertise and knowledge to address the key issues facing a local government. Participatory planning processes can often succumb to the pressures of being all-inclusive, thereby reducing the value of the output and subsequent outcomes (Innes, 2004; Innes and Booher, 2004). Thus, the selection of stakeholders for inclusion in the process is critical to ensuring the quality of the process, and its outcomes.

Conversely, the stakeholder identification process runs the risk of placing value judgments on the knowledge and expertise of individuals and groups able to contribute to meaningful dialogue in the policy development process (Innes, 2004; Goldstein and Butler, 2010; Faehnle and Tyrväinen, 2013; Goldstein *et al.*, 2013; Shin and Lee, 2017). Exclusion can potentially hinder the process at a later stage, just as inclusion of stakeholders whose knowledge expertise may be ill-suited to the policy challenges being addressed can be counter-productive. The collaborative process has evolved to acknowledge this challenge. Within the process, there is the recognition that planning is a dynamic and on-going process that will require the inputs of varying stakeholders (Innes, 2004). Thus, there is flexibility regarding who is included in the process and what stages (Innes, 2004; Goldstein and Butler, 2010).

Even after key stakeholders have been identified, local governments are faced with balancing the power dynamics that will ultimately emerge in a collaborative process and the costs of engaging in the process (Healey, 1998b). Consensus will not be achieved without disagreement (Healey, 1998b; Innes, 2004; Innes and Booher, 2004). This is where public engagement, in meaningful ways can potentially add value to the process. The normative objective of local government is to address the needs of the citizenry, to whom they are accountable via elected processes, and in the case of civil servants their duty to serve the public

(Heywood, 2004; Brand and Gaffikin, 2007; Hawkins and Wang, 2011; Shin and Lee, 2017). Input from the public is important in collaborative planning, especially in the identification of problems that need to be addressed; as it can draw attention to issues of which policy makers were unaware, and highlight potential narratives for collaboration. Moreover, it can serve as a barometer for determining the knowledge that needs to be disseminated into the public realm such that policy comprehension is optimised.

The literature demonstrates the immense value of engaging in comprehensive and participatory planning processes. However, the process is time consuming (Innes, 2004). Local governments need to balance the benefits and costs of engaging in the intensive process in the short run with the long-term benefits (Faehnle and Tyrväinen, 2013). In the time that it takes to complete the process, the challenges facing the urban environment may have progressed and evolved beyond those addressed in the initial plan (Innes, 2004). Further, in the context of climate change planning, time presents a challenge. Adaptation of the urban environment to the impacts of climate change needs to catch up with climate change itself. Therefore, engaging in a comprehensive approach that strives to include all stakeholders is potentially a hindrance in the development of climate change policies. However, collaborative planning processes in theory narrow the scope, and focus on meaningful knowledge and expertise. It is a dynamic and responsive process, that is selective of who is engaged in the process; the objective is not to be all encompassing, but to acquire knowledge from the 'right' sources that benefit and contribute to outputs and outcomes (Agger and Löfgren, 2008; Hawkins and Wang, 2011; Faehnle and Tyrväinen, 2013). The value of the outcomes and outputs, lies in the quality of information gathered, the expertise used in the process. Careful selection of experts reduces the costs of the processes and maximises its utility.

As discussed, collaborative planning is not solely about including everyone and achieving consensus on a plan; rather, it is focused on integrating stakeholder knowledge into the policy development process (Goldstein and Butler, 2010; Morton *et al.*, 2012). Further, collaborative planning is about knowledge gains, and using knowledge to achieve mutual benefits. Power is not in the dynamic, equity in the process is; as the focus is on networking, exchanging expertise to collaboratively address a policy issue (Heywood, 2004; Agger and Löfgren, 2008; Faehnle and Tyrväinen, 2013). While conflict may arise, it is a valuable asset in expanding knowledge and producing cohesive and comprehensive policy. Debates on key policy issues promote discussion and therefore active problem solving, an important characteristic in addressing climate change in urban environments

Another consideration for collaborative planning processes, that was briefly mentioned, is the temporal nature of the process. As has been discussed, collaborative planning is an ongoing process, where issues lead to actions and outcomes, which in turn produce new points of collaboration (Innes, 1996, 2004, Healey, 1997, 1998b). It is a dynamic process. In the discussion of consensus building, the issue of maintaining consensus was presented. As consensus building is an aspect of collaboration, it follows that maintaining interest in the collaborative process is also a concern (Allmendinger, 2002) In the overall process, the willingness to maintain the action of collaborating is subject to the willingness of stakeholders to continue to engage in the process with urban policy makers (Allmendinger, 2002). Engagement can be influenced by various factors depending on the background of the stakeholder. For politicians, their engagement is likely to follow political cycles and may be dependent on their likelihood of maintaining their political positions (Healey, 1997). For citizens, it may be a matter of interest and their sense of contribution (Healey, 1997). If perhaps citizens perceive that their ideas are not being included, or their values conflict they perhaps may choose to discontinue their participation in the process. Further, considering the proliferation of social media and the evolution of technology this may have implications for the ways in which citizens engage with government. In the context of this research, the rise of 'smart' cities, where technology is employed to address urban challenges and aid governments in the delivery of services, i.e. e-government, technology presents both opportunities and risks for policy makers, particularly in the realm of engagement. The local authorities of Dublin have already embarked on a smart cities initiative, while in Canada cities across the country are competing for Federal Government funding to develop their smart cities initiatives. For planners, who are assumed to be the initiators and drivers of collaborative process, their continued engagement can be affected by numerous factors from: political changes and funding to ultimately their perceptions of the success of the process (Healey, 1997). Ultimately, collaborative planning is a long-term process that has built on the experiences of previous planning practices, its success in yielding policy that will address the challenges that cities face now and in the future is still being understood.

An operational framework for developing climate change resilience policy

As mentioned collaborative planning was the framework used to analyse the formulation of policy that addresses the impacts of climate change in the urban environment. Collaborative planning presents itself as a viable tool; that can inform and guide the policy development process, especially for local governments operating under a mode of adaptive governance (Pitt and Bassett, 2014). As adaptive governance calls for adaptability in the actions and roles of government in the policy making process, collaborative planning provides a complementary tool for achieving the objectives of adaptive governance (Agger and Löfgren, 2008; Goldstein and Butler, 2010; Faehnle and Tyrväinen, 2013; van de Ven *et al.*, 2016). As a dynamic process, collaborative planning can potentially enable the formulation of resilience-based climate change adaptation policy. Further, the process of collaborative planning is reflective and evaluative; continuous assessment of outputs and outcomes are critical (Morton *et al.*, 2012; Faehnle and Tyrväinen, 2013). In other words, adapting and responding to the changes that emerge and evolve in the policy context is a priority.

Given a narrative from which to collaborate with meaning and value, cities can develop climate resilience policies that are effective responses. There are potentially several avenues through which urban policy makers can collaborate with experts in a range of fields and respond to climate change. How cities identify these narratives and the avenues is likely to depend on a city's unique attributes and characteristics. Embarking on a collaborative process though, as has been discussed, is not a prescriptive process as previous planning practices have been. That said, there are general considerations that can be given to the process. Healey's (1997) guidelines have been discussed above (Box 2.2): below are those put forth by Faehnle and Tyrvainen (2013), based on their evaluation of collaborative processes in practice. Their work is in line with the endeavour to demonstrate that identifying narratives that support the collaborative development of resilience-based climate change policy will enable the development of a net of policies that achieve resilience to climate change in urban environments in the long run (Rodin, 2014). In their criteria for collaborative process, they outline the following priorities:

- Set knowledge building as the priority.
- Take into account stakeholder perspectives.
- Take into account the administrative setting.

(Faehnle and Tyrväinen, 2013)

The outcome then to be achieved and evaluated is the decision to develop policies that have been informed by the knowledge gained in the process of consultation. In short, grounded policy that encompasses the shared values and objectives of stakeholders and is achieved by a process rooted in sound consensus building.

Considering these priorities and the guidelines for planners put forth by Forester (Box 2.1) and Healey (Box 2.2), it is evident that collaborative processes require leadership that is able to guide the process in an equitable manner. Thus, while collaboration is about the inclusion of stakeholders, it is dependent on the skills of planners and policy makers to balance various roles.

The role of policy makers and planners in collaborative planning for climate change

For collaborative processes in the urban environment clarity of roles is important, as the success of the process is dependent on the building of consensus on issues and how to address the issues. A clear understanding of the roles of all stakeholders is needed. Throughout this chapter it has been stated that all stakeholders have value in the process and an equitable say. However, the planner plays a critical role in the process; their role has been discussed in Forester's work.

Forester (1994 and 1999) highlights that whilst planners are experts on the urban environment based on their theoretical knowledge, in practice their job is more than translating theoretical understandings of planning into practice. They are in the collaborative process simultaneously mediators, negotiators, translators, leaders, advocates, teachers and students. The ability to adapt and switch between these roles is critical to a planner's success (Forester, 1994, 1999, 2012). Forester consistently emphasises that an effective planner can read situations and suggests alternatives for responding. His advice for planners emerges from the recognition that while democratic processes aimed at including stakeholders are valuable, they can be messy and unpredictable. In other words, while theory suggests action based on an ideal world, practice operates in reality, where planners are tasked with getting things done (Forester, 1994).

Planners and policy makers will be faced with stakeholders who may be rational, however as Forester (1990 and 1994) highlights, these individuals and groups are not all knowing. They will have feelings, and they will possess histories and memories, made up of suffering, risks, losses, betrayals that they may perceive to be the fault/responsibility of planners. Failure to acknowledge these histories can hinder the collaborative process, just as dwelling on past 'wrongs' can. Planners face the challenge of acknowledging past perceived wrongs, present issues and future action (and potential issues). The key here lies in acknowledgement and using the power of acknowledgment to build trust with stakeholders; by first acquiring knowledge on issues, then identifying common ground from which all stakeholders can agree to move forward with policy actions. Therefore, the planner engages in diplomacy to achieve practical action. Forester (1994) suggests this is achieved through a mindset of 'learning'. Creating opportunities for stakeholders to teach planners about the ways issues impact them, which can be through formal or informal channels: public meetings, drinks, social media, face-to-face, and third parties, are a few of the suggested means of engagement (Healey, 1997, 1998b; Forester, 2012). The objective is to learn and acquire knowledge on what are the perceived threats and vulnerabilities and how these issues can be addressed effectively in local political contexts (Forester, 1994; Allmendinger, 2002; Allmendinger *et al.*, 2003).

Whilst collaborative planning process in theory ideally strives for the removal of power in favour of democracy, there is still power at play. There is the possibility of power dynamics emerging through various mediums, which were discussed in the section on consensus building. For example, as participation is emphasised to be a democratic and equitable process, there is the inherent risk that the 'loudest' voices are heard (Allmendinger, 2002). These are not necessarily informed voices (Habermas *et al.*, 1974). However, recognising that a process is democratic presents an opportunity for planners to disseminate knowledge such that voters make informed votes and make decisions for or against a policy reformation based on acquired knowledge. An emphasis of Forester's work is that planners should be conscious of the words they use in posing questions to stakeholders and in delivering their message to stakeholders (Forester, 1994, 1999). The words they use will be guided by process and ultimately evolve throughout the process, as planners are continuously building meaning with stakeholders to achieve collaboration and consensus. This is a process of exploration and discovery for planners and stakeholders alike with the goal of building a resilient city which is demonstrated by the cities discussed, in the following chapters.

References

Adger, W. N. (2006) 'Vulnerability', *Global Environmental Change*. Pergamon, 16(3), pp. 268–281. doi: 10.1016/J.GLOENVCHA.2006.02.006.

Agger, A. and Löfgren, K. (2008) 'Democratic Assessment of Collaborative Planning Processes', *Planning Theory*, 7(2), pp. 145–164. doi: 10.1177/1473095208090432.

Alexander, E. R. (2001) 'The Planner-Prince: Interdependence, Rationalities and Post-communicative Practice', *Planning Theory & Practice*. Routledge, 2(3), pp. 311–324. doi: 10.1080/14649350120096848.

Allmendinger, P. (2002) *Planning in Postmodern Times*. Taylor & Francis (RTPI Library Series). Available at: https://books.google.ie/books?id=nt2AAgAAQBAJ.

Allmendinger, P., Tewdwr-Jones, M. and Morphet, J. (2003) 'Public Scrutiny, Standards and the Planning System: Assessing Professional Values within a Modernized Local Government', *Public Administration*, 81(4), pp. 761–780. doi: 10.1111/j.0033-3298.2003.00370.x.

Arnstein, S. R. (1969) 'A Ladder Of Citizen Participation', *Journal of the American Institute of Planners*. Routledge, 35(4), pp. 216–224. doi: 10.1080/01944366908977225.

Van Assche, K. and Lo, M. C. (2011) 'Planning, preservation and place branding: A tale of sharing assets and narratives', *Place Branding and Public Diplomacy*, 7(2), pp. 116–126. doi: 10.1057/pb.2011.11.

Barnett, J. and Adger, W. N. (2007) 'Climate change, human security and violent conflict', *Political Geography*. Pergamon, 26(6), pp. 639–655. doi: 10.1016/J.POLGEO.2007.03.003.

Barton, H. (2009) 'Land use planning and health and well-being', *Land Use Policy*. Pergamon, 26, pp. S115–S123. doi: 10.1016/J.LANDUSEPOL.2009.09.008.

Betsill, M. and Bulkeley, H. (2007) 'Looking Back and Thinking Ahead: A Decade of Cities and Climate Change Research', *Local Environment*. Routledge, 12(5), pp. 447–456. doi: 10.1080/13549830701659683.

Botkin, D. B. and Beveridge, C. E. (1997) 'Cities as environments', *Urban Ecosystems*, 1(1), pp. 3–19. doi: 10.1023/A:1014354923367.

Bowen, K. J., Friel, S., Ebi, K., Butler, C., Miller, F. and McMichael, A. (2012) 'Governing for a Healthy Population: Towards an Understanding of How Decision-Making Will Determine Our Global Health in a Changing Climate', *International Journal of Environmental Research and Public Health*, 9(1), pp. 55–72. doi: 10.3390/ijerph9010055.

Brand, R. and Gaffikin, F. (2007) 'Collaborative Planning in an Uncollaborative World', *Planning Theory*. SAGE Publications, 6(3), pp. 282–313. doi: 10.1177/1473095207082036.

Bulkeley, H. and Betsill, M. (2005) 'Rethinking Sustainable Cities: Multilevel Governance and the "Urban" Politics of Climate Change', *Environmental Politics*. Routledge, 14(1), pp. 42–63. doi: 10.1080/0964401042000310178.

Burton, P. (2009) 'Conceptual, Theoretical and Practical Issues in Measuring the Benefits of Public Participation', *Evaluation*. SAGE Publications Ltd, 15(3), pp. 263–284. doi: 10.1177/1356389009105881.

Campbell-Lendrum, D. and Corvalàn, C. (2007) 'Climate Change and Developing-Country Cities: Implications For Environmental Health and Equity', 84(1), pp. 109–117. doi: 10.1007/s11524-007-9170-x.

Carter, J. G. (2011) 'Climate change adaptation in European cities', *Current Opinion in Environmental Sustainability*. Elsevier, 3(3), pp. 193–198. doi: 10.1016/J.COSUST. 2010.12.015.

Carter, J. G., Cavan, G., Connelly, A., Guy, S., Handley, J. and Kazmierczak, A. (2015) 'Climate change and the city: Building capacity for urban adaptation', *Progress in Planning*, 95, pp. 1–66. doi: 10.1016/j.progress.2013.08.001.

Castán Broto, V. (2017) 'Urban Governance and the Politics of Climate change', *World Development*, 93, pp. 1–15. doi: 10.1016/j.worlddev.2016.12.031.

Castán Broto, V., Oballa, B. and Junior, P. (2013) 'Governing climate change for a just city: challenges and lessons from Maputo, Mozambique', *Local Environment*, 18 (January 2015), pp. 678–704. doi: 10.1080/13549839.2013.801573.

Corburn, J. (2009) 'Cities, Climate Change and Urban Heat Island Mitigation: Localising Global Environmental Science', *Urban Studies*, 46(2), pp. 413–427. doi: 10.1177/00 42098008099361.

Cote, M. and Nightingale, A. J. (2011) 'Resilience thinking meets social theory: Situating social change in socio-ecological systems (SES) research', *Progress in Human Geography*. SAGE Publications Ltd, 36(4), pp. 475–489. doi: 10.1177/0309132511425708.

Davoudi, S., Shaw, K., Haider, L., Quinlan, A., Peterson, G., Wilkinson, C., Fünfgeld, H., McEvoy, D. and Porter, L. (2012) 'Resilience: A Bridging Concept or a Dead End? "Reframing" Resilience: Challenges for Planning Theory and Practice Interacting Traps: Resilience Assessment of a Pasture Management System in Northern Afghanistan Urban Resilience: What Does it Mean in Planning Practice?', *Planning Theory and Practice*, 13(2), pp. 299–333. doi: 10.1080/14649357.2012.677124.

Duit, A. (2016) 'Resilience Thinking: Lessons for Public Administration', *Public Administration*, 94(2), pp. 364–380. doi: 10.1111/padm.12182.

Ernstson, H., Leeuw, S., Redman, C., Meffert, D., Davis, G., Alfsen, C., Elmqvist, T., Orleans, Á. and Town, Á. (2010) 'Urban Transitions: On Urban Resilience and Human-Dominated Ecosystems', pp. 531–545. doi: 10.1007/s13280-010-0081-9.

Faehnle, M. and Tyrväinen, L. (2013) 'A framework for evaluating and designing collaborative planning', *Land Use Policy*. Pergamon, 34, pp. 332–341. doi: 10.1016/J. LANDUSEPOL.2013.04.006.

Flyvbjerg, B. (2012) 'Why Mass Media Matter to Planning Research: The Case of Megaprojects', *Journal of Planning Education and Research*. SAGE Publications Inc, 32(2), pp. 169–181. doi: 10.1177/0739456X12441950.

Folke, C., Carpenter, S., Elmqvist, T., Gunderson, L. and Walker B. (2002) 'Resilience and Sustainable Development: Building Adaptive Capacity in a World of', 31(5), pp. 437–440. doi: 10.1579/0044-7447-31.5.437.

Folke, C. (2006) 'Resilience: The emergence of a perspective for social–ecological systems analyses', *Global Environmental Change*. Pergamon, 16(3), pp. 253–267. doi: 10.1016/J.GLOENVCHA.2006.04.002.

Folke, C. (2007) 'Social-ecological systems and adaptive governance of the commons', *Ecological Research*, 22(1), pp. 14–15. doi: 10.1007/s11284-006-0074-0.

Forester, J. (1990) 'NO PLANNING OR ADMINISTRATION WITHOUT PHENOMENOLOGY?', *Public Administration Quarterly*. SPAEF, 14(1), pp. 55–65. Available at: www.jstor.org/stable/40861466.

Forester, J. (1994) 'Bridging Interests and Community: Advocacy Planning and the Challenges of Deliberative Democracy', *Journal of the American Planning Association*. Routledge, 60(2), pp. 153–158. doi: 10.1080/01944369408975567.

Forester, J. (1999) 'Reflections on the future understanding of planning practice', *International Planning Studies*. Routledge, 4(2), pp. 175–193. doi: 10.1080/13563479 908721734.

Forester, J. (2006) 'Exploring urban practice in a democratising society: opportunities, techniques and challenges', *Development Southern Africa*. Routledge, 23(5), pp. 569–586. doi: 10.1080/03768350601021814.

Forester, J. (2012) 'Learning to Improve Practice: Lessons from Practice Stories and Practitioners' Own Discourse Analyses (or Why Only the Loons Show Up)', *Planning Theory & Practice*. Routledge, 13(1), pp. 11–26. doi: 10.1080/14649357.2012.649905.

Foss, A. (2016) 'Divergent responses to sustainability and climate change planning: The role of politics, cultural frames and public participation', *Urban Studies*. SAGE Publications Ltd, 55(2), pp. 332–348. doi: 10.1177/0042098016651554.

Friedmann, J. (2005) 'Globalization and the emerging culture of planning', *Progress in Planning*. Pergamon, 64(3), pp. 183–234. doi: 10.1016/J.PROGRESS.2005.05.001.

Galvão, L. A. C., Edwards, S., Corvalan, C., Fortune, K. and Akerman, M. (2009) 'Climate change and social determinants of health: two interlinked agendas', *Global Health Promotion*, 16(1_suppl), pp. 81–84. doi: 10.1177/1757975909103761.

Geddes, A., Adger, W., Arnell, N., Black, R. and Thomas, D. (2012) 'Migration, Environmental Change, and the "Challenges of Governance"', *Environment and Planning C: Government and Policy*. SAGE Publications Ltd STM, 30(6), pp. 951–967. doi: 10. 1068/c3006ed.

Goldstein, B. E., Wessells, A., Leiano, R. and Butler, W. (2013) 'Narrating Resilience: Transforming Urban Systems Through Collaborative Storytelling', *Urban Studies*. SAGE Publications Ltd, 52(7), pp. 1285–1303. doi: 10.1177/0042098013505653.

Goldstein, B. E. and Butler, W. H. (2010) 'Expanding the Scope and Impact of Collaborative Planning', *Journal of the American Planning Association*. Routledge, 76(2), pp. 238–249. doi: 10.1080/01944361003646463.

Gotham, K. F. and Campanella, R. (2010) 'Toward a Research Agenda on Transformative Resilience: Challenges and Opportunities for Post-Trauma Urban Ecosystems', *Critical Planning*, Summer (December), pp. 9–23.

Habermas, J. (1964) 'The Public Sphere: An Encyclopedia Article', *New German Critique* 3, pp. 49-55

Habermas, J. (1970) 'Towards a theory of communicative competence', *Inquiry*. Routledge, 13(1–4), pp. 360–375. doi: 10.1080/00201747008601597.

Habermas, J., Lennox, S. and Lennox, F. (1974) 'The Public Sphere: An Encyclopedia Article (1964)', *New German Critique*. Duke University Press, (3), pp. 49–55. doi: 10.2307/487737.

Hawkins, C. V and Wang, X. (2011) 'Sustainable Development Governance: Citizen Participation and Support Networks in Local Sustainability Initiatives', *Public Works Management & Policy*. SAGE Publications Inc, 17(1), pp. 7–29. doi: 10.1177/10877 24X11429045.

Healey, P. (1992) 'Planning through debate: the communicative turn in planning theory', *Town Planning Review*, 63(2), p. 143. doi: 10.3828/tpr.63.2.422x602303814821.

Healey, P. (1996) 'The Communicative Turn in Planning Theory and its Implications for Spatial Strategy Formation', *Environment and Planning B: Planning and Design*, 23(2), pp. 217–234. doi: 10.1068/b230217.

Healey, P. (1997) *Collaborative Planning: Shaping Places in Fragmented Societies*. UBC Press (Planning, environment, cities). Available at: https://books.google.ie/books?id= psW_hMb3AH8C.

Healey, P. (1998a) 'Building Institutional Capacity through Collaborative Approaches to Urban Planning', *Environment and Planning A: Economy and Space*. SAGE Publications Ltd, 30(9), pp. 1531–1546. doi: 10.1068/a301531.

Healey, P. (1998b) 'Collaborative planning in a stakeholder society', *Town Planning Review*, 69(1), p. 1. doi: 10.3828/tpr.69.1.h651u2327m86326p.

Healey, P. (2002) 'On Creating the "City" as a Collective Resource', *Urban Studies*, 39(10), pp. 1777–1792. doi: 10.1080/0042098022000002957.

Healey, P. (2003) 'Collaborative Planning in Perspective', *Planning Theory*, 2(2), pp. 101–123. doi: 10.1177/14730952030022002.

Healey, P. (2004) 'Creativity and Urban Governance', *disP – The Planning Review*. Routledge, 40(158), pp. 11–20. doi: 10.1080/02513625.2004.10556888.

Healey, P. (2007a) 'Cities where planning is valued ...', *Planning Theory & Practice*. Routledge, 8(3), pp. 287–291. doi: 10.1080/14649350701531896.

Healey, P. (2007b) 'On the Social Nature of Planning', *Planning Theory & Practice*. Routledge, 8(2), pp. 133–136. doi: 10.1080/14649350701324342.

Healey, P. (2009) 'In Search of the "Strategic" in Spatial Strategy Making', *Planning Theory & Practice*. Routledge, 10(4), pp. 439–457. doi: 10.1080/14649350903417191.

Helm, D. (2008) 'Climate-change policy: why has so little been achieved?', *Oxford Review of Economic Policy*, 24(2), pp. 211–238. doi: 10.1093/oxrep/grn014.

Heltberg, R., Siegel, P. B. and Jorgensen, S. L. (2009) 'Addressing human vulnerability to climate change: Toward a "no-regrets" approach', *Global Environmental Change*. Pergamon, 19(1), pp. 89–99. doi: 10.1016/J.GLOENVCHA.2008.11.003.

Heywood, P. (2004) 'Collaborative community planning', *Australian Planner*. Routledge, 41(3), pp. 30–34. doi: 10.1080/07293682.2004.9982367.

Holling, C. S. (1973) 'Resilience and Stability of Ecological Systems', *Annual Review of Ecology and Systematics*, 4(1), pp. 1–23. doi: 10.1146/annurev.es.04.110173. 000245.

Huang-Lachmann, J. T. and Lovett, J. C. (2016) 'How cities prepare for climate change: Comparing Hamburg and Rotterdam', *Cities*. Elsevier B.V., 54, pp. 36–44. doi: 10. 1016/j.cities.2015.11.001.

Innes, J. E. (1996) 'Planning Through Consensus Building: A New View of the Comprehensive Planning Ideal', *Journal of the American Planning Association*. Routledge, 62(4), pp. 460–472. doi: 10.1080/01944369608975712.

Innes, J. E. (2004) 'Consensus Building: Clarifications for the Critics', *Planning Theory*. SAGE Publications, 3(1), pp. 5–20. doi: 10.1177/1473095204042315.

Innes, J. E. and Booher, D. E. (1999) 'Consensus Building as Role Playing and Bricolage', *Journal of the American Planning Association*. Routledge, 65(1), pp. 9–26. doi: 10.1080/01944369908976031.

Innes, J. E. and Booher, D. E. (2004) 'Reframing public participation: strategies for the 21st century', *Planning Theory & Practice*. Routledge, 5(4), pp. 419–436. doi: 10. 1080/1464935042000293170.

Kenzer, M. (1999) 'Healthy cities: a guide to the literature', 11(1), pp. 201–220.

Krizek, K., Forsyth, A. and Slotterback, C. S. (2009) 'Is There a Role for Evidence-Based Practice in Urban Planning and Policy?', *Planning Theory & Practice*. Routledge, 10(4), pp. 459–478. doi: 10.1080/14649350903417241.

Kythreotis, A. P. and Bristow, G. I. (2017) 'The "resilience trap": exploring the practical utility of resilience for climate change adaptation in UK city-regions', *Regional Studies*. Routledge, 51(10), pp. 1530–1541. doi: 10.1080/00343404.2016.1200719.

Laurian, L. (2009) 'Trust in planning: Theoretical and practical considerations for participatory and deliberative planning', *Planning Theory and Practice*, 10(3), pp. 369–391. doi: 10.1080/14649350903229810.

Laurian, L. and Shaw, M. M. (2008) 'Evaluation of Public Participation: The Practices of Certified Planners', *Journal of Planning Education and Research*. SAGE Publications Inc, 28(3), pp. 293–309. doi: 10.1177/0739456X08326532.

Mark, S. (2013) 'Resilience: a Conceptual Lens for Rural Studies?', *Geography Compass*, 7(9), pp. 597–610. doi: 10.1111/gec3.12066.

McKay, S., Murray, M. and Hui, L. P. (2011) 'Pitfalls in Strategic Planning: Lessons for Legitimacy', *Space and Polity*. Routledge, 15(2), pp. 107–124. doi: 10.1080/13562576. 2011.625222.

Mees, H. (2017) 'Local governments in the driving seat? A comparative analysis of public and private responsibilities for adaptation to climate change in European and North-American cities', *Journal of Environmental Policy & Planning*. Routledge, 19(4), pp. 374–390. doi: 10.1080/1523908X.2016.1223540.

Miller, F., Osbahr, H., Boyd, E., Thomalla, F., Bharwani, S., Ziervogel, G., Walker, B., Birkmann, J., Van der Leeuw, S., Rockström, J., Hinkel, J., Downing, T., Folke, C. and Nelson D (2010) 'Resilience and vulnerability: Complementary or conflicting concepts?', *Ecology and Society*, 15(3). doi: 10.5751/ES-03378-150311.

Morton, C., Gunton, T. I. and Day, J. C. (2012) 'Engaging aboriginal populations in collaborative planning: an evaluation of a two-tiered collaborative planning model for land and resource management', *Journal of Environmental Planning and Management*. Routledge, 55(4), pp. 507–523. doi: 10.1080/09640568.2011.613592.

Mumford, L. (1961) *The City in History. Its Origins, Its Transformations, and Its Prospects*, New York (Harcourt, Brace & World) 1961.

Norris, F. H., Stevens, S., Pfefferbaum, B., Wyche, K. and Pfefferbaum, R. (2008) 'Community Resilience as a Metaphor, Theory, Set of Capacities, and Strategy for Disaster Readiness', *American Journal of Community Psychology*, 41(1–2), pp. 127–150. doi: 10.1007/s10464-007-9156-6.

Pendall, R., Foster, K. A. and Cowell, M. (2010) 'Resilience and regions: building understanding of the metaphor', *Cambridge Journal of Regions, Economy and Society*, 3(1), pp. 71–84. doi: 10.1093/cjres/rsp028.

Pickett, S. T. A., Buckley, G., Kaushal, S. and Williams, Y. (2011) 'Social-ecological science in the humane metropolis', *Urban Ecosystems*, 14(3), pp. 319–339. doi: 10. 1007/s11252-011-0166-7.

Pisano, U. (2012) 'Resilience and Sustainable Development: Theory of resilience, systems thinking and adaptive governance', *ESDN Quarterly Report*, (September), p. 51. doi: 10.1017/S1355770X06003020.

Pitt, D. and Bassett, E. (2014) 'Innovation and the Role of Collaborative Planning in Local Clean Energy Policy', *Environmental Policy and Governance*, 24(6), pp. 377–390. doi: 10.1002/eet.1653.

Pizzo, B. (2015) 'Problematizing resilience: Implications for planning theory and practice', *Cities*, 43, pp. 133–140. doi: https://doi.org/10.1016/j.cities.2014.11.015.

Poortinga, W. (2012) 'Community resilience and health: The role of bonding, bridging, and linking aspects of social capital', *Health & Place*. Pergamon, 18(2), pp. 286–295. doi: 10.1016/J.HEALTHPLACE.2011.09.017.

Proust, K., Newell, B., Brown, H., Capon, A., Browne, C., Burton, A., Dixon, J., Mu, L. and Zarafu, M. (2012) 'Human health and climate change: Leverage points for adaptation in urban environments', *International Journal of Environmental Research and Public Health*, 9(6), pp. 2134–2158. doi: 10.3390/ijerph9062134.

Rees, W.E (1997). 'Urban Ecosystems the human dimension' *Urban Ecosystems* 1 pp. 63–75. https://doi.org/10.1023/A:1014380105620.Rees, W. and Wackernagel, M. (1996) 'Urban Ecological Footprints: Why Cities Cannot Be Sustainable – and Why They Are a Key To Sustainability', *Environmental Impact Assessment Review*, 16(96), pp. 223–248.

Rodin, J. (2014) *The Resilience Dividend: Being Strong in a World Where Things Go Wrong.* Public Affairs. Available at: https://books.google.ie/books?id=E7GMAwAAQBAJ.

Romero Lankao, P. and Qin, H. (2011) 'Conceptualizing urban vulnerability to global climate and environmental change', *Current Opinion in Environmental Sustainability*. Elsevier, 3(3), pp. 142–149. doi: 10.1016/J.COSUST.2010.12.016.

Rosenzweig, C., Solecki, W., Hammer, S. and Mehrotra, S. (2010) 'Cities lead the way in climate-change action', *Nature*, 467(7318), pp. 909–911. doi: 10.1038/467909a.

Rutter, M. (2012) 'Resilience as a dynamic concept', *Development and Psychopathology*. Cambridge University Press, 24(2), pp. 335–344. doi: 10.1017/S0954579412000028.

Rydin, Y. (2012) 'Healthy cities and planning', *The Planning Review*, 83(4), pp. xiii–xviii

Rydin, Y., Davies, M., Dávila, J. D., Hallal, P. C., Hamilton, I., Lai, K. M. and Wilkinson, P. (2012) 'Healthy communities', *Local Environment*, 17(5), pp. 553–560. doi: 10.1080/13549839.2012.681465.

Rydin, Y., Bleahu, A., Davies, M., Dávila, J. D., Friel, S., de Grandis, G., Groce, N., Hallal, P. C., Hamilton, I., Howden-Chapman, P., Lai, K. M., Lim, C. J., Martins, J., Osrin, D., Ridley, I., Scott, I., Taylor, M., Wilkinson, P. and Wilson, J. (2012) 'Shaping cities for health: complexity and the planning of urban environments in the 21st century', *The Lancet*, 379, pp. 2079–2108.

Schulz, A. and Northridge, M. E. (2004) 'Social Determinants of Health: Implications for Environmental Health Promotion', *Health Education & Behavior*. SAGE Publications Inc, 31(4), pp. 455–471. doi: 10.1177/1090198104265598.

Shin, H. and Lee, K. (2017) 'Participatory governance and trans-sectoral mobilities: The new dynamics of adaptive preferences in the case of transport planning in Seoul, South Korea', *Cities*. Elsevier Ltd, 65, pp. 87–93. doi: 10.1016/j.cities.2017.01.012.

Smit, B. and Wandel, J. (2006) 'Adaptation, adaptive capacity and vulnerability', *Global Environmental Change*. Pergamon, 16(3), pp. 282–292. doi: 10.1016/J.GLOENVCHA.2006.03.008.

Spirn, A. W. (2014) 'Ecological Urbanism: A Framework for the Design of Resilient Cities (2014) BT – The Ecological Design and Planning Reader', in Ndubisi, F. O. (ed.). Washington, DC: Island Press/Center for Resource Economics, pp. 557–571. doi: 10.5822/978-1-61091-491-8_50.

Termeer, C. J. A. M., Dewulf, A. and van Lieshout, M. (2010) 'Disentangling Scale Approaches in Governance Research', *Ecology and Society*. Resilience Alliance Inc., 15(4). Available at: www.jstor.org/stable/26268216.

Tewdwr-Jones, M. and Allmendinger, P. (1998) 'Deconstructing Communicative Rationality: A Critique of Habermasian Collaborative Planning', *Environment and Planning A: Economy and Space*, 30(11), pp. 1975–1989. doi: 10.1068/a301975.

Tol, R. S. J. (2009) 'The Economic Effects of Climate Change', *Journal of Economic Perspectives*, 23(2), pp. 29–51. doi: 10.1257/jep. 23.2.29.

Turner, B. L, Kasperson, R., Matson, P., McCarthy, J., Corell, R., Christensen, L., Eckley, N., Kasperson, J., Luers, A,. Martello, M., Polsky, C., Pulsipher, A. and Schiller, A. (2003) 'A framework for vulnerability analysis in sustainability science', *Proceedings of the National Academy of Sciences*. National Academy of Sciences, 100(14), pp. 8074–8079. doi: 10.1073/pnas.1231335100.

United Nations Human Settlements Programme (UN-Habitat) (2016) *World Cities Report 2016 – Urbanization and Development: Emerging Futures*, *International Journal*. doi: 10.1016/S0264-2751(03)00010-6.

van de Ven, F., Snep, R., Koole, S., Brolsma, R., van der Brugge, R., Spijker, J. and Vergroesen, T. (2016) 'Adaptation Planning Support Toolbox: Measurable performance information based tools for co-creation of resilient, ecosystem-based urban plans with urban designers, decision-makers and stakeholders', *Environmental Science & Policy*, 66, pp. 427–436. doi: 10.1016/j.envsci.2016.06.010.

Walker, B., Holling, C., Carpenter, S. and Kinzig, A. (2004) 'Resilience, Adaptability and Transformability in Social – ecological Systems', *Ecology and Society*, 9(2), p. 5. doi: 10.1103/PhysRevLett.95.258101.

Watts, N., Adger, W., Agnolucci, P., Blackstock, J., Byass, P., Cai, W., Chaytor, S., Colbourn, T., Collins, M., Cooper, A., Cox, P., Depledge, J., Drummond, P., Ekins, P., Galaz, V., Grace, D., Graham, H., Grubb, M., Haines, A., Hamilton, I., Hunter, A., Jiang, X., Li, M., Kelman, I., Liang, L., Lott, M., Lowe, R., Luo, Y., Mace, G., Maslin, M., Nilsson, M., Oreszczyn, T., Pye, S., Quinn, T., Svensdotter, M., Venevsky, S., Warner, K., Xu, B., Yang, J., Yin, Y., Yu, C., Zhang, Q .,Gong, P., Montgomery., H. and Costello, A. (2018) 'Health and climate change: policy responses to protect public health', *The Lancet*. Elsevier, 386(10006), pp. 1861–1914. doi: 10.1016/S0140–6736 (15)60854–6.

Whittemore, A. H. (2014) 'Phenomenology and City Planning', *Journal of Planning Education and Research*. SAGE Publications Inc, 34(3), pp. 301–308. doi: 10.1177/ 0739456X14536989.

Wilkinson, C. (2011) 'Social-ecological resilience: Insights and issues for planning theory', *Planning Theory*, 11(2), pp. 148–169.

Yiftachel, O. and Huxley, M. (2002) 'Debating Dominance and Relevance: Notes on the "Communicative Turn" in Planning Theory', *International Journal of Urban and Regional Research*. Wiley/Blackwell (10.1111), 24(4), pp. 907–913. doi: 10.1111/ 1468-2427.00286.

Yohe, G. and Tol, R. S. J. (2002) 'Indicators for social and economic coping capacity – moving toward a working definition of adaptive capacity', *Global Environmental Change*. Pergamon, 12(1), pp. 25–40. doi: 10.1016/S0959-3780(01)00026-7.

Younger , M., Morrow-Almeida, H., Vindigni, S. and Dannenberg, A. (2018) 'The Built Environment, Climate Change, and Health', *American Journal of Preventive Medicine*. Elsevier, 35(5), pp. 517–526. doi: 10.1016/j.amepre.2008.08.017.

Zimmerman, R. and Faris, C. (2011) 'Climate change mitigation and adaptation in North American cities', *Current Opinion in Environmental Sustainability*. Elsevier, 3(3), pp. 181–187. doi: 10.1016/J.COSUST.2010.12.004.

Zolli, A. and Healy, A. M. (2013) *Resilience: Why Things Bounce Back*. Simon & Schuster. Available at: https://books.google.ie/books?id=n90b-I0hgU8C.

3   Responding to climate change

Formal to informal

Collaborative climate change policy development in cities

> Cities are kind of ground zero with respect to environmental issues. Senior governments are too far away whether it's provincial or federal. They can make some big broad sweeping policies, like the carbon tax ... has been a really nice policy. But, to actually make a difference on the ground and connect with individuals and communities, it has to be local government and I think this government realised that.
>
> (Interview 1, Vancouver)

Between April 2015 and June 2016, 35 interviews with key stakeholders in Glasgow, Vancouver, Portland and Dublin to understand the scope of climate change responses and how they are developed were undertaken. The policy makers provided valuable insight into the process of developing climate action plans with actionable policy. Critically, it was evident that there are two processes at work in the development of policy, the formal and the informal. Discussed first are the formal processes that guide the policy development process, in which the institutional and organisational structures appear to play a significant role in the capacity of cities to engage stakeholders. Each city is presented individually to highlight the differences that have contributed to their capacities. Following from this is a discussion of the informal practices employed by these cities to develop policy, specifically collaborative planning in practice. Collaboration, beyond public consultation, with stakeholders to develop and implement policy appears to be, in practice, something beyond what is formally required by statutory guidance. As such, it has largely been an initiative led by urban policy makers themselves, based on their recognition of its value for achieving buy-in from the public. Furthermore, collaboration seems to have highlighted the need to address long-standing challenges facing each of these cities, particularly relationship building, accountability, ownership, trust, learning, and failure, which may act as barriers to cities developing and implementing policies to achieve resilience to climate change. The chapter concludes with lessons of practice from these cities that may be used to inform practice in other cities, which critically were applied in developing the climate change action plans for the Dublin Local Authorities (DLAs).

Glasgow

> The new plan, I can show it to you on the phone, its 58 pages. And you can read it in an hour and a half, which is great. So, it makes a heck of a difference that you can read it quickly. The new plan is all about policies and taking the detail into supplementary guidance, or the documents that can help you look at things. It is a different way of doing. So, when we look at having a lead policy that is about place. Place is important and that's the thing that we want to lead off on, and then everything else will flow from it. Glasgow before that did an awful lot of trying to draw lines around things. Here be this, here be that.
>
> (Interview 1, Glasgow)

Glasgow recognises that it is a unique city, claiming to be the birthplace of the industrial revolution (Glasgow, 2010); the city has experienced its share of challenges as it has grown and evolved. Since becoming one of the Rockefeller Foundation's 100 Resilient Cities,[1] Glasgow is taking the opportunity to transform itself 'from the carbon-belching centre of a global economic revolution to the low carbon smart city of a new, greener future' (Glasgow City Council, 2015). Being selected as a resilient city is not the sole driving force for Glasgow's actions on climate change. Glasgow City Council is responsible for a broad remit including: planning, health, social assistance, parks, lighting, roads, education and schools. Given this, Glasgow has endeavoured to use its capacities to integrate climate change into all areas, a process that is not without challenges and lessons (Interviews, Glasgow, 2015). Through its Climate Change Strategy, which was developed using the social determinants of health, and City Plan 2, Glasgow has evolved its policies and is now forming a development plan that incorporates the lessons and the insights it has gained from these processes into its future policies. Moreover, the Scottish Government has been instrumental in enabling Glasgow City Council to develop and implement climate change policy. Formally, under statutory law Glasgow City Council is required to produce development plans every five years, which are then submitted to the Scottish Government for review and approval. At the time of the interviews (June, 2015) the Council had submitted its new plan for approval by government. In this plan the council tested the new guidance provided by the Scottish Government intended to enable planners to develop and implement actionable policies, as demonstrated by the following excerpts. (The new plan has been approved and released and has retained its brevity and focus on main issues and supplementary guidance.) It should be noted that the quote opening this section was in reference to restrictive zoning, while the first quote here is regarding the use of maps as a tool for identifying areas where activities and programmes are happening; in other words, areas for potential collaboration:

> The Scottish Government put together a body that is trying to get us back to design led, back to diagrams and less words, because what has happened in

the planning profession in the last 20–25 years, is people have forgotten that they used to draw maps, and lay maps and make analysis and decisions based on maps....

(Interview 1, Glasgow)

We have a statutory obligation to produce a development plan every 5 years ... in the past every issue was up for debate. Even if something was working and you are going to carry it through, everything was open for somebody to come throw all their arguments at it. And in the past the same people came back every 5 years. So, what the Government said was you are running to debate new issues. If something is working you are not going to change direction, you don't need to say anything in your main issues report. For example, in the main issues report climate change stuff would come through. It was published in October 2011. It started for the first time to say there is a major issue with flooding and drainage, this is the issue and this is what we want to do. There was a major issue about the urban environment, about how it contributes to climate change mitigation and adaptation and all that had come through in the 5 years since the last plan. They are new issues, these are the issues, and this is how we think we are going to address them. This is our preferred way of dealing with it. This is our option. Main issues report said new issues, give the community your preferred way forward or we want you to do something else. So, people could make comments on the main issues report.

(Interview 1, Glasgow)

In support of this, the Scottish Government is encouraging local authorities to reduce the length and breadth of plans, by allowing for local government to not re-iterate all policies and actions to address issues. Rather, the Scottish Government is asking for a main issues report, with the local council's preferred actions that can be debated. In doing this, it has allowed for Glasgow City Council to reduce its plan to 12 policies. To achieve this, the city set additional parameters for staff responsible for developing the 12 policies, i.e. a two-page maximum for a policy with a supporting background paper. The background papers have then served as the basis for supplementary guidance to the main plan. While supplementary guidance still requires a review by the Scottish Government, the process is significantly shorter; which allows for Glasgow City Council to nimbly respond to changes in not only Scottish Government policies, but European Union legislation and other international policies.

The beauty of supplementary guidance is if European legislation changes or UN says, 'we are going to do something' or Scottish Government legislation changes, we just pull the supplementary guidance back off the shelf and tweak the bit of it that needs to be tweaked, stick it out for 6 weeks consultation, deal with any of the reps that either agree or disagree report back to committee and send it back to Scottish Government. So, we can reshape guidance in about a 2-month period. It means that we don't have anything static sitting there.

(Interview 1, Glasgow)

Beyond giving Glasgow the capacity to respond nimbly with supplementary guidance, shifting the details to supplementary guidance enables a detailed debate to occur at an appropriate time. There is also recognition of the need for adaptive responses. This shift has permitted urban policy makers to focus on emerging issues and making the city resilient to climate change. This is critically important when one considers that climate science is showing that climate change impacts are rapidly evolving and intensifying. Policy makers need the ability to respond nimbly.

> Unless it is something happening in your backyard most people don't engage. So the main issues report although it is saying, 'Do you want to deal with climate change? Yes, we want to deal with climate change.' It wasn't about where you wanted to deal with it, because that was coming through the plan or something else. What we have said by stripping most of the stuff out of the plan, and making the plan more high level, you can have the details debated when we do the supplementary guidance and you start to see things happening, 'yeah, that's happening next door to me!' or 'that's happening around the corner' and you can have the debate and hopefully, in a calmed down manner. Because what was happening with local plans before, although government thought it was planning a document, more and more developers were bringing lawyers and it was turning into a legal argument rather than a debate about space. So what the government is trying to do is say, 'Right, let's have a debate about space, let's have only those new discussions if you have the argument back and forth about a site facing, and you had it every 5 years for the last 20 years why bother having it again?' That debate is gone unless it has been a complete change in circumstances. That site is still going to be housing? There's no point in consulting on that.
>
> (Interview 1, Glasgow)

> In the last 13 years things have really progressed, especially in Scotland. A lot of green issues and a lot of legislation have come forward, on climate change. And, we, through restructuring we've actually taken on a fairly significant chunk, well, we've taken on a whole department. Sustainable Glasgow sits within that wider environmental health. The team's remit ranges from air quality modeling through to climate change through to all sorts of green projects.
>
> (Interview 4, Glasgow)

The support given to Glasgow City Council by the Scottish Government has been beneficial to enhancing the capacity of the council in developing policy and having debates that add value to policy. Thus, the institutional structure has played a role in enabling Glasgow to 'test the waters' (Interview with Planner, Glasgow City Council, 2015). The institutional structure of Glasgow City Council (Figure 3.1) has also lent to Glasgow's policy development capacity and ability to collaborate with a range of stakeholders. The Sustainable Glasgow Board is chaired by council leaders, and 'brings together influential people from across the city, private and public partnerships' (Interview with Planner, Glasgow City Council, 2015) to develop collaborative solutions to challenges facing Glasgow. In addition to restructuring, Glasgow is benefiting from becoming one of the 100 Resilient Cities, a program which requires that cities have a chief resilience officer who reports directly to the mayor. This also suggests that participation in city-led initiatives that foster the exchange of ideas for responding to urban challenges empowers urban policy makers.

> The [mayor] is very open. He has been very engaged. He is the reason we have created the structure. Our chief resilience officer has a direct reporting

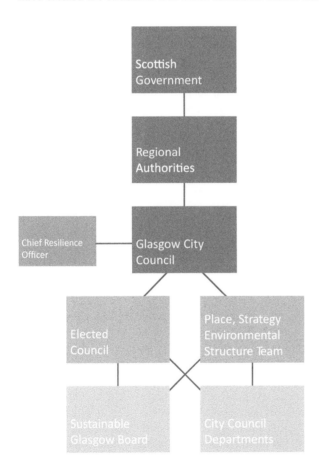

Figure 3.1 City of Glasgow's organisational structure.

line to him, which no other officer apart from executive directors have. I don't know if you know about the structure of the council. We've got our officers, employees, paid to deliver on the manifesto and then you have got your political structures. The officers are only the directors and assistant directors; they have a direct reporting line to the mayor, or council leader. The chief resilience officer is not part of that family, but he still has a direct reporting line. So that, I think, represents the fact that there is an acknowledgement that this is an extremely important agenda.

(Interview 2, Glasgow)

We are only at the start of the journey. We are starting to kind of talk in different languages. One of the reasons there was a bit of reshuffling. In development, they created the team called, 'place strategy and environmental structure'. There are 4 or 5 of us, but they needed a team that said, 'we are the one that is going to pull this together. We are the one that, ok you live there, come and talk to us and we will put you in touch with that person over there. You can concentrate on your stuff and we are going to try and make sure that place and policy actually works.'

(Interview 1, Glasgow)

Ultimately, in addition to Government support, Glasgow appears to be benefiting from an institutional structure that prioritises and supports the responses of local governments to climate change. Further, according to interviewees, Glasgow has taken this opportunity and created an organisational structure that supports the development of collaborative policies that respond to climate change by all departments within the council with the objective of creating a city that is people-centric.

Vancouver

One of the reasons I took the job with the city was it had a 4-day week, and one of the reasons they had a 4-day week was to reduce people commuting to work for pollution. And they came up with that in the 70s.

(Interview 1, Vancouver)

Vancouver has a reputation for being a city that is environmentally conscious (Interview 1, Vancouver, 2015). Residents of Vancouver protested the development of a highway through the core of the city in the 70s, and the city is the birthplace of the campaigning organisation Greenpeace (City of Vancouver, 2015). The City of Vancouver is unique in that it is governed by its own charter and is able to enact policy without approval from regional authorities, unlike other cities in the province (Interview with Director, City of Vancouver, 2015). Vancouver influences the standard for federal building codes and in turn provincial building codes, which are then followed by other municipalities (Interview 1, Vancouver, 2015). The institutional structure within which Vancouver operates allows the city somewhat more autonomy in the policy development process, compared to other municipalities across the region, which are guided by the regional authority, Metro Vancouver. Interestingly, the plans that were discussed with interviewees, the Greenest City Action Plan, the Healthy City Strategy, and Climate Action Plan, were initiated at the city level; and the plans were not required by higher levels of government (i.e. Metro Vancouver, or the Province of British Columbia), Vancouver embarked on its climate change journey willingly. This is because the city recognises its position as an opportunity, and sees its capacity as a brand for being a leader in green policy; critically there is a keen awareness of the responsibilities the city has:

> [Vancouver has] 10,000 employees, a $1 billion dollar budget, we own all roads. We have $6 billion of real estate; we have water, sewers, and almost 5,000 pieces of equipment in our fleet. We have shops, operations, and parks … City of Vancouver is a big brand, we are known all over the world.
>
> (Interview 1, Vancouver)

> I think the structure here is really conducive to the system. Having a very senior staff person, who is a champion, is helpful. And having a plan with targets approved by council is helpful.
>
> (Interview 2, Vancouver)

From speaking with interviewees, there is a sense of collective responsibility that runs through the organisation that is reflected in the city's structure. Formally, the City of Vancouver's organisational structure places an emphasis on environmental policy. Under the current government, which ran on a platform of making Vancouver the Greenest City, the Mayor created a sustainability group that oversees the work of all city departments. This group is overseen by the Deputy City Manager who was hand picked by the Mayor. The Deputy City Manager has been placed above all the department directors, and the role involves tracking the entire city's metrics on sustainability. As such, if a department is not achieving its targets, agreed upon in the Greenest City Action Plan, the Deputy City Manager has the ability to approach a director on behalf of council and ask for action. Box 3.1 discusses Vancouver's organisational structure and provides a rationale for the structure adopted by council and an example of how it has been applied. With this structure in place, sustainability and climate change are not placed under the prerogative of a specific department but made front and centre – the responsibility of the whole organisation. A clear message is sent by council to staff and citizens that addressing climate change and sustainability are important issues. Further, to support this organisational structure the council created a task force to support the work of the sustainability group.

The role of the sustainability group is primarily to oversee the implementation of the City of Vancouver's Greenest City Action Plan (GCAP), through policy and projects, and vitally the monitoring and evaluation of these policies and projects. The sustainability group has a responsibility to report transparently to council and the broader public on the progress of the targets laid out in the

Box 3.1 Vancouver's organisational structure

INTERVIEWEE: When this council came in, [Mayor] shortly after hired [Deputy City Manager], who was the environmental person for the City of Chicago. He was the top environmental sustainability person with the City of Chicago, and he was in his 20s. And then [Mayor] hand picked him to come lead the sustainability group for the City of Vancouver and place him as Deputy City Manager. He is actually above the Director of Engineering, the Director of Planning, the Director of Parks and so forth. He is the one that ultimately tracks all the metrics that all the reporting goes through. And if an action on the Greenest City isn't happening, i.e. parks board isn't doing something, and the sense of staff is that there is just not enough will and they're not really making it happen. If it hits that point it will go up to [Deputy City Manager]. Then [Deputy City Manager] can talk to the director of parks and say look this is important, this is a council priority, make it go. So, they have made this structure, where sustainability is not tucked over in engineering or off to the side, it has a lot of clout.

INTERVIEWER: Has it happened where you have had to escalate?

INTERVIEWEE: Yes, it happens.

INTERVIEWER: Can you give an example?

INTERVIEWEE: One of the adaptation priorities, the city developed a citywide storm water plan. And the storm water plan was meant to do more than just take water and pipes. It was meant to create rain gardens and infiltration systems and treat water quality and add more than just pipes. So engineering is doing that. They have a consultant; they have the draft report. And this is a project I am supporting, I am the sustainability person working on it, but it has taken a lot longer than it should. The draft report was kind of weak. It did not have strong recommendations; it didn't have an action plan. It was sort of a literature review, and a tool kit of things you can do. It didn't have much teeth to it. I had to talk to my director and say, 'We've got this draft. I don't think [Deputy City Manager] is going to be happy; this is not going to do what we want it do.' So [Deputy City Manager's] office schedules a meeting and we talk about what the plan is doing, and what it is not doing, and what it needs to do. And in some cases engineering might have valid concerns about why they can't do X, Y, and Z, but that conversation is had. There's a clear message that this is important and it needs to deliver on what everyone is expecting it do.

(Interview 2, Vancouver)

GCAP. Therefore, it produces an annual progress report using a green, yellow and red system to indicate progress: green being good, yellow being moderate, and red being poor (Interview, City of Vancouver, 2015).

The City of Vancouver has created an organisational structure (Figure 3.2) that supports its objectives of becoming the 'Greenest City by 2020'. Through its structure the city has created an internal environment that calls for accountability by all city staff to the plan, which in turn, has enabled the city to engage with stakeholders outside the city's administration.

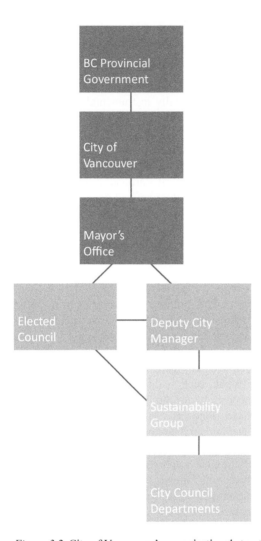

Figure 3.2 City of Vancouver's organisational structure.

Portland

In the bubble that looks like utopia, Portlandia, but outside the bubble, it looks like any other place that is struggling.

(Interview 5, Portland)

We're a city that if you compared it to other large cities. We don't have a strong organising culture here. We are not like a Chicago, where organising is a skill that is a job, it's a life.

(Interview 4, Portland)

The City of Portland is known for its environmental image; in the 90s it was the first city in the United States to develop a formal climate change plan (Interview, Portland, 2015). However, it was not until 2001 that the plan was revisited and reformulated.

> Portland was the first city to develop a formalised climate plan and it started in 1991 ... the Bureau Director was really instrumental in getting the first plan drafted. I think she was an intern, when it was drafted and she did a lot of work on it. There used to be an energy office. That does not exist anymore, that merged into the Office of Sustainable development. So that plan was the first one and the energy office worked with other bureaus within the city and it was only the City of Portland at that point that came up with a bunch of actions to put into the plan and goals. Then in 2001 the city joined Multnomah County, and then we started to work on an update to the 1991 plan. Then there was another update in 2009 and now we are in the midst of doing another update for 2015, for the climate action plan. Now it's the city and county coming together.
>
> (Interview 1, Portland)

Similarly to Vancouver, the City of Portland is governed by its own charter, and therefore can for the most part set its own policy. However, its policies are influenced and limited by state and federal policies, and its remit is not as far reaching. The remit of the City of Portland extends to development, environmental management, emergency services (police and fire), parks and recreation and equity. The development of a comprehensive plan such as the Portland Plan and the Climate Action Plan are the primary responsibility of the Bureau of Planning and Sustainability within the City of Portland. Portland's institutional structure is different from Glasgow and Vancouver, as Figure 3.3 demonstrates; the Bureau of Planning and Sustainability is embedded within the organisation. There is no entity that oversees the implementation of the plan's actions by all departments within the city. However, the Climate Preparation Strategy, which was also discussed with the interviewees, unlike the comprehensive plan was not a document used to determined city-wide policy on climate change, but to guide internal actions. An interview with key policy makers in the Bureau of Planning and Sustainability described how the Climate Preparation Strategy is intended to be used:

> This goal, this is our action. Because they are more like work plans for city employees and county employees, they have to do and they don't even have funding necessarily backing the actions... and some of them, on purpose, are aspirational. So, it keeps us moving in the direction we want to go. But so then afterwards, when we are on the implementation stage, each one of the bureaus or employees that are working on whatever the action is, needs to do the work what needs to happen to make it happen; going through the budget process, getting it funded, notifying whatever stakeholders need to be notified. Working with whatever stakeholders need to be worked with.
>
> (Interview 1, Portland)

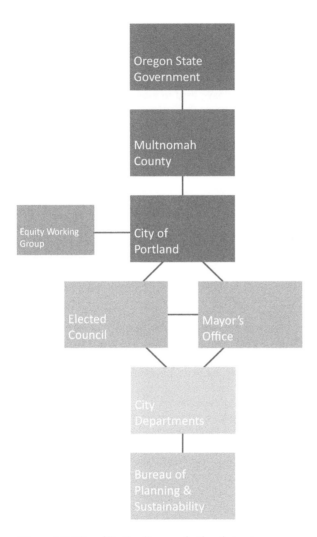

Figure 3.3 City of Portland's organisational structure.

It has served as an internal document by which the city could set its own targets in relation to climate change. Building on the document and shifting the focus beyond the city's departments, the city is working with Multnomah County to engage citizens on climate change through the Climate Action Plan. Multnomah County is the county within the State of Oregon in which Portland is situated. The county is responsible for education, health, and housing for the Multnomah county region, and as such its remit is far greater than the City's. Further, there is recognition by planners that in partnering with the County, Portland will increase its capacity and change its approach to planning and yield a more thoughtful plan with actions that are deliverable.

Box 3.2 Portland's evolving planning process

We used to do a planning approach that was more, 'the planners or policy makers are going to develop a draft and we are going to take it out to a community open house or advisory group.' Something that is very reactionary, and say we want your input in our plan. I think we have tried to move to something that is a bit more integrated, so that we have groups that are more than just advisory groups. They are people, community members or representatives from other organisations, public agencies sitting with staff in a room, helping develop things. The shift that you are, we are talking about, here's our 27,000 actions, ok, let's just talk about the issues. What should we be addressing? In a more one-on-one way. That fundamental shift is really important.

(Interview 2, Portland)

We have an equity specialist in our bureau who has a lot of really good connections throughout the community, especially with communities of colour. She is on board, really well connected. We use her a lot. Then there are a bunch of different kind of newspapers that are directed towards different communities that will write something about the plan and then we will do a lot of translated materials.

(Interview 1, Portland)

In 2001, the county joined them for a local plan, it was really ground breaking and now I look back, it was very simple operation, nuts and bolts. The year 2009 is really when I came into the work. It was first kind of major re-work where we took account of the co-benefits of health and broad-brush strokes of how climate aligns with a lot of different community outcomes and values. This process meant to be sort of a long-term goal of reducing emissions to 80% from 1990 levels by 2050, but really focused on three-year actions. So, every three years, the city and county would go back and update. We've actually taken five, almost six years to do it and have now made it a five-year plan. Because, not only is it just administratively challenging to get together something that has so much breadth in terms of staff engagement and community; we have expanded it so much to bring stronger elements of health and liveability and equity and also bringing in the dual dimensions of mitigation and adaptation. Any one of those number of conversations deep dive and just the work took a long time to get off the ground. We envision now every five years doing a full update and every year doing a progress report on how we are doing; both how we are delivering actions and how we are going to measure, we are equitably putting our values into practice.

(Interview 3, Portland)

Portland has created an equity working group that is outside the City's official structure, but links the work of the city and county. Similar to Glasgow and Vancouver there is an individual who is accountable for the work of the group. Ultimately, Portland has created a structure that aims to address the barriers it has to engaging stakeholders within city departments and those outside.

Dublin

While Dublin is comparable in population (approx. 523,000) and geographical size (117 km²) to Vancouver (approx. 615,000 pop. and 115 km²), Portland (approx. 639,000 pop. and 380 km²) and Glasgow (approx. 598,000 pop. and 178 km²), a key difference is that the city is the capital of its country. As such, central government is located in Dublin, and more or less 'all roads lead to Dublin' (Interview, Dublin 2015). There are other factors to consider beyond Dublin's position as a capital city, in its process of developing policy collaboratively to respond to climate change. Thus, this section discusses the institutional structure that shapes Dublin City Council's capacity for developing climate change policy. Consideration is also given to the planning context in Ireland, as being a city in a highly centralised state; planning laws are set by National Government. As public consultation is a cornerstone of planning in Ireland, the benefits and challenges of engaging the public are discussed.

Institutional structure

In Ireland, the Planning and Development Act 2000 (and subsequent amendments) set by the National Government regulates planning by all local authorities in Ireland. Where the perceived challenge lies for Dublin is that it is the largest local authority in Ireland with a population density of over half a million in the city, and 1.3 million in the Dublin Region. (The Dublin Region or County Dublin includes the neighbouring local authorities of Fingal County Council, South Dublin County Council and Dún Laoghaire-Rathdown, which Dublin works closely with and are currently developing their climate change action plans together).

> Dublin or the Dublin Region, if you take the three surrounding authorities, its about 40% of the population. It has about 50% of gross national product; it is an enormous block.... We have a much bigger share of GDP than say London has of the UK. There would be very few cities or city regions that have a dominant share of the local economy. I think that is a factor. There was a discussion on the possibility of a mayor for Dublin, and it didn't go ahead. I think they would be reluctant to have a mayor with real powers, because it would almost be a threat to central government.
>
> (Interview 1, Dublin)

> I think cities internationally have a huge amount of power. In Ireland, in contrast to international policy practice our powers are a lot less. In the UK, the powers of cities while they are increasing in recent years, there is a lot more power being divested down to cities. Compared to other European Union countries, the powers are fairly limited. What powers do we have? We have the planning system, and we can set higher standards in our development plan. We have influence over transport policy. Although in Dublin, the main transport decisions are made by the National Transport Authority.

We work with them to implement new transport measures. And that is a success story, because most of the money we're investing in transport in Dublin is going into cycling.

(Interview 11, Dublin)

As suggested by the above Dublin is unique in Ireland due to its concentration of population and contribution to gross domestic product (GDP). Interviewees alluded to the fact that being subject to the same planning legislative framework as other local authorities with smaller populations was a barrier to Dublin's capacity to affect real change. As one interviewee stated, 'Dublin is a state city as oppose to a city state', suggesting that instead of being able to set the example for others, it is controlled by Central Government. However, interviewees consistently stated that a directly elected mayor would shift this dynamic, as the mayor would be elected with a mandate to affect change. Conversely though, considering the emphasis of collaborative planning on stakeholder engagement and the study by Cheng and Daniels (2003), on the spatial correlation to collaboration, Dublin's status as a state city is perhaps a benefit to collaborative efforts. This will be discussed later. First though, it is important to consider Dublin's current remit and its relationship to Central Government (Figure 3.4).

As a local authority, Dublin City Council has responsibility for development, spatial planning, economic development, waste, recreation, culture, social housing, and flood management, as stated in the excerpts above. In other areas, such as roads and transportation the city collaborates with state bodies, such as the National Transport Authority. Considering the size of Dublin relative to other cities and its status as a hub of Ireland's economic growth, interviewees suggested that these are nominal powers (Box 3.3 and Box 3.4). Interviewees emphasised that the increasing shift of policy remits to Central Government, most recently with creation of Irish Water, were counterintuitive in light of the trend of comparable cities such as Manchester and Glasgow in the United Kingdom being given broader remits, where similar planning laws exist. Further, policy areas such as transport, water, and energy, that interviewees viewed as important to Dublin's capacity to respond to climate change, the centralisation of power has increased the number of agencies with whom Dublin City Council must engage to collaborate on policy with, especially in the area of climate change adaptation.

At the time of the interviews the Department of Environment, Community and Local Government (now the Department of Housing, Planning and Local Government) was responsible for addressing climate change (climate change is now the remit of the Department of Communications, Climate Action and Energy), and they successfully saw the passing of the *Climate Action and Low Carbon Development Act 2015* in December 2015, which sets out how Ireland is to respond to climate change. There is a focus on an all of government approach, as responding to climate change involves all sectors, other departments and semi-state bodies. However, the role of local authorities in the Act is not as significant as it could be, rather it is more about supporting the implementation of sectorial adaptation plans and enabling communities. Figure 3.4 illustrates the

Box 3.3 Dublin City Council's power

INTERVIEWEE: There was always a slightly inferior relationship to Government. Government particularly in the late 1970s up until recently we stopped having significant taxes on homes and therefore Local Government was very dependent on Central Government for funding. Particularly for capital funding for big projects. So we have always had to go with our hat and say can we have money for this, can we have money for that?

INTERVIEWER: Oliver Twist in a way

INTERVIEWEE: The type of gruel we get, is usually agreed. And then signed off by the councillors. In theory the councillors agree to everything. But in practice are often signing off on decision that has already been made.

INTERVIEWER: How much influence as a councillor, do you have in shaping the Dublin City Development Plan?

INTERVIEWEE: Physical planning and spatial planning is an area, its one of the few strong powers that the city council have. But plans are getting more complex; the wording of those plans is complex. It's becoming increasingly difficult to influence those plans because of their growing complexity, so we are at a draft city development plan stage. My colleagues and I, we would have put in maybe 50 or 60 motions to amend the plan. Some of those got passed and some of those didn't.

INTERVIEWER: What kind of motions?

INTERVIEWEE: A lot of them would have related to issues around climate. A motion that we would have a target to reduce emissions from the city by 3% every year. Over the course of the plan. A motion to seek higher building standards in new buildings to go to the passive house standard. Motions that we would prioritise walking and cycling. That we would put walking in the transportation hierarchy for the city, which was agreed. Those motions come up before the full city council of 63 members, the manager gives his advice, agrees some of them, disagrees with others, sometimes the councillors overrule the manager, sometimes the group of councillors say, 'no we are not going with this'. So, I have to make sure any motions I put forward have the approval of my colleagues. I have to get the manager to agree with my point of view. But sometimes we overrule the manager, by way of voting. And at the moment we have a draft city development plan we're inviting the public's views on that, and it will come back to us with the publics views and manager's views and we will vote on it again. And eventually we will have a plan that sets out the broad vision and some detailed specifics for what the shape of the city will be over the next 6 years.

INTERVIEWER: What are the challenges in getting your fellow councillor to agree with you, or getting the manager to agree with you?

INTERVIEWEE: Our Chief Executive would probably have a strong pro-development bias, because development brings in development levies and rates in other words taxes to the city. And they would be cautious of any undue imposition of higher standards. Fairly similar to [how] the car industry resisted safety improvements over the years. Safety belts are going to add a thousand dollars to the sticker price of a car; people don't want them. Same with passive house building standard are going to raise the price of new housing by 5% why are we doing this? Putting walking and cycling first? Cars are the lifeblood of the city. And then one of the nice things there is a lot more evidence base research in recent years. So, the NTA looked at who's coming in to shop in the middle of town and we discovered twice as many people were coming by bus as by car and they were spending twice as much as those who travelled by car. Suddenly, that shattered the idea that the car drivers needed to be put first because their purchases were much more than buses. But we can set targets for reducing emissions from the city, from the bubble that is the city by 3% a year. But we don't have the tools to implement that. And we can't knock on somebody's door and say 'your emissions are higher than the level allowed in the city'.

INTERVIEWER: What are ways around not having those tools though?

INTERVIEWEE: The work-arounds, as I say, are the carrots of offering grant aid, which can be quite useful. We can change the way we manage traffic to prioritise public transit, walking and cycling. We can provide support for energy users in the city, and we provide funding to the City of Dublin Energy Management Agency (Codema) and Codema is funded by three of the four Dublin local authorities. And they provide research and assistance to the local authorities, but also to the industrial users, institutions around the city and if its got energy in the title, Codema is probably trying to get into that space to help you use less of it. Or use it more efficiently. So that's one of the ways in which we can tackle energy.

(Interview 10, Dublin)

Box 3.4 Power and engagement: Politicians, civil servants and citizens

INTERVIEWER: What could government do to get better engagement and less up in arms engagement?

INTERVIEWEE: Well, there isn't a mass movement among the population to take action on climate change I haven't come across it. There's actually good engagement with the politicians. You can, or I can pick up the phone I could phone a local politician and explain a problem to him, now it could be something trivial and he will take action. This is one of the people sitting in the parliament. So it's a very, there's huge access to the politicians. Even government ministers will go back to their constituencies and they will hold clinics, they will be in a little office and people will come in.... There's huge engagement, but, nobody going into those clinics saying, 'you do something about climate change!'

INTERVIEWER: What about the civil servants and their capacity, and then the citizens?

INTERVIEWEE: Civil servants can't rock the boat, they have to ensure the whole thing, the show keeps on the road, and that we meet our obligations, that's it.... When you talk to them they all understand the science and they say, 'yes we know, but what can we do? Like people buy cars, I can't stop them buying cars. This isn't Russia or wherever you could do that, North Korea. We can't tell people what to do.' So they're operating within the reality of what can be done.... They're dealing with political realities all the time and while attempting to keep a functioning society, such that the minister is happy as well. They wouldn't be free to come out and say come up with their own policies. They can go to the minister, and say we have this target for 2020, and we better do something in this area, and then they may get the ok to go ahead and spend some more money on something. But they certainly can't make something up on their own. And this is where that expert body on climate change, because they are separate from the civil service, they are supposed to have freedom to come up with more policies. But it has to go back into the government departments after that and then they will decide what they are going to do.

(Interview 16, Dublin)

In relation to the awareness of the implications of climate change amongst central government, another interviewee highlighted that leadership and collaborative work is needed to bring awareness to the impacts and potential responses to climate change.

INTERVIEWER: How do you get policy makers to see the broad picture, how do you get them to see that policies are connected?

INTERVIEWEE: If you can introduce some joined up work, my own view.... It takes leadership, it takes a mandate, and if you want to call it crudely, it takes incentivisation. The mandate for that level of co-operation really has to come from the Taoiseach or the prime minister. Ideally if you want to get that joined up working, you have to them reporting in some fashion back into the Taoiseach's department, leadership can be exhibited by him in terms of giving a mandate to a group to operate on that basis and then what you have to really consider is how you can encourage. If it is stick and carrot methods to get that cooperation.... So, if you want to call the directors of public health, the leaders of the local education authorities, the leaders of the health authority, the leaders of the local environment authority have to sit around the table and they are allocated from central and location a certain pot of money and then they have to collectively agree how they are going to spend that, so that forces them to come to the table and they don't get to discharge those funds, until they actually agree a plan for the city or for the county or the region.... The other way is you have it, 'It is my job to actually cooperate with you', if I work in the Department of Health part of my portfolio or part of my benchmarking is against the degree of contact I have had with other government departments. How I have been able to interact with them. What I can show at the end of the year. How many engagements we have had. What work we have done cooperatively. What goals and targets we've addressed collaboratively. Then your performance [is] bench marked against those criteria. So its not just there should be a working group on, an interdepartmental group on the environment.... But there are actually indicators of successful addressing of the issues that you are doing on a joined-up cooperative, worked out plan and basis.

(Interview 15, Dublin)

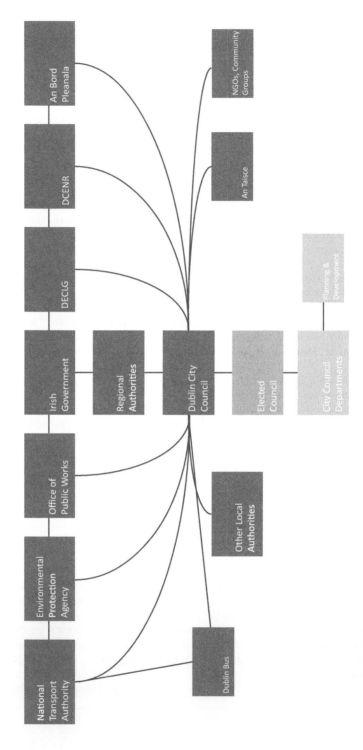

Figure 3.4 Dublin's organisational structure.

various state and semi-state actors that Dublin City Council works with to respond to climate change, and other urban issues.

Emerging from Box 3.3 is an understanding of the challenges Dublin City Council faces in developing policy. The number and diversity of stakeholders that council needs to engage with creates complexity for the policy development process, especially when power and capacity are decreasing and dependence on central government is increasing (Box 3.4).

As with other local authorities, Dublin is dependent upon Central Government for financing (Box 3.3 and Box 3.4). Specifically, Dublin, (and all local authorities) is dependent on the ability of the Department for Environment, Community and Local Government (now in 2018, the Department of Housing, Planning and Local Government) to acquire funds from the Department of Public Expenditure and Reform. If Dublin City Council had the capacity to raise funds it would enable policy makers to initiate policies and projects that address climate change, the unfortunate reality is that they do not. Funding and financing therefore was viewed as a challenge for policy making. Further as demonstrated in Box 3.3 and Box 3.4, there is a perception that the policy tools for implementing climate change adaptation measures are not in the hands of local authorities, and to some extent, not in the hands of civil servants at higher levels of government. Box 3.4 illustrates another factor of policy making that, while a benefit to the planning system, collaboration is also a challenge: the capacity of individuals to speak directly with ministers in charge of various departments. This access and transparency is valuable in that, as highlighted by interviewees, citizens can engage with government directly through ministers on issues relevant to them. However, the challenge is that climate change is not yet a pressing issue for citizens, but fortunately it is for government, as demonstrated by the creation of a Climate Change Action Group. In theory, this group is to be separate from government, and have the mandate to form policy recommendations on climate change, which it will then put forth to Central Government. However, as the second excerpt in Box 3.5 highlights there needs to be a structure that supports productive and beneficial collaboration that permeates throughout all government departments and levels of government. Interviewees, though, expressed concern that the increasing centralisation of power is creating greater challenges for responding to climate change as opposed to aiding it. As the last excerpt in Box 3.5 highlights and aligns with Box 3.4, there is a history of grassroots bottom-up political action that is rooted in 'getting a piece of the pie' for individuals, that is at odds with the purpose of local government, due to ministers being focused on responding to individuals. Therefore, the capacity of Dublin City Council to influence and have impact on climate change policy through the powers they have (i.e. spatial development and land-use) is minimised due to apparent policy contradiction by Central Government (Interview, Dublin 2015).

Box 3.5 Impacts of centralisation and the political system on local power

Dublin is what we call a primary city ... in a way Dublin is a state city, as oppose to a city state like Singapore. And that may be lost to some extent because it is a third of the population and the government sits in Dublin. All roads lead to central Dublin. So it's true that it is very centralised. Power is very centralised and even within government power is centralised in the four people who comprise the Department of Finance.

(Interview 21, Dublin)

The idea that we will achieve our climate change targets by just regulatory measures ... that is the real issue. This is a much more complex.... The reality is that we have increasingly less sort of impact or influence... we are subject to ministerial direction.... Let's suppose we said that all new development in the city was to meet housing energy passivity, which is carbon neutral. It is possible to build a unit that is neutral using heat pumps. I would be directed by the department not to do it. Secondly, the consequence would be that no one would want to build in the city. Then you would have people working in the city, living much further out.... We have to be very careful of superficial policies intended to achieve particular goals.

(Interview 1, Dublin)

Local government, well first of all its not local government, I mean at one level you can say local authorities have unique democratic mandates, and on that basis, at the end of the day members exercise very significant control over a variety of areas, even though it's a strong managerial system. But it's quite clear that central government doesn't really value that and increasingly more and more functions have been taken from local authorities. If you look back 50 years, all social welfare, all health, were run by local government.

(Interview 2, Dublin)

There are areas where the council can influence and doesn't control. And in the last 5 years, the areas of influence of the council have reduced greatly. Water has gone to Irish Water; the Dublin Transportation Authority has been integrated into the National Transport Authority (NTA). The rates, money collected by households, taxes have been transferred from the council to the national body. So, a lot of these functions and sources of income have been removed from the direct control of the city and moved to the Central Government... The city council has far less authority in Dublin, than it would in some other countries. In terms of energy, some cities generate energy and sell it and control the energy distribution systems, say for example district heating. They would have revenues from that. Dublin is very dependent on the Central Government for revenues.

(Interview 21, Dublin)

How we must review our development plans. For a city that is a capital city of a half million population, the making of the city development plan is no different in process and procedure than Leitrim County Council, but the issues that we face are far more severe and challenging than Leitrim's. It is also one of the few pieces of public policy which is a reserved function of the elected members.... We live in a highly centralised state. Most of what we do is laid down in government by government. We're also not a taxation authority, we can collect rates, which is service charges but we cannot collect tax. The only people that can collect tax are central government. So that funding of local government is still a big issue.... For the most part we are dependent on central government for funding. In making the development plan ... the executive makes recommendations to elected members, the elected members consider it, and in considering it they engage with a debate with the public, it goes on public display. But you can manipulate a debate. I would argue that, you are asking me the question about consensus. I think there are some very well-organised organisations, who are fairly well up to speed on the whole use of social media, and can exploit the situation and have been very successful at leading debate and winning the debate with elected members.

(Interview 2, Dublin)

Barriers here, the Irish political system, we are very clientelist. We don't ultimately think we own the political system. Because we were not independent for a long time and therefore the role of the political system is to get you something from the system that you don't quite own. Therefore, what the local TD does, is provide that, gets a slice of the pie.... Its foundation was in the 19th century with Daniel O'Connell and Parnell and these amazing bottom up movements, that didn't own, they were nationalist ... they created this alternative, sub structure of local representation, fighting for catholic emancipation fighting for land rights, fighting for freedom. So our culture, political cultural is a very strong bottom, connected to local ward, not as tied to the establishment.

(Interview 20, Dublin)

Planning context

While the centralisation of power has changed the capacity of Dublin City Council, it still has the ability to shape the city through planning. The statutory planning obligations that Dublin is beholden to are the same as all other councils around the country, as the following excerpts in Box 3.6 illustrates.

Before discussing the implications of statutory guidance on Dublin's capacity, it is important to acknowledge the context of the county/city development plan. There are several planning documents to which local government development plans are connected. The first is the National Spatial Strategy (NSS), which during the time of these interviews was being revised to become the National Planning Framework (NPF), which was completed in February 2018 and sets out the vision for Ireland's growth to 2040. The NSS was intended to guide growth in Ireland, however, a challenge with the NSS is that it was too detailed and consequently became the reference document for planning (Interview, Dublin). The new NPF, Project Ireland 2040, is still detailed and is endeavouring to redistribute growth to other parts of the country. There is nominal hope in

---

Box 3.6 Planning a capital city

We live in a very centralised government system. Everything comes down from Central Government. The difficulty we have in this city is that we are not just a capital city, but also the seat of government is located in the capital city. So, from a political, from a power point of view, most, a lot of the authority rests with central government not with local government, as in the city. When we are making a development plan we are making it based on legislation that has been drafted by Oireachtas and set down in regulations. We have to follow the set legal process and procedure, because it is required to do it, because it is the law that we must do it. One thing that you will notice is that Dublin, I suppose is unique in so far that, it is the largest urban area in the country, it is a capital city, but procedures for making the development plan for Dublin City are no different from the procedure for making the development plan for the smallest rural authority, Leitrim. There's no difference. The time lines in making development plans and the time that is available for consultation is exactly the same for Dublin City as it is for the small rural authorities.

(Interview 2, Dublin)

Ireland is a very centralised system. National Government has a lot of power and influence and Dublin City Council doesn't have the power, that I think, that it should to be able to build communities.

(Interview 4, Dublin)

The realities of the last 5 years, we've been in survival mode. We've had to cut our expenditure and our employment by 25%. An awful lot of things we would have liked to be doing, we weren't able to do, because of the pressure on our budget.

(Interview 4, Dublin)

We don't control education, police, social services, very limited in reality. We have a major role to play in recreation, culture and amenities. We do a lot of things there. Obviously, we have land-use plan and development control, major functions there. We've major functions in housing, particularly social housing.... Roads and traffic. But it would be very relative.

(Interview 2, Dublin)

---

that responding to climate change is addressed, however, there is focus on solutions that rely on engineering and economics. The NPF, as in the case of the NSS, in turn will shape the eight Regional Planning Guidelines, which are being revised in 2018 to Regional Spatial and Economic Strategies, that set out strategies for regional growth, which must also be considered in local authority development plans. Then within the development plans, local authorities have local area plans and economic development plans. As the following excerpt discusses, public consultation is a requirement for all plans as part of their development process. A challenge for Dublin in public consultation is not only the size but the diversity of the population.

Local government reform in the Republic risks reducing involvement in the development plan rather than increasing it. Because now you got the local economic and community plans. You will probably have consultation fatigue and also people wondering what is this plan that the local authority is doing, what it does differently to the development plan. I am sure they will come together at some stage, but now you are onto consultation on regional strategies, you are then going to have consultation on the successor to National Spatial Strategy (NSS), and people don't see deliverables from plan. So, you are going to get to the point where people are saying, 'what are all these plans? What is the point of them? Is it just people doing plans for the sake of doing plans?' That probably goes back to streamlining them and making these as straightforward as possible. Final point of this answer, I think the National Planning Framework succeeding the NSS, is the next best opportunity we have to get people engaged in planning. You look at the Scottish model, very short document, broad-brush maps. This is what is going to development, there is going to be stuff over in this part of the country. There is going to be this infrastructure, linking stuff up. Dublin is going to grow to this size. That is probably potentially something that people can engage with. Or get excited about if you present it properly. If you keep it straightforward and if you keep account of that high level strategic thing.

(Interview 6, Dublin)

Acknowledging that development plans are situated in the context of both national and regional plans, it is evident that formulating the development plan is a challenging task. While the city can produce a comprehensive development plan, that plan is subject to national legislation determined by the DHLGP. Local government can influence and shape the city through local area plans for specific areas of the city; this was emphasised by interviewees in DHLGP to be a key capacity of the city. However, there was little focus on the local area plans by interviewees in Dublin City Council. This is perhaps because even local area plans run into roadblocks that can result in the plans being objected to by residents, and potentially appealed and brought before An Bord Pleanála (a unique feature of the Irish planning system that allows for third party appeals). What is clear is that the timescales for planning are not suited to Dublin's size, demographic make-up and physical characteristics.

Dublin is expected to follow the exact same timelines for producing a development plan that sets out the priorities for the city, as a town with a population of 10,000. This is seen as statutory barrier (Box 3.6) and was emphasised by interviewees to be a hindrance to the city's operational capacity and ability to affect change by developing policies that address Dublin's urban challenges. Furthermore, as the following excerpt discusses, it creates confusion around the roles of local government and central government; which in turn has created hesitation to go beyond, due to the risk of legal proceedings that have the potential to further curb the capacities of council.

Media generally look at what is Dublin doing? And then Dublin becomes the benchmark; you become answerable for planning policy for the entire country. They won't ask Leitrim County Council, or they won't ask Limerick County Council. They will ask Dublin City Council, what are you doing about this? Because we are the capital, we are the seat of government. There is a bit of confusion between the role of central government and local government on broad planning issues. And we often become the body responsible for answering on what are central or national kind of policies that is number one. You were asking about what we are doing about it. We have to be conscious of the fact, when I say a statutory process, what does that mean? A legal process. We ended up in court the last time around on the last development plan. We were brought to court on the basis that property owners, those owners of institutional lands, felt aggrieved at the fact that we were bringing in policies that were curtailing the development potential of their lands. Now in this country the right of the owner of the land is enshrined in the Constitution. So, the landowner in this country has fairly significant kind of rights, so when we are making the development plan we are governed by the regulation. But, we know that we have to also be cognisant of the fact that the whole issue of consultation, communication is changing and there's a whole new social media world out there. But we have to be very clear that we don't exceed where we can go.... But the regulations need to be reviewed to take consideration of the growth of social media and to integrate those into the development plan process, rather than us kind of having two parallel systems. Look, we have to do public display in the library here, because that is what we've always done, but we know that nobody will probably come look at the plan for the duration that it is there, for the 10 weeks.

(Interview 2, Dublin)

Thus, interviewees from within the city did not acknowledge the city's capacity to shape the city through local area plans. This is likely due to the tendency for planning to fall into the trap of becoming a legal debate; not a debate about space and liveability, which would be more conducive to a local government being able to meet the needs of citizens effectively by providing services. Rather interviewees focused on the absence of functions that they do not have, highlighting the increasing loss of responsibilities as a key barrier to the city's abilities to deliver services to citizens. The recent loss of water services to Irish Water was held up as an example of how a service that the city had provided effectively has been centralised and created a gap in service as demonstrated by the following excerpt:

We've lost utilities, Irish Water was set up, that may even backfire on them.... Even if there are arguments, everything they say is about economies of scale. You have 31 local authorities; they must be inefficient. That is completely spurious. We are the largest local authority.... We lost water services; we've been providing water services for 150 years. Some of the schemes that transformed Dublin, the engineering schemes bringing water from Round Wood. Round Wood was built in the 1860s and [an] extraordinary piece of civil engineering brought water, piped, gravity fed to most of the city.... It was a major part of what we were, despite the constant moaning we delivered high quality water in the city, free of charge to point of delivery 24/7 and there were very few interruptions. Now, the problem was when we lost our rates base in the 70s, we were supposed to be compensated by Central Government, but that never really happened. The state took on the capital funding and the capital funding proved inadequate, so we weren't maintaining the pipe distribution network. So there was a major investment deficit. We have one single integrated wastewater management and water supply system. Its not as if we have four competing local authorities.... The problem was lack of investment to renew the pipe network and to develop new sources. I accept down in the country there were a plethora of small inefficient plants.... You can't have two people running the water services, we are currently their contractor but that's not sustainable.

(Interview 1, Dublin)

Public consultation

It is clear that public consultation is a key feature of planning and policy making in Ireland. Public consultation creates the perception of transparency, but transparency and accessibility are not the same. As such, public consultation is for those who know about it, not for those who need to be consulted and heard. How the city formally engages with the public and overcomes the challenges, specifically lack of engagement, calls for an understanding of the process for public consultation in Ireland.

The public consultation process for the formulation of the development plan is set out in statutory guidelines produced by the DHLGP. The guidelines set the procedures for mandatory public consultation and the corresponding timeline. This presents several challenges for planners and policy makers in Dublin. As has been mentioned, the guidelines are the same for all local councils in Ireland, irrespective of population or social and economic factors. For Dublin, as the largest city, the economic and political centre of Ireland, the guidelines according to interviewees are limiting, in that people, citizens, rarely engage in the development plan process, primarily because they do not have time or do not understand the process and its purpose (Box 3.7). Again, it is worth noting that all processes in planning in Ireland, such as public consultation are transparent. However, as the excerpts in Box 3.7 show, that transparency does not necessarily translate into participation, as there are challenges with accessibility of information. In other words, whilst Ireland may have transparent governance, it is not accessible to everyone, but primarily to those who understand the system. Which raises the question of how Dublin City Council can increase participation and engagement if the information, as transparent as it is, is inaccessible to the

---

Box 3.7 The consultation process: communicating with the public

We hold local workshops to explain the plan, when the plan goes out on display, people can submit material. So, anybody we get, the material that comes, that influences the final document would be from statutory bodies, organised groups and locally organised groups, individuals, and you get the comments back via the elected representatives. There are multiple strands. Let's say before the 2000 Act … it was a much more basic, there was no pre-draft opportunity to comment.

(Interview 7, Dublin)

Often people aren't terribly interesting in planning until they find out the building next door is about to be redeveloped and they suddenly become aware of or conscious of the restrictions, the limitations of the planning process and they have lots of things to say, but they never said it during the development plan process. Because it wasn't an issue then.

(Interview 2, Dublin)

People say, 'look give us a break.' We've major problems of homelessness to deal with; the economy is recovering. We've had 7 or 8 years of austerity. I think its been very difficult to engage people but there is a general issue of engaging people in anything that is long term. And the nature of the political cycle, it is very difficult to engage politicians. And there's short term problems to get engagement on long term issues, and its not just climate change....

(Interview 1, Dublin)

Its another problem of civic education, people in Ireland. This is terrible to say so, but you asked me for my relative experience. There's an issue with how you join up broad policy implementation and all those things you hear about Ireland, that clientelism. All those things are a result of the disjoint between policy and the individual case, whatever is an individual, an emotional case, that trumps policy every time and our media is full of it.

(Interview 3, Dublin)

Consultation at the moment is tokenistic and at the end of the day the vested interests have a sway. The government is doing a consultation on transport. It's not going to annoy the road industry.... The consultation process as we have it at the moment is not properly communicating the issues to the public at large and it is very often, tokenistic. The consultations we are having a number of consultations on sectorial mitigation, plans for climate change. Those have been done internally by different government departments and then there's supposed to be an overall coordinating role.... There's no communication of the urgency or scale of the issues. And there's no real, public engagement, in the process, because you are dealing with highly technical documents, that would be beyond a lot of people outside those specialist areas.

(Interview 17, Dublin)

citizens from whom city council needs to hear? Further, as indicated by interviewees, urban policy makers face the challenge of stimulating interest in planning, when attention spans are short and media has the capacity to sway public
opinion.

Recalling the excerpts earlier in this chapter in Box 3.4 and Box 3.5, the
ability of the citizen to speak directly to ministers and politicians is a trait of the
Irish political system and can impact upon the planning process, namely through
elected councillors, as elected councillors represent the voice of citizens and
simultaneously are the information conduits. They are tasked with explaining
policy decisions to citizens, and with conveying citizen expectations to policy
makers. This proximity to citizens enables Dublin City Council's elected
members to respond, as will be discussed. However, remaining a member of
council is dependent on the ability of councillors to secure votes. Consequently,
their ability to influence policy is dependent on their capacity to balance informing constituents of what is needed with addressing what their constituents want,
such that they secure votes. The competition for votes creates challenges for
councillors, while there is an understanding of what is 'good' for the city, vying
for votes may lead to councillors having to sacrifice their vision for the city or an
area to retain their seats as discussed in Box 3.8 below. This is an area that is not
exempt from the centralisation of power.

Box 3.8 Engaging with the public: a councillor's view

INTERVIEWEE: I find the hardest thing about the whole planning process is that
there is nobody that stands up for the people who haven't moved into an area,
but will as soon as they build the houses. Or there is nobody standing up for
future generations, the only political pressure is from people who are already
living in a place, and they generally don't want any change.

INTERVIEWER: How do you address that?

INTERVIEWEE: An incremental approach is what I found to be sensible. So, I push
as far as I can, when I can, when I get an opportunity.... Consultation is a real
challenge for us. I was there at a public consultation meeting on the development out in Ballymun about three weeks ago and I turned up to it and there
wasn't one single solitary member of the public. I just sat there for an hour
with the official from the council – sat there for an hour. There wasn't a single
person from the public who turned up to it.

INTERVIEWER: Hypothesis as to how come?

INTERVIEWEE: I don't think we do a great job of promoting it or publicising it,
there was an ad in the newspaper. We should have been writing to all the
community associations. The city council have a ton of connections... resident's associations, energy groups, arts, we have all of these contacts, I don't
think we did a great job of contacting them.... Its still very difficult.... The
more local the issue is. The more likely you are going to get engagement. If
it's a national spatial strategy. Nobody gives a d***. If it's a city development
plan, you get a few people commenting. It's a local area plan; everybody
wants to know what is going on in their local area.

Overcoming fear:

INTERVIEWEE: This is a plot [of] land that has been lying idle for 50 years.... It has been available for 50 years to build houses on. There's been 2 or 3 proposals over the years, but its never quite happened. So, the council are looking to try to get this developed, this is just a rough plan of what they would like to do. Here they want to create connections to the various communities around it.... Now [name] She's a MP she used to be in my party ... she put out a letter to all the houses saying that this appalling.... She called a public meeting 200 people turned up, said, 'those 4 councillors trying to say it's not a bad thing'. Nearly got hung from the rafters, because they don't want these connections through their estate.... The traffic is just really bad, they feel if those connections are coming through, traffic is so awful in their estates, it will be even worse if you let people drive through.... But their thing is you can hardly get your car out of the drive around here. 'If you let another 700 homes here drive through our estate its going to be hell'.... There are no traffic problems; they have the most minor traffic problems you would come across. They think its hell.... It was designed like this with a road that would have let it through, but the people said no way, so they built a wall across here, and then these houses were built and it was designed to allow them to drive into the next estate, but the residents said no way so they built a wall across ... I got an email today from a resident, basically saying, 'don't let them do that to me.' ... So what do I do as an elected official? Would I be an elected official much longer if I do what is right? ...

INTERVIEWER: How do you balance this?

INTERVIEWEE: You try and compromise.... When the public meeting part of the meeting was over I spent 2 hours, talking to everyone; there were 200 people ... I went to every single table, there was at least some trust, they know me from the area, they like me. Trying to persuade them. But fear is a very powerful emotion, whereas logic and calmed reason saying that the more entrances and exits, the more the traffic is dispersed. If you trying to focus it down to one or two entrances and exits, you are piling on the traffic and it is not fair to the estate ... I try and persuade people as best I can. But if it comes to the crunch and they are too angry you just have to go with them.

INTERVIEWER: What are good proxies?

INTERVIEWEE: There are a few things I am trying to persuade them.... Their worry is that this is a really busy road here and it's very difficult to get into this part of the city. So, they think everybody is going to cut in ... I am going to try and say, maybe we can make this is.... We are not supposed to do this, we could make this a 10 km zone, or we could make it a zig zag, so its really painful to drive through the area.... It makes for [a] child friendly environment. It makes for reduced driving and its very good. But if you want to increase cycling and walking, you need that permeability. But that is the difficulty in getting that permeability. I know I should be doing it. I will try to persuade and encourage, I might have to give [in] and vote against permeability and that will break my heart, but that is [the] kind of situation you find yourself in.... But because fear is a powerful emotion that will get you votes.... She will get 75% of the votes in this area, by promoting the wrong things, damaging her area she will get 75% of the votes, by damaging future generations. That is what my frustration is, there's nobody, there's no political recompense for doing the right thing, for standing up for future generations, and the people who live here in 2 years time. I cannot get their votes, and when they move in, in 2 years time they won't come to me and thank me for standing up for them, they won't know its something that happened in the past. It will just seem trivial, that's a real problem. And what has made it easier is that my colleagues on the council are more concerned about the housing situation, they are sticking with me on this so far. They are looking to me, what are we going to do [name], it is my estate I did grow up here. They are not going to get a huge amount of votes here anyway. They are kind of looking over here and saying we will follow you. Even from different parties. Like [name], you make the decision. We will back you. Which is good.

(Interview 10, Dublin)

This excerpt demonstrates not only the challenges (the politics of fear) with securing votes, but the level of understanding that citizens have with regards to the functions of Dublin City Council. Over the course of the interviews, it became apparent from interviewees that the public does not have a full understanding of the functions and capacities of Dublin City Council. The reason for the lack of understanding is perhaps due to the history of Ireland and Dublin, which has possibly contributed to a lack of engagement with council and government, as there is a lack of clarity in the roles of central, regional and local governments. Further, citizens may not be concerned or, interested in, and have expectations with regards to the actions of the city. Lastly, as the timeline for public consultation is determined by central government, consultation for all local authorities occurs around the same time, lending itself to consultation fatigue.

Organising for climate leadership

From interviewing stakeholders it appears that the institutional structures within which planners and policy makers work is important to their capacity to develop policies. Further, considering these cities collectively, there was a common theme to achieving policy success, leadership. Throughout the interviews in each city it was apparent that leadership was key in the success of developing and implementing climate change policies. Leadership could be by an individual (i.e. deputy city mayor, chief resilience officer) or a group of individuals (i.e. leadership roundtables, working groups), and either within the local government or outside. Key to leadership, as demonstrated by the excerpts in Box 3.9, is the commitment to addressing climate change and the accountability that leadership would take for policies. Formally, it is evident that each of these cities has created an environment that fosters their ability to lead in the development of climate change policy. Glasgow and Vancouver have more clearly developed mechanisms for reporting back on policies, particularly with their sustainability

Box 3.9 Leadership for aspiration

Portland

INTERVIEWEE: We've created a plan that in theory leads to a really wonderful future. We are the only ones that can get in its way. We are the only ones that can do it and prevent it from happening. I don't know what will prevent it other than losing the relationships, that people don't see themselves as part of the solution.... If we talk about walkable communities and park development, and transit access and quality housing, affordable housing, then we will bring people in. If we are talking about pipelines to employment, people win. If we talk about educating folks around this work they define, and align with how they learn and what they value, then people will stay engaged. I think that has been the biggest challenge around this....

INTERVIEWER: So the community and county, Portland, their job is to maintain open channels and to not be a barrier onto itself?

INTERVIEWEE: Absolutely, I think it's the [name]'s and the [name]'s of the world that track this, you know. The people stay engaged and understand. I think one of the questions that came up in a meeting, 'Is this a legal document?' This isn't, there is no recourse, if we don't do anything in there, and it doesn't really matter, other than the world collapses. There's nothing that binds us other than, goodwill; other than communities wanting to be part of the discussion.

(Interview 4, Portland)

Vancouver

We have very good leadership, it was chaired by the city manager. Great support of the staff at the city of Vancouver. In the way they took discussion and were able to turn, sometimes I wonder how they could do this, the discussion was so broad, to distil them down to draft goals. It wouldn't have happened if we didn't have the great support from the City of Vancouver to bring people together. The people around the table were very sophisticated people. If you do something like this you are always going to get advocacy groups who may want one thing in the plan. But these were all leaders who understood how to move things forward. So, I think they brought the right people together.

(Interview 5, Vancouver)

So the most important part of any type of large policy decision that is made is you need to have someone in charge or a small group of people in charge to agree that this is important and we need to do it. The most important thing was the change in government and I've been through multiple governments here in the City of Vancouver. They were all good and they all wanted to make the city a good place. I've never worked for a bad city council. Every city council has their slight priorities; they are all left or right of centre. But when this city council came in they had a singular vision, no pun intended, to do something green to actually make a difference and I think they realised – I don't know who the brain trust is, whether it's the mayor or other groups. I think they realised that cities, (and they were ahead of their time, 'cause a lot of people realise this now). Cities are kind of ground zero with respect to environmental issues.... The most important thing is having a very senior champion who says this is important – go find a way to do it. That is what they did. So once that fuse was lit, the next piece they did which I think is brilliant.... They brought keenly objective third-party groups, which was called the blue ribbon panel or Greenest City Action Team. This was scientists, leaders and academics from schools and health professionals. They brought them together and supported them and said, 'Tell us what you think based on your experience would make this city the greenest in the world. What do we have to do?' They came up with these very broad ten actions.... The staff took it back and made it into an operational plan and tried to put realistic targets in it.... We didn't pick easy targets because we are not going to hit them all. We picked targets we thought were aspirational to a point but also realistic. So people, who are actually going to have to make this happen, which is staff throughout the city mostly, and our partners weren't going to throw their hands in the air and say, 'this is impossible, we can't do this'. We wanted people to feel this was achievable but not easy. That is where the alchemy comes in, the magic, you need to inspire people to something that is out there, but not so far-fetched that they are just going to walk away.... There is no international award for the greenest city. It's an aspirational goal.

(Interview 1, Vancouver)

Glasgow

As a city-wide strategy it is not just going to be the city council which is quite different for us. It's very important to have a steering group. Hence we've got a multi-agency steering group with lots of different partners involved so that everyone can collectively input into that process. City council will obviously facilitate a bit of a lead in it, in terms of resourcing it and going out and actively engaging with people. But by all means, all of our partners will be playing a part. I suppose in the initial stages the city council has a bit of an organisational role to play, to keep things ticking. The idea would be that as time goes on, the process becomes more established, it would be kind of collaborative. It's a collective project and will continue.

(Interview 4, Glasgow)

groups positioned to oversee and bring together stakeholders. Portland is still evolving in this regard, however, historically it has had mayors who have progressed the agenda of climate change. Now as they move forward there is an awareness of the need for reporting mechanisms that strengthen accountability to policy actions, for which the Equity Working Group is intended to be the leader. While the Dublin Local Authorities are in the midst of this process, they are benefiting from the experience of these cities (and others). Reporting out on progress in addressing climate change is not an easy feat; how do you monitor progress on something when the targets keep changing as the climate changes? Leadership therefore needs not only be accountable, but adaptive and responsive; prepared to change course and open to new ways of doing things.

Leadership for each of the cities, while an important aspect of formal organisational structure, is not limited to an individual given 'power' to oversee development and implementation, but expands to leadership teams, both internally and externally. Interviewees highlighted that a challenge with formal plans is that they contain a breadth and scope of goals, and actions that may not succeed. However, leaders who are committed to the goals and targets of plans can play a valuable role in the successful uptake of policy, by driving the vision, being pragmatic in the development of policy, and bringing people together to build relationships that move policy forward.

Collaboration in practice: informal practices and the policy process

Recalling the work of Forester (1994, 1999, and 2012), Healey (1998, 2001, and 2004) and Innes (2004) in the arena of collaborative planning has demonstrated that as a practice, collaborative planning sees the engagement of stakeholders in a dialogue to address planning issues and complex problems and thus, create policy solutions. Through this process, planners take on various roles, from facilitators and educators to mediators and leaders (Forester, 1999, 2012). The process is intended to be inclusive and to give voice to citizens, but it is not without challenges, namely conflict. Collaborative planning is in theory an 'ideal' model, as it calls for stakeholders to come together, in spite of their differences, and work to address problems and create solutions that can be supported by all. In practice, the realities of collaborative planning may vary from theory as practice is subject to a variety of variables that may impact on the ability of planners and policy makers to engage with stakeholders; some of which Healey and Forester acknowledge: histories, beliefs, perceptions of stakeholders and perhaps others that are unknown. In short, the unpredictability of 'life' may shape practice more than theory can anticipate, something that each of these cities demonstrated as they sought to build trust, and relationships.

An objective of this book is to contribute to the understandings of collaborative planning in practice and the theoretical understanding of it. This section discusses the experiences of Glasgow, Vancouver and Portland in collaborating with a range of stakeholders to develop policy, which in large part occurs beyond the formal processes and practices of policy development. The section begins with a discussion of the aspects of Healey's, Forester's, and Innes' work that formed the questions posed to interviewees. Following this, the themes of relationship building, trust, equity and learning related to collaborative planning that emerged in the interviews will be discussed. Then the lessons from practice are discussed, namely the importance of time, acknowledgement and accountability, engagement, and the role of not knowing and learning from failure.

From theory to practice, applying collaborative planning

Each of the case study cities indicated that they engaged a range of stakeholders from internal partners to external partners, i.e. other levels of government, community-based organisations, advocacy groups, experts in climate change and citizens. How, though, did their engagement in practice reflect the theoretical tenets of collaborative planning? The questions posed to interviewees sought to gain insight into how policy makers engaged with stakeholders by asking first for a description of the plan development process, then moved towards questions about who was engaged and how. The questions were open ended to allow for stories of practice to emerge that could be analysed within a critical collaborative planning framework.

Collaborative planning theory, as discussed is concerned with the engagement of stakeholders in a manner that gives stakeholders a voice, considers the context in which policy is being developed, and strives to produce outcomes that are inclusive (Healey, 1998). As collaborative planning evolved from the work of Habermas on 'ideal speech', which was concerned with the ability of the public to have a voice in the formation of policy, communication is a key element of collaboration and is further developed by Forester who emphasises the meanings of language used in communication (Habermas *et al.*, 1974; Healey, 2002; Forester, 2012; Whittemore, 2014). Communication, in conjunction with relationship/trust building, openness, and knowledge sharing are key to engaging stakeholders in collaborative processes. Further, Healey in her work on collaborative planning highlights that trust and openness are valuable in growing networks and increasing knowledge exchange between stakeholders. However, theoretical understandings differ from the realities of practice, which is acknowledged by Healey in her emphasis on the 'how' and 'where' these opportunities for collaboration occur, and Forester in his emphasis on the influences on interaction that stem from location, place and set-up of a room, which can determine 'the success' of collaboration.

Across each of the cities there was recognition that changes needed to occur in relation to engagement processes and who was engaged in the process, as discussed in Box 3.10. What is interesting in these stories is that each of these cities is developing an engagement process that is outside the realm of their formal processes and statutory objectives. There is an effort by urban policy makers to seek out stakeholders and find novel ways and places to engage stakeholders, particularly citizens.

Engagement through relationships, leadership, and time

Collaborative planning is an ongoing process, and as such its value to formal policy development processes that cities engage in for the purposes of developing comprehensive plans is found in its call for building relationships with stakeholders. Collectively, interviewees in all three cities echoed the sentiment that the process of developing plans can fall short in effective engagement (Box 3.11). Furthermore, each city has recognised the value of engaging communities and they are employing new methods for engagement with the intent to build relationships with stakeholders, such that dialogue for policy development is ongoing, an important aspect of responding to climate change in cities.

Box 3.10 Engagement in practice

We, actually our planners, for the west end plan, which is Davie Street. They did one night where they went on a bar crawl with a local drag queen just to talk to people about the plan and what was happening. Because they knew people weren't going to come out to their meeting, they went to where they were and where the community they really needed to hear from were. Then also by having a drag queen there, who is part of that culture. It's a cultural ambassador. It is a welcoming in.

(Interview 3, Vancouver)

One of the things that came out fairly strongly [from the European Green Capital Bid] was that we had a bit of work to do around communication and engagement with our citizens and other people around green issues. So as part of the [our own Green] year we've actually focused on four groups: tourists, people coming into the city, citizens and a specific focus on young people. And we are trying events and various seminars bringing things to the city or sponsoring and endorsing other things, which would hit these definite target areas. We are trying to link with people and put more messages out there.

(Interview 4, Glasgow)

I just met with our library group. We have one of the most active libraries in the country, second busiest to NYC. Really well used, and they understand that a library is not just about books, but about services and connecting people.... They do a summer reads program, that is one opportunity to have some reading and work-shopping around [the] public curriculum... There are a lot of opportunities to engage in language around heat risk, and heat liveable wellness, which is what we are really concerned about. People are recognising heat-related illness, under-standing where they live and the built environment ... if you are an older adult, you are at risk, and if you have children in the house you are at risk. So trying to connect with those vulnerable communities through libraries.

(Interview 3, Portland)

Technology is providing a new path to engagement that previously did not exist; for example in the case of Vancouver using social media yielded an unanticipated amount of interest and engagement around the Greenest City Action Plan. The City of Vancouver as a result has a social media coordinator and strategy that feeds into the policy process. Technology appears to be emerging as a tool for engagement that each of the cities is grappling with. It represents both an opportunity and a challenge. There is an art to balancing the information that is gained through the process with what is feasible, as well as the opinions. With increased engagement via technology there is a need to harness information in clear and transparent ways. In one sense, cities in using social media open themselves to increased demands, criticism and render themselves more accountable to their actions (or inaction). However, the value of technology and social media lies in its ability to engage people who would not have previously interacted with the city. It is a tool for relationship building and trust building.

Box 3.11 Effective engagement of citizens

… We've been going about this all wrong. And that is true of a lot of community-led processes. There's good intent, the approach is fundamentally alienating just by virtue and a lot of it is time and resources. You want to get something done; having a slow process of bringing people into the conversation and building a long-term partnership is a very different thing. I think what has to happen is … more deliberative engagement processes have to happen slower.

(Interview 3, Portland)

The Scottish Government is recognizing that the actual program that sits behind the development plan is starting to become the key tool for getting people connected, and driving and delivering together. So what we can do from a planning perspective is make sure we highlight the key challenges and issues, look at them spatially, and try to make an intelligent analysis of what is going on … and bring it all together.

(Interview 1, Glasgow)

It got to more people than our last consultation did. It is really difficult to engage, we normally get the usual suspects. So what this [consultation] tried to do was say, here are the main points. There were 50-odd post cards that we gave out on how to comment. A summary document on which anyone could say anything. Here's a post card, you fill it in and post it back to us. You could also fill it online. We tried to make it as easy as possible.

(Interview 1, Glasgow)

Vancouver is in a slightly different position and faced with the need to sustain engagement.

I think this is the biggest public consultation the city has ever done. Some 30,000 people through all different channels, through the typical open house engagement, through to social media forms, Facebook and Twitter, and online discussion, for feedback on the plan.

(Interview 2, Vancouver)

We went to the public and engaged 35,000 people through open houses, workshops, you know everything from small table top meetings to huge online consultation asking people what do you think about this? It was amazingly a success. I think there was this latent demand to, 'What can I do to make a difference?' Probably the only downfall that came out of this, is once we got input from the public and from this committee, the public were still there going, 'What can we do now? What is next? How can we support this?' And we didn't have an answer for them.

(Interview 1, Vancouver)

Furthermore, as in the case of Vancouver it is a tool for public education on what the city is doing, the challenges the city faces, and how citizens can engage with the city.

There is recognition that engagement of a range of stakeholders beyond formal processes is needed for policy development, and implementation. Reflective of collaborative planning practice, the data gathered in the interviews highlighted the importance of relationship building and trust building as a condition for engagement with stakeholders. For Innes (2004), and Forester (2012) this is about planners and policy makers cultivating an awareness of sensitivities, and histories that may have meanings for the stakeholders that create barriers to engagement. In Portland, Vancouver and Glasgow, there was evidence of planners and policy makers being confronted with histories that have affected present day policy making (Box 3.12). Further, interviewees demonstrated a keen awareness of how their race and socio-economic status played a role in interaction with stakeholders; especially vulnerable groups, whom all three cities acknowledged were challenging to engage in the dialogue on climate change. Therefore, a keen awareness of audience and context in the engagement process, has led planners to recognise that, 'there are times when you are the messenger and times when you are not' (Interview 3, Portland 2015).

Collaborative planning calls for leadership that is fluid, not held solely by one individual, but shared, meaning that those involved in the collaborative process have the opportunity to be a leader. Interviewees were not asked directly about leadership, but the topic of leadership arose when asked about lessons that cities could teach each other and what enables cities to develop policy. Consistently,

---

Box 3.12 Confronting negative histories

Equity talks a lot about relationships, and sort of understanding your positional authority. Understanding, if you are a white person and want to be an advocate for people of colour, there are things you can do and there's things you shouldn't do, times you should be the messenger and [times you should] not.

(Interview 3, Portland)

Underpinning our ability to respond to even climate change and environmental shocks is health inequality, poverty, deprivation. They are the biggest challenges we face. Through this piece of work we've recognised that there are people we need to reach out to and speak to and understand what their particular perception is, what their challenge is. We are about to embark on a big consultation period for this, through which we've identified that we need to work with other agencies in the city as a way of doing that. Because as a council you kind of have a perception that a lot of time there is a parent–child relationship going and people often distrust the nature of that relationship. So we are working through other agencies; volunteering agencies, housing associations in the city, the NHS, police, and fire to reach these communities.... It's almost an ongoing thing.

(Interview 2, Glasgow)

leadership, either in the form of a team, or a champion was emphasised as a key driving force of policy. In relation to public participation and engagement in collaborative planning this fluidity supports the capacity of stakeholders, particularly individuals and communities to actively address their challenges with their solutions, as they have intimate knowledge of the impacts (Cohen and Schuchter, 2013). In other words, supporting ownership of policy actions. However, enabling and empowering stakeholders to be leaders is not without conflict, particularly in relation to power, in that collaboration as demonstrated by these cities and research (Cohen and Schuchter, 2013) calls for power in the form of hierarchy to be broken down.

In the literature critiquing collaborative planning, particularly in relation to conflict and consensus building, a key criticism is power (Allmendinger *et al.*, 2003; Innes *et al.*, 2007). The argument is that in the process of attempting to collaborate through consensus building it is inevitable that a struggle for power will occur, by means of the metaphorical 'loudest voice' winning (Healey, 1997; Innes *et al.*, 2007) and by the perception of parent–child relationships as demonstrated in the excerpts in Box 3.12. Contradicting this is the call for a 'benevolent' leader or team of leaders by interviewees that endeavours to actively listen to all voices while balancing the need for action. This is perhaps in light of the recognition that historically, the formal process of public consultation has leant itself to enabling the 'shouty voices', or the usual suspects to dominate the decision-making process. An opinion that consistently arose in all three cities, as demonstrated by the quotes below discussing how engagement is changing. What the excerpts illustrate is the recognition that a sense of power, or rather capacity, needs to be nurtured in citizens to achieve public participation in collaborative processes. In other words, as Mandarano (2015) cites in her research, echoing Arnstein (1969), that public participation increases when local government increases confidence in citizens that their engagement makes a difference; that government does not hold power over citizens, but seeks to empower citizens:

> What we are trying to do is get more community involvement.... There's supplementary guidance, which is about community consultation. The community saying, 'Yeah that feels comfortable'.... The reason they are doing things like charrettes is because it is a different way of engaging the community. We are trying different ways to get 'not-the-usual' suspects. Talking about things that matter to them. So instead of talking about the whole city, it is let's talk about an area that you know.... What we think we are going to do is take it down to the local level. We are going to take all the maps, and lay them. We are going to take our own space back, the drainage map, the vacant and derelict land map, put them all in one document and then we are going to hand it to community planning, and they are going to use their networks and go, 'this is the story of your spaces. This is what all these different bodies are saying they are going to do. Is that what you want them to do? What is important to you?'
>
> (Interview 1, Glasgow)

A technical advisor perspective, in general, there are a range of stakeholder or range of people that would have information that would be beneficial to this decision. They're probably limited by our institutional knowledge, as to where those groups are. So we have defaulted, going back to the same group. I think that, that is an area where we need to have those relationships to know, 'oh, there's a new group that formed, it is a local non-profit that has expertise in tree equity'.... And I don't necessarily always know that. From a broad participatory perspective, we do look at who's participating in a public process. If we do survey ... where we have the ability to collect demographic information, we look at that and try to see how reflective it is of the overall community and identify gaps. 'Hey, we are not hearing from the Asian American community, can we do direct outreach to try to get those voices in the process?'

(Interview 2, Portland)

Leadership is not about holding power, but about managing power and ensuring 'equity' and 'opportunity'. Leaders in these cities endeavoured to create conditions that would build trust with people, thereby signalling to people that their opinions and knowledge have value for the policy development process and implementation. Succinctly, according to interviewees, leadership equated to ownership of problems and solutions, within the organisation and by communities with whom cities are working. Without communities and citizens being part of policy development process, responding to problems, such as climate change, it was acknowledged that policies created by the city would fail. Buy-in from communities is contingent upon their participation as leaders and the role of the city is to facilitate the conditions in which communities and stakeholders can come together.

Relationship building, trust building, empowering a sense of ownership and leadership are challenging for cities. Whilst acknowledgement of past wrongs, history and understanding circumstances of stakeholders can overcome barriers to these challenges, interviewees unanimously emphasised time as an important aspect of building relationships, fostering leadership and developing policy. Time, in the context of climate change planning, is a challenge. There is an argument that climate change is a pressing need that urgently requires action now. Yet the interviewees' reference to time is more with regards to policy development processes being deliberate and considerate. There appears to be a view that time is an investment, particularly with regards to building relationships and trust to achieve engagement in the short and long terms. Further, time is valuable in developing policy, as it allows for policy makers to take stock of problems identified by various stakeholders and how they can be solved efficiently, and collaboratively. The value of time spent engaging in a deliberate and considered process, is demonstrated by the excerpt presented here describing an engagement process with aboriginal groups around health issues in Portland.

You pay for relationships. One of the best ways for government to build goodwill in communities is to fund the programs, projects and services that those communities want. And to do it in ways that are respectful. That allows the flexibility for those communities to define what that looks like. We have some work, the future generations collaborative. Run out the [place]. It's Native American health. I don't know all the details. But the whole thing, I mean it is a white woman that is coordinating it.... She's a staffer to these elders, the Wisdom of Elders Group Who are literally defining, 'you want to talk to us. You want to do this work to affect our diabetes you are going to do it like this. We are going to have a long time for relationships building. We don't give a s*** about your budget timeline. Ask for more money. Because for these 9 months we are going have relationships. We are going to have food. You are going to understand our history, and then we get over to what you want to try to teach us'. It is a wonderful example. And now you see these women and men working with [name], who is the coordinator and it's amazing. If you talked to her a year and a half ago, she would say how frustrating it was and how she wasn't the right person for this; that, there was too much trauma and too much history.... If you look now.... That same group of folks we can talk to on any number issues. They are going to engage with us in ways that they never would have before. So whether its emergency planning or climate change or health outcomes, criminal justice, it doesn't matter the whole portfolio of what we do. That investment here is going to pay dividends a decade, two decades from now. These are folks who have built relationships and trust. Which is a long way of saying you pay for these relationships. And the communities are better for it, because they are building their own capacity to solve their own problems. Which then is our obligation. Then the taxpayers'. It's good government. In theory.

(Interview 4, Portland)

Taking the time to engage in a deliberate and considered process that is collaborative serves another purpose; it allows for policy makers to discover a focal point for collaboration. Identifying a narrative, as has been argued in this research enables collaboration around the development of resilience-based climate change policy. Narratives provide a unifying vision for policy makers to engage stakeholders from citizens to higher levels of government. Vitally they facilitate ownership of problems and solutions. Before this can happen, though, policy makers need to identify a unifying narrative from which to begin dialogue with stakeholders. As each of the cities demonstrate this is a process that calls for meaningful engagement with citizens

Finding a narrative

At the outset, before interviewing policy makers, a hypothesis was made that identifying a narrative that holds value for stakeholders could provide a focus for collaboration on climate change policy development. The case for narratives is rooted in the research and literature on resilience building and collaborative planning. The rationale for narratives, as opposed to finding issues and concerns of stakeholders, is that resilience building is an on-going process that requires long-term active engagement. What has emerged from discussions with interviewees is that narratives that acknowledge place-specific challenges are needed for engagement and collaborative policy development, and to allow urban policy makers to build trust and relationships with stakeholders allowing new narratives to evolve. Interviewees (Box 3.13) point towards the consideration of narratives that revolve around people, their needs and values, and place: succinctly, narratives need to be tangible and concrete.

Box 3.13 A focus for engaging on climate change policy

In terms of public, I think not so much, and I think that, that is something where for instance we now have this partnership with Vancouver Coastal Health (VCH). I think they can play a role in getting involved. For instance, if there is an engagement process around bike lanes ... having someone, like the Ministry of Health, say, 'I support this plan. It has these potential health benefits.' I think can really help. I think health is something that is really concrete and tangible for a lot of people. Whereas climate change is not. Planning speak is also sometimes not very accessible. It's not something people can wrap their head around in a tangible way. I think coming from a health perspective people get it. They get, 'I don't want my kid to be obese and not have physical activity. I don't want to feel like I am socially isolated'.... The actions that we are putting forward as part of the Healthy City Strategy do help climate change. It does help with planning a better environment. But if we frame it under a health lens it resonates in a lot bigger way for residents than if you came at it from a different angle.

(Interview 4, Vancouver)

We can't talk about water resources; they got to find those places where they can. What's really interesting, much of the work disaster resilience folks are trying to do in terms of engaging local community, neighbourhood emergency teams, where they are building capacity.... We don't need a great big word. We need to understand where this work is taking place under different names, and where it aligns. And if it means not calling it climate change, making sure it is not alienating conversations. I am actually for it. I think there is a time and a place where you need to talk about climate change.

(Interview 3, Portland)

The people we engaged with are the people who probably are older people, who had a vested interest in the community. People who weren't interested in the community or didn't appear to be interested.... There was a barrier, it was obvious through the kind of demographics of the people who wanted to engage and people who were engaged that there was a gap and what we need to understand is who are these people, and why aren't they engaged with this. And I think the problem is they don't want to be engaged for other reasons. There are underlying things. So then how do we get engagement with long term thinking about risk and resilience if there's underlying things? ... Lack of education, bad education, bad experience, bad social, poverty, deprivation, perception of government.... People who come in and talk with them are generally police, agencies; ... it's kind of the hierarchy of needs. It's the things at the bottom. If they aren't there, it's almost like, is climate change something or resilience something at the top of that? How do you engage with people at the top level, when there's stuff at the bottom? That is the problem.

(Interview 2, Glasgow)

There's been a lot of chat around volunteering, as a kind of good indicator. It shows people's basic needs are being met and they've got something to give back.... Certainly something around volunteering might be close enough; it's a close step to being a kind of balanced city, for health and wellbeing. Cause there's sort of mental health issues here as well. People feeling included in their community. Having that community cohesiveness as well. It's an interesting one. But there's been some thought around it.

(Interview 4, Glasgow)

On a focus for policy, it was also stated by interviewees that a singular focus could be limiting.

We've moved from sustainability, as our kind of core guiding principle, to an explosion of sustainability, so we are being a lot more explicit about sustainability. It doesn't just mean environmental sustainability, it is economic sustainability, it means social, it means climate, it means health. And I think that, that shift is helpful as far as setting future agendas but then it also kind of opens up a world and makes it more complicated.

(Interview 2, Portland)

What is interesting about the narratives chosen by each city is how they emerged. Glasgow used health and the social determinants of health (SDH), Vancouver used branding as the 'Greenest City', and Portland used equity. Interviewees were asked how these focuses emerged for policy and formed the narratives used to engage stakeholders. The responses highlighted the importance of identifying a narrative that is place-based that would 'spark' the policy dialogue and debate. Critically, in all three cities the initial narrative introduced urban policy makers to the inherent problems with policy making in its formal form. Consequently, the process of identifying narratives for collaboration forced urban policy makers to acknowledge the 'hopes and concerns' of stakeholders, permitting them to engage in dialogue with stakeholders and find new narratives for on-going engagement.

So they started with the Greenest City Action Plan, we approached them about the Healthy City Strategy, but the two overlap a lot. I just think the healthy city initiative is broader, it has the opportunity to resonate with the population because people are always interested in things that might adversely impact their health or improve their health.

(Interview 5, Vancouver)

The process underlying the evolution of each city's narrative is important, as they show that engagement needs to be done in a considered and deliberate manner and done respectfully. Vancouver's Health City Strategy emerged from the Greenest City Action Plan, from the recognition that the environment in which people live plays a role in their health. Vancouver recognises that it is blessed with a natural environment that endows the city with clean air and water, and permits people to live and to lead healthy lifestyles. As such, protecting that endowment is at the core of the Greenest City Action Plan and the Healthy City Strategy. A key difference with these two plans is their development; public engagement on the Greenest City Action Plan was broad, the team responsible for the Healthy City Strategy did not invite public comment in a similar manner, perhaps as a lesson learned. Instead, for the Healthy City Strategy, the city worked with Vancouver Coastal Health and carefully selected a group of 30 community leaders, who were respected in the broader community and there-fore, able to represent people. This was beneficial in engaging and building rela-tionships with key groups whose health is of concern, i.e. the aboriginal community and the homeless. This shift demonstrates how a focus can be used to identify challenges that can then serve as a focus for on-going collaboration. For example, during interviews it emerged that Vancouver faces challenges with social cohesion/loneliness. Now, the city is taking action to address this by ensuring citizens have access to green spaces for recreation, which incidentally helps the city address climate change. There is an acknowledgement that often one action can address multiple problems and it is about maximising these bene-fits and opportunities.

> The Single Outcome agreement basically, all cities or councils in Scotland are tasked with developing a single or a set of a few goals that all of the ser-vices in the city will work towards. In Glasgow one of them is around health. Basically, everything we should be doing, we should be looking at improving the health of the city.... The Glasgow Effect basically, the life expectancy rate in Glasgow is much lower than other cities and neighbour-ing authorities. No one really knows why that is, lack of education, health. We don't really know the problem and there [have] been so many studies into why Glasgow is affected more than other comparable cities, like Man-chester, Leeds and Liverpool. There's a big problem and we don't neces-sarily know what it is. I think driving all of that is a will to improve health.
>
> (Interview 1, Glasgow)

Glasgow's policy development process in some regards is the reverse of Van-couver's, in that its approach to climate change began with health and the social determinants of health (SDH), and is now focused on the city as a whole. In choosing to study Glasgow's policy development process, it was recognised that the city's decision to use the SDH as the foundation for its Climate Change Strategy may have emerged from Glasgow's pre-existing population health challenges, namely its high mortality rates and low life expectancy. The value (and lessons) for Glasgow in developing its climate change strategy around the SDH is that the process revealed the need for planning to return its focus to people and place. Consequently, Glasgow embarked on a branding exercise to engage citizens, which resulted in the slogan 'People Make Glasgow', a theme that is now embedded in its policy development. For Glasgow, the focus of policy is people, and creating a place that meets their needs and makes them resilient to climate change. As in Vancouver, the process highlighted a need to engage specific groups, to be strategic about engagement:

> Health was a good focus and it kind of went with our sustainability lens that we were looking at. Health and well-being with the social aspect of it, and then we had other themes addressing the economic pillar and the environmental pillar. In Glasgow, people are such an important asset. Health and well-being have to be at the centre for people to be at the centre of it. It was felt by the city council that it was important, that it couldn't be … a theme on its own…. A lot of the actions that were recommended under it should be under the other themes, to make sure that there would be ownership of them. So, that is why it became … the overarching theme…. The team working quite closely with the Glasgow Centre for Population and Health used a lot of research. We used a lot of that evidence base to write the document…. When it went to senior management for approval, they seemed to be happy with it. And at different stages of the consultation, we sort of got validation as a sign of progress. People seemed to be happy with it. We trusted the evidence and we trusted people's input that this was the right thing to do. For the city, at the time.
>
> (Interview 3, Glasgow)

During Portland's engagement process, the city discovered its need to address social inequity, leading to its focus on equity. For Portland, the focus for policy has been equity, and using an equity lens to address climate change, as the argument has been made through environmental justice that climate change adversely impacts vulnerable groups the most. In the process of engaging stakeholders for the development plan, the scope of the city's challenges with inequity stemming from race, and poverty became apparent. For policy makers and stakeholders alike it became apparent that addressing climate change was simultaneously an opportunity for addressing inequity, an issue that is an emerging challenge for Portland. For policy makers in Portland, inequity in health has emerged as an equity issue, and as such it has informed the city's need to develop policies that address health and climate change simultaneously.

> The equity work, I think, naturally is rooted in public health. I don't know if our climate action work would be able to describe the reasons for equity without public health information. Public health has the story, it has the connectivity, and everybody understands being hot. I mean everybody understands things that impact your health, your housing conditions, how far,

what your street is like, how many trees you have. There's an intrinsic or intuitive, there's a deep level of understanding around when we talk about health. So for me, health provides and will provide the connection of how we talk and move people in a very emotional way.

(Interview 4, Portland)

Each of these cities have shown that identifying a narrative that has meaning for stakeholders is a point from which to begin collaborating on policy. Engagement does not happen in the absence of recognising the needs of the community or citizens for whom policy solutions are intended. In order for stakeholders, particularly citizens, to engage with cities on climate change policy they need to understand the relationship between the issues, the policy responses and their lives, and also how they as individuals can contribute to the solutions. In other words, 'hope value', and as such each of these cities has the means to support stakeholders in taking actions to help their cities become resilient to climate change.

Resilient communities own the solutions to the problems they face. Resilient communities have the power to make decisions. You know there's the old adage to environmental justice, 'the community that speaks for itself best protects itself.' I think that is what resilient communities look like. They understand their problems; they have ownership, or collective ownership. They're not necessarily responsible for the solutions but they can help drive them.

(Interview 4, Portland)

Creative engagement: setting the path for life long relationships

How are cities setting the course for building relationships that will sustain engagement in policy dialogue? This is a question that yielded unique and practical answers for overcoming the challenges and barriers to building relationships, to empowering communities with a sense of ownership, and to fostering leadership.

In Vancouver, CityStudio emerged as an endeavour to engage with the city's six main post-secondary schools; to create a programme where students can gain real world experience relevant to their studies. The program has evolved into a highly valuable tool for the city to address issues that simultaneously benefits students wanting to make their city a better place by providing them with the opportunity to work with the city. Students and city staff can approach each other with ideas and problems that they would like to be addressed and the student work to create a solution. The program has yielded successes and failures, from 'Keys to the Street' to bonfires, both aimed at addressing a key issue for the City of Vancouver, social cohesion.

The other one that we did, it started off as something called C3, campus city collaborative and the intent was to somehow get all the universities in the city working together and kind of after a lot of dancing, what we landed on was a project called CityStudio. That has been really successful. And we are CityStudio, the city and the six schools are looking at what the next phase of that is going to be. It's been hugely successful. There's been ten thousand student hours put towards Greenest City Projects. It is such a symbiotic relationship because … the city gets work done related to the Greenest City, that we would either have to hire a consultant for if we didn't have internal expertise or capacity to do. And the students get real world project experience that they can put on their resumes and also learn from and learn what it is like to work with municipalities. One of the priorities for us, how do you get work done in a bureaucracy. It's not easy all the time. So that's a really good project. And there are two main sides to CityStudio. One side called the partner courses, which functions similar to a co-op. Your traditional co-op where the city would say up at 10.… For example, I am thinking of transit issues and they are going to close a street, and it's going to impact traffic but I don't have time to do the work. I can put forward as a CityStudio project. CityStudio will review the project. 'Yeah I know BCIT has a transit course and it lines up perfectly with this, I'll go talk to the instructor and see if they want to take the project for one year.… The other half is the studio project where they bring in 20 students every semester, fall, spring and summer semester.… We kind of sit down with them, here are the big issues the city is working on. They go off and develop their own projects.

(Interview 1, Vancouver)

As mentioned, in developing the Greenest City Action Plan, the city ran into the unique issue of citizens asking what more they can do to help the city. A response to this latent demand has led the city to embark on its Green and Digital Demonstration Program. This program is mutually beneficial to business owners and the city. For the city it allows them to engage with business owners, and for business owners it gives them the opportunity to have their product tested and reviewed by a recognised brand, 'The City of Vancouver'.

The Green and Digital Demonstration Program (GDDP) came out of the Greenest City Action Plan as one of the projects to support the green economy. It kind of lingered for a while, until I started working here, and I looked up how come nobody is doing the project. So, I took it on and got in front of council and it was approved by Council last July. We launched it last September. And what the project is the City of Vancouver, as a corporation big 'C', big 'C' city; little 'c' is community, as a corporation is huge.… There's hundreds if not thousands of fledgling green businesses looking for ways to demonstrate their products, and either kind of do a little bit of a beta test, or 'my product is good it's been tested it works fine, but I need some marketing 'oomphs' and the City of Vancouver is a big brand'. We are known all over the world. If they can go to their investors, or to their potential buyers and say, 'City of Vancouver is using my product and you can go talk to the city and they will tell you about my product and why they like my product', it will help them develop and grow as a green business. So the intent of this program is to work with inner procurement system to allow businesses to demonstrate their products on city assets. Those assets could be vehicles, roads, buildings, could be staff. One of the companies we are working with has an electric assist bicycle that is fully enclosed. It looks like a smart car, three wheels, called 'Velo Metro'. Really cool company. They are going to use a very similar system as a car-to-go. It would be a one-way car share, except it's a bicycle, and it's enclosed so you put your groceries in there, you can do it in a suit in the rain. It's perfect for Vancouver, but you are riding a bike, not driving a car. And its power assist so you are not getting all sweaty in your suit, but you can adjust the power assist you can make it really difficult or really easy. And so they are just developing the prototype and they are trying to get investors but they need someone to actually use their bikes, try them out. So they approached us through this program. We have staff that go to meetings, we have staff who ride bikes to meetings all the time, we have staff who use a car-to-go or Modo car share. We could use your bikes. So the program is kind of the bureaucracy in the background that makes sure there is insurance in place and legal agreements and the risk is managed appropriately and everything is done.

(Interview 1, Vancouver)

When reviewing Glasgow's plans the novel 'Sow and Grow Everywhere' (SAGE) project, a policy action to address vacant sites with urban greening, was earmarked for further discussion with interviewees. During the interviews, this program was discussed in greater detail. The program has evolved, and has demonstrated a means through which the city is building relationships between stakeholders and making the city about people and place:

SAGE was a pilot. So what we've got in Glasgow is called stalled spaces. That said, in order to improve the environment we've got so many vacant and derelict land, brownfield sites, across the city and some of our most deprived communities are living beside this horrible environment. There's metal fences, stuff abandoned in it, there's guard dogs. It is horrible, it doesn't feel safe, and it is not nice. These are development sites. We are not going to turn them into open space, we are not going to take them out of development, but we want to do something different.... What Glasgow did was say, 'actually you are trying to brand that, it's actually about growing spaces. We'll do something called stalled spaces, which is bigger, because not all of these vacant sites, will the community grow on them, they may want a temporary play area, performance area....' What we did was set up a kind of per form or a legal agreement that made it easier for community to go to the private land owners and say, 'look sign this land over to us, we acknowledge it's not taking away your development potential'.

(Interview 1, Glasgow)

The city's wide range of responsibilities lends itself to collaboration with other agencies. As such, it has worked with organisations such as the Glasgow Centre for Population Health, to develop policies, namely its climate change action plan, which was based on the social determinants of health. Further, they work with the National Health Service and Fire Service to formulate their community planning policy. There is an effort to learn from these organisations and incorporate their practices into policy set by the council. A story of practice provided in the interviews highlights the manner in which the city is looking to build connections through connections:

> For example, I was speaking to a fireman. He's quite senior, a manager in the fire brigade. And he's saying they've actually got a scheme where once a week they actually go out and play football with community groups. And it is about being a friendly face and about becoming part of the community rather than on the edge of the community. And its things like that little schemes that make a big difference. They are about gaining trust; they are about people. Allowing people to open up to you. And that way you can kind of share your agenda with them, and receive their agenda too. It's a two-way thing. Its things like that, that we are going to hopefully start looking at through the resilience strategy.
>
> (Interview 2, Glasgow)

Another practice example in relation to climate change is the city's endeavour to engage a vulnerable community on issues of flooding.

> [Name] is an area that abuts onto the countryside. It's almost like a village in itself. Physically it is very cut-off from the city. There is one road that leads to it, and that road floods a lot. They've got a lot of problems in that area. There's a very deprived area; a lot of vacant and derelict land. A lot of gangs in that area as well. It's a challenging area. Small area, but a challenging area. There's actually a community group that was set up, actually ten years now, called [Name]. Now we did some work not too long ago, recently we're still doing work with [Name], specifically to make [Name] a more climate resilient community. We've worked, we've gone in through the [Name], which is basically like a community enterprise, but it's been set up to work with residents in the area. To try and develop their understanding of climate change risk and also almost develop [an] integrated action plan. So, the council and communities work together.... We did an exercise where we walked through the streets where we tried to engage with people that way.
>
> (Interview 2, Glasgow)

We did an exercise where we got people to draw their vision of the future. So, a really simple exercise. What is a more sustainable, and a better future for [Name]? One guy literally drew a kind of vegetable patch that he was working on. And for him that was something that excited him and it was something that he was empowered to do, it was a very real thing. So some people were drawing these big pictures of people holding hands, kind of wind turbines on top of buildings. But his was a very real thing. I think it's that, finding very real things that excited people and these kind of community gardens, I think they are great opportunities and I've seen it work really well. I think its finding opportunities rather than you know, 'we're scaring people'.

(Interview 2, Glasgow)

Portland's capacity in terms of its remit is significantly less than Vancouver and Glasgow. Despite this the city works within its constraints, and the city is working to strengthen its own internal ability to implement the Portland Plan. This was reflected in its efforts to engage over 20 agencies outside the city in the development of the Portland Plan to create a common vision. Beyond the Portland Plan, specifically the Climate Action Plan (CAP), planners worked with other government departments to create plans that were collectively developed. The quote below illustrates the engagement of stakeholders in developing the health policies in the plan.

... this is the start of having multi-partner groups that were developing the plan. We had nine different technical action groups (TAGs).... The one I chaired, or facilitated, on health food and safety we had folks from Multnomah Health Department, The Policy Bureau, Oregon Public Health. All these different agencies and as well as community members who had a particular interest in health. We tried to weave those pieces together from the get go. Rather than developing something and having everyone sign on to it. So, these other plans. The comprehensive plan and the climate action plan, are, well, the CAP is directing the city and county and it is adopted by resolution by the city and county.

(Interview 2, Portland)

The city and county are also benefiting from empowering community groups to undertake work. The work undertaken by these groups is playing a role in the city's development of ongoing engagement by having a dialogue with youth around climate change.

There's a community organisation called APANO (Asian Pacific Association) ... they are working with the city, doing neighbourhood revitalisation in an area called the Jade District. And as part of that the youth engagement component we have in our office a woman that is doing a climate or health workshop, and so she is working with their youth organiser to organise culturally specific youth workshops around educating and informing, trying to find opportunities for kind of youth projects around climate change. Also working with schools in other settings. She did workshops with one of the schools around climate health and environmental justice. This one in the Jade District is at their community farm their community room. So it's about being on the ground.

(Interview 3, Portland)

The examples from practice presented here are a small sample of what each city is doing to engage citizens, and to build relationships and awareness of how citizens can play a key role in the delivery of climate change policy. Cities are using other methods to engage citizens beyond these that have yielded success. Vancouver used social media in its engagement for the Greenest City Action Plan, which led to the city finding additional avenues through social media to engage citizens, for example, its annual city bird competition using Twitter to educate people on the different bird species in Vancouver which contribute to biodiversity, and to vote on their favourite. Green education figures prominently in Glasgow and Portland as a means to educate younger generations, and to build lifelong commitment to the environment. Constructing these policies has taught policy makers in each of these cities lessons that are valuable to the policy dialogue around cities responding to climate change, and enabling cities to 'leap frog over each other' and become the greenest city.

Note

1 The Rockefeller Foundation's 100 Resilient Cities was pioneered by the Rockefeller Foundation, and is dedicated to helping cities around the world become more resilient to the physical, social and economic challenges that are a growing part of the 21st century – www.100resilientcities.org.

References

Allmendinger, P., Tewdwr-Jones, M. and Morphet, J. (2003) 'Public Scrutiny, Standards and the Planning System: Assessing Professional Values within a Modernized Local Government', *Public Administration*, 81(4), pp. 761–780. doi: 10.1111/j.0033-3298.2003.00370.x.
Arnstein, S.R. (1969) 'A ladder of Citizen Participation', *Journal of the American Institute of Planners,* 35(4), pp. 216–224.
Cheng, A. S. and Daniels, S. E. (2003) 'Examining the Interaction Between Geographic Scale and Ways of Knowing in Ecosystem Management: A Case Study of Place-Based Collaborative Planning', *Forest Science*, 49(6), pp. 841–854. doi: 10.1093/forestscience/49.6.841.
Cohen, A. K. and Schuchter, J. W. (2013) 'Revitalizing Communities Together', *Journal of Urban Health*, 90(2), pp. 187–196. doi: 10.1007/s11524-012-9733-3.
Forester, J. (1994) 'Bridging Interests and Community: Advocacy Planning and the Challenges of Deliberative Democracy', *Journal of the American Planning Association,* 60(2), pp. 153–158.
Forester, J. (1999) 'Reflections on the future understanding of planning practice', *International Planning Studies*. Routledge, 4(2), pp. 175–193. doi: 10.1080/135634799 08721734.

Forester, J. (2012) 'Learning to Improve Practice: Lessons from Practice Stories and Practitioners' Own Discourse Analyses (or Why Only the Loons Show Up)', *Planning Theory & Practice*. Routledge, 13(1), pp. 11–26. doi: 10.1080/14649357.2012.649905.

Glasgow City Council (2012) *Climate Change Strategy and Action Plan*, November 2010

Habermas, J., Lennox, S. and Lennox, F. (1974) 'The Public Sphere: An Encyclopedia Article (1964)', *New German Critique*. [New German Critique, Duke University Press], (3), pp. 49–55. doi: 10.2307/487737.

Healey, P. (1997) *Collaborative Planning: Shaping Places in Fragmented Societies*. UBC Press (Planning, environment, cities). Available at: https://books.google.ie/books?id=psW_hMb3AH8C.

Healey, P. (1998) 'Collaborative planning in a stakeholder society', *Town Planning Review*, 69(1), p. 1. doi: 10.3828/tpr.69.1.h651u2327m86326p.

Healey, P. (2002) 'On Creating the "City" as a Collective Resource', *Urban Studies*, 39(10), pp. 1777–1792. doi: 10.1080/0042098022000002957.

Innes, J.E. (2004). "Consensus Building: Clarifications for the Critics', *Planning Theory*, 3(1), pp. 5–20.

Innes, J. E., Connick, S. and Booher, D. (2007) 'Informality as a Planning Strategy', *Journal of the American Planning Association*. Routledge, 73(2), pp. 195–210. doi: 10.1080/01944360708976153.

Mandarano, L.A. (2015) 'Civic Engagement Capacity Building: An Assessment of the Citizen Planning Academy Model of Public Outreach and Education', *Journal of Planning Education and Research*, 35(2), pp. 174–187.

Whittemore, A. H. (2014) 'Phenomenology and City Planning', *Journal of Planning Education and Research*. SAGE Publications Inc, 34(3), pp. 301–308. doi: 10.1177/0739456X14536989.

4 Lessons for collaborative planning from practice

Introduction

Collaborative planning, as discussed in Chapter 2 is the theoretical framework used to analyse the policy development process in Glasgow, Vancouver, Portland and Dublin. It is evident that planners and urban policy makers recognise the value of collaborating with diverse stakeholders to formulate climate change responses that will make cities and citizens resilient to present and future impacts of climate change. Engaging with stakeholders in collaborative processes has for urban policy makers emphasised the importance of addressing the social and economic impacts of climate change, not just the physical, through policies that consider the lived experiences of stakeholders. In working with stakeholders, interviewees in all four case study cities were able to develop policy responses that addressed climate change and that responded to stakeholder concerns. For example, in Vancouver the process of introducing protected cycle paths throughout the city addressed concerns of safety for cyclists while providing a solution for achieving a modal shift in transportation. With their focus on equity, Portland addressed a challenge for lower-income families, costly energy bills, while reducing energy demands (fossil fuel use) via its weatherisation of homes program. While in Glasgow, the 'Glasgow Effect' led policy makers to create policies that sought to improve the health of citizens by increasing green spaces, which also provided flood adaptation. Glasgow, Vancouver and Portland have all been able to create institutional structures that define responsibilities and ownership for policy development, implementation and monitoring in support of their efforts. For these cities, to engage in collaborative processes with a range of stakeholders, it is evident that an institutional structure that supports adaptive governance, permitting stakeholders to take the 'lead' on policies and programs, facilitates collaborative action. (The Dublin Local Authorities (DLAs) are embarking on a process to create an organisational structure that will in theory enable them to achieve their climate change action plans within the parameters set out by the Irish National Government.)

Institutional structures and narratives are not the sole key to success. Emerging from the stories of practice is the importance of five key aspects: ownership, the role of the planner, leadership, technology, and narratives in collaborative processes. In each of the case study cities, ownership emerged as the foundation of collaborative planning processes, and is connected to the other four key aspects: ownership's role will be discussed in the context of each, to begin a discussion of the evolving role of the planner in practice from Forester's ideas to the policy maker's ideal of themselves, which involves a more explicit awareness of one's identity. Building on the role of the urban policy makers is the challenge of leadership in collaborative planning, which is investigated and reframed in the context of ownership of 'problems and solutions' and empowerment. How policy makers can potentially address the problems and solutions with technology is then examined: the benefits and challenges technology presents for engagement and collaboration, and how it can increase capacity for policy dialogue.

Finally, the narratives used by the case study cities to engage stakeholders in collaborative policy development processes. Of importance here is identifying a narrative that has value, but also fosters ownership, such that stakeholders are imbued with a sense of agency.

Role of the policy practitioners: from Forester to self-cognisant

Narratives for policy dialogue not only opened the doors for collaboration, they drew attention to the role of policy makers, specifically their positionality and identities. What has emerged is that while the 'right' narrative is beneficial to opening the doors to dialogue, policy makers need to be open to acknowledging and taking ownership of history (cultural, and legacies of past governments), negative perceptions, and lack of knowledge, and be prepared to take risks, innovate and fail. From the experience of practitioners, it is important that policy makers recognise past wrongs in order to build trust and relationships with stakeholders that will enable dialogue on policy issues to happen.

There is an emphasis in Forester's work on understanding and building empathy with stakeholders and finding concerns and common ground from which to collaborate. The key here lies in using acknowledgment to build trust by acquiring knowledge of issues facing stakeholders, then identifying common ground from which all stakeholders can agree to move forward with policy actions (Forester, 1994; Shipley and Utz, 2012). The planner is to engage in diplomacy to achieve practical action through a mindset of 'learning' (Forester, 1994). Learning can be facilitated by creating opportunities for stakeholders to teach planners about how issues impact them, which can be through formal or informal channels: public meetings, drinks, social media, face-to-face and third parties are a few of the suggested means of engagement (Healey, 1997; Forester, 2012; Shipley and Utz, 2012). The objective is to learn and acquire knowledge on what are the perceived threats and vulnerabilities, and how these issues can be addressed effectively (Forester, 1994).

> I think the main thing is that we should ... be humble and open to listening to other people's experiences and views. We also did a lot of work with

other local authorities. Some of them were part of a network, so sharing experiences there as well helped us. From my perspective its being open to other ideas and other perspectives and other experiences rather than setting out with one objective, that's very wretched of us. And I think Glasgow, that's being open with sharing and reinventing things and being creative and using people to do that.

(Interview 3, Glasgow)

Planners and policy makers alike were working to find ways of engaging with stakeholders, especially those who have tended to be on the periphery of policy development. For urban policy makers in Glasgow, they recognised that they were not hearing from the residents of Lambhill. For Portland and Vancouver, it is various ethnic groups and for Dublin, it is the 'transient population' and the vulnerable that urban policy makers needed to engage. All the cities were faced with the question of how to overcome these barriers and engage with these groups in meaningful ways to develop and implement policy. One approach to addressing this barrier was to increase the accessibility of information available to citizens. For example, in Vancouver and in Portland this meant translating various documents into multiple languages to reach various ethnic groups. However, an emphasis of Forester's work is that planners should be conscious of the words they use in posing questions to stakeholders and in delivering their message to stakeholders. As the messages are affected by the words used to convey the message, in choosing the 'wrong' words a message can become lost. Therefore, while translations provide information the under-standing of the message depends on the complexity of the words chosen. It is acknowledged that 'planner-speak' (and 'policy-speak') potentially alienates citizens and other stakeholders; whereas choosing words that are understood is more effective in conveying a message; it also demonstrates authenticity in wanting to engage.

The self-cognisant planner

Building on this, the interviewees echoed Forester's (1994 and 1999) view that the role of a planners is to be not only experts but simultaneously mediators, negotiators, translators, leaders, advocates, teachers and students. While inter-viewees shared this view in regards to their role, they added an element of 'whom'. This referred to the meanings or perceptions of their identities held by stakeholders, and how that impacts upon the delivery of policy messages. Box 4.1 presents the awareness of the 'meanings' that their individual identities play in the process of developing policy. As such, communication is not just the words or the 'role' they take on, but the nonverbal aspects of 'who' they are that play a role in engagement and policy development. In order for ownership of policies to occur, the stakeholders need to feel involved, and to have been involved in the process, which may be impacted by 'whom' the messages are delivered. Perceived inequity could result in an unwillingness to co-operate by stakeholders. This element of reflecting on one's identity progresses Forester's idea of the deliberate planner (Forester, 1999; Allmendinger, 2002).

In Glasgow, Portland, and Vancouver, the importance of building trust and building relationships stood out as a key factor in the capacity of policy makers to engage with the communities and citizens they needed to work with in the development of policy. Simultaneously, there was recognition of the barriers to the building of that trust. For all cities a barrier was distrust in the actions of local government (and often government in general). The roots of this distrust varied for each city, but there were common themes for example: history, institutional racism, and inequity. There was a general acknowledgement that in order for this barrier of distrust, and its associated barriers of inequity and racism to be overcome, planners and urban policy makers would need to go into the communities and understand the root causes and the solutions people desired and sought. However, there was sensitivity to the meanings attached to their position as a policy maker within city 'X', and who they might represent simply by nature of their physical appearances, e.g. skin colour, socio-economic status and the associated meanings, that was discussed by interviewees (Box 4.1).

In forming this awareness of who is delivering the messages or who is communicating with stakeholders, there was an emphasis that humility and acknowledging that they, the policy makers, do not have all the answers, is needed for engagement. This self-critique or self-awareness adds to collaborative planning theory. Whilst collaborative planning theory calls for planners to reflect on the histories, and the culture of the stakeholders; there is little emphasis on the planner or policy maker to 'check' their own values, their personal histories, their ethnic and socio-economic backgrounds, and how their perspectives may affect engagement (Forester, 1994, 1999; Healey, 1998b; Lake and Zitcer, 2012; Pitt and Bassett, 2014). Interviewees consistently emphasised the value of admitting to 'not knowing' the lived experience of stakeholders due (possibly) to their own race and socio-economic status. As such, being open to learning about the lived experiences of citizens is a valuable tool for engagement. This according to interviewees (Box 4.1) is strengthened by their ability to reflect upon and understand their personal lived experiences. In essence, planners and policy makers are recognising the value of being 'vulnerable' with the 'vulnerable' in order to engage. Further, recognising that vulnerability in the context of climate change, those who are perceived to be vulnerable may not view themselves as vulnerable (Box 4.2). In other words, being open and transparent, allows stakeholders to be open and engage in a deliberate and considered dialogue about problems and solutions. Moreover, it is about finding the places and opportunities for trust and relationships to be built such that dialogue can occur and local government and citizens can engage in collaborative problem solving (Box 4.3).

When interviewees were asked what their city could teach other cities going forward in developing their climate change action plans or plans in general there was a call for openness, humility, and vulnerability which were presented as valuable policy 'tools' (Box 4.3). A critical aspect in this is not only acknowledgement and ownership of past actions by the city, but also future

Box 4.1 Who is delivering the message?

Understanding their values or their goals, what the stresses are in the community and trying to reframe with that mind. But a lot of it I think, this is one of the tensions that I have, early on I felt like, maybe I have to check my own sense of power and privilege, I need to help these groups, through *good intention.*

(Interview 3, Portland)

If you are a white person and want to be an advocate for people of color, there are things you can do and there's things you shouldn't do, times you should be the messenger and [times when you should] not. Understanding where those are, and making sure that you are advocating authentically, that you care about these issues and that you are ready to be responsive.... What are your vision and values, what is your lived experience? How are you checking your own privilege? How are you informing yourself about the lived experience in your community? There are a lot of resources out there. It takes time and energy to invest yourself to do that.

(Interview 3, Portland)

There's strategies to build towards that place, I have been sitting around these tables in theory representing low income communities of colour. It's like why are you talking to me? I'm making six figures in a job as a director. Why do you think I am going to have the perspective of the Latino community out in Cully? But it's been folks like me that they've relied on to show up, because they have to.

(Interview 4, Portland)

I had to carry the mantle as the leading equity voice, which is uncomfortable ... I'm a privileged white guy. What does that say? But again, this goes back to how do we sequence. You could have used the equity working group to increase the capacity of the technical awareness and understanding of people who are more directly, represent the impacted communities.

(Interview 5, Portland)

It is looking at what can communities do for themselves and *empowering* them to have budgetary control over the decisions that are made in their area as well. So it's working with all those sorts of things and getting in with, with various channels and various groups that people work with.... It's really a hard thing to reach people who are more maybe disconnected, who maybe don't attend kind of community things. Don't attend groups. It's one of those difficult things and they are the people we want to reach out to. It's kind of on-going. It's not one that is going to go away. But it's one we are committed to.

(Interview 2, Glasgow)

The communities that are more vulnerable are the ones that need to be engaged, because they are less likely to come forward and participate. They don't have the confidence at times to do so. And also feel the power to participate, they are already quite resilient. I know coming to the vulnerable and telling them how they can change their behaviour might not be taken that well, if they feel that they might not have that much to contribute. So we need to think about how to do that.

(Interview 3, Glasgow)

Box 4.2 Vulnerability in a changing climate

An individual or group's vulnerability to climate change and climate-related disasters is thus influenced by the complex array of social, economic, political and environmental factors operating at a variety of levels that in combination affect vulnerability. Consequently vulnerability is not evenly distributed across society, and some individuals, households or groups are likely to be disproportionately affected by climate change or disasters.... Interestingly most vulnerable people do not perceive themselves to be vulnerable – they instead refer to vulnerability in terms of 'weakness', 'problems' and 'constraints'.

(O'Brien, 2008, p. 14)

Box 4.3 What can your city teach other cities?

It's learning as you go. We've got a lot of experience with doing this. If you look at things like the Commonwealth Games. That was an example of how we've worked really well with communities to develop, to regenerate areas and develop. Develop a different approach and it's an example that has worked.

(Interview 2, Glasgow)

I think that the ability to regenerate ourselves by drawing on our culture, heritage, is something we can really share with other cities.... It's about drawing on your strengths. It's about drawing on what makes you a unique city, and celebrating that, and that's allowed us to regenerate ourselves as a city. Being an innovative city and regeneration by celebrating what we are good at, are two things. They're things that I think make us strong when we are facing these challenges in terms of climate risk and climate change.

(Interview 2, Glasgow)

This might sound like a really basic thing, but *not to plan, not to solve problems* yourself. It has to be a collaborative, integrated relationship and an integrated plan of action. And that's why this piece of work is taking us so long. We could have locked ourselves in a room and developed a resilient strategy for the city. Which is probably like five years ago, ten years ago we might have done that. But we are trying to do something that sounds straightforward, but it is different, in the fact that it is *asset led*. I think people have to be involved in everything you do. If you want it to be a sustainable meaningful change.

(Interview 2, Glasgow)

The golden way is being *100% honest*. Don't try to hide anything; people aren't stupid. So when we were dealing with buildings owners' associations, we deal with developers, we deal with construction guys. When we start thinking about changing a policy we sit down with them first.

(Interview 1, Vancouver)

Talk to people, get objective opinions, get the public's opinions, come up with realistic targets. Behind all those targets have to be actions to make them real.

The most important thing is the accountability. You have to report out. You have to continuously be putting yourself in the spotlight, whether you look good or not. Here's how we are doing and yeah, we are doing ok here, this isn't so good, and you will notice in the updates. So this is the plan, every year we issue updates. This is not all roses. There's pieces in here that say we are not doing very good, that's really important because *we learn, and the rest of the world learns from mistakes.*

(Interview 1, Vancouver)

I think once you become involved, intimately involved, in a project, you develop a *sense of ownership over it.* So that is something we definitely felt with our public outreach... On Facebook and Twitter, people were having conversations with each other and identifying. It seemed like people had an affinity to the Greenest City brand.

(Interview 3, Vancouver)

The other part is you bring your life, professional experience to the table as a decision maker. It is a group of people, the experiences of that group collectively shape the work. If there's not constantly new faces. The nature of this work is changing so fast, you constantly need to have new people coming to the table with new ideas on how to approach it. I mean I feel sort of constrained in my thinking at times. I really have to talk myself out and say, 'No, there is another way'.... So keeping it fresh and lively.... What we can teach other cities? I feel like we need to bring a lot more *humility.* I think we have been humbled as a region. As we start to take a more thoughtful approach to where this is working and where it is not. I think some of the conversations, we have had to date are sort of around recognising that, serving as a check and challenge, using our privilege as a being recognised as a leader to call out our challenges. Helping us find a deeper way to engage in our work.

(Interview 3, Portland)

It would be convening different people. It would be a much more slower and deliberate process in terms of first hearing communities, setting the course, and this is a much more of a process than staff and smart people coming up with the bulk of material, the steering committee is a check for permission and it's just a different way to engage people.

(Interview 3, Portland)

There's the idea, an expression down in the Southwest of Ireland, the 5/8th job. If you are doing a job and you are 5/8th right you are over half way done and that's good enough. And there's also the idea that when you, you can spend more effort covering up a mistake than actually trying to rectify it. People are reluctant to admit their errors. Whereas in Sweden you'd read a book and the name of the book would be the mistakes we made. Whereas, here you'd never find it. The name of the book would be the success we've had. So there's that. I suppose its *transparency.* That is very hard. Its quite normal when the government commissions a report from a consultant with public money, that the report is not released to the public, or at least not released until its too late.

(Interview 21, Dublin)

actions. Learning from failure is valuable to future policy development, as the reasons for failure provide opportunities for re-shaping policy and finding new pathways. Further, failure provides an opportunity to demonstrate transparency and accountability, and critically, a willingness to learn from experiences.

Emerging from the experience of urban policy makers is an acknowledgement that collaborative policy development does not equate to successful policy outcomes. Rather, success is defined by planners and stakeholders collaborating to innovate, and take risks that may succeed or fail, but ultimately that either outcome is owned by planners and stakeholders alike. In doing so, future collaboration will allow for stakeholders to learn together and share their experiences, thereby developing policies that are owned by all, and critically, foster relationships with stakeholders. Collaborative planning for climate change needs to be a 'slower and deliberate' process, such that engagement is sustained through development, implementation, and evaluation of policies, and fosters meaningful engagement and sustained ownership of successes and failures. Furthermore, as highlighted in Box 4.3, innovation is enabled by bringing new stakeholders in, leading to new policy ideas and responses; this also reflects the feedback loops between resilience, adaptive governance and collaborative planning in Figure 2.1, where new threats, and solutions are continually identified as policies are developed, implemented and monitored. This deliberate and considered approach was demonstrated by the case study cities, through actions to deliberately engage communities, for example Vancouver's pub-crawl with a drag queen, Glasgow's stalled spaces, and Portland's aboriginal engagement initiatives. Moreover, as demonstrated in Box 4.4, planners themselves need to share their knowledge with each other and stakeholders to build dialogue; further, planners can create the conditions that facilitate dialogue between stakeholders and fosters their ownership of problems and solutions. The excerpt echoes Forester's view of planners being: mediators, negotiators, translators, leaders, advocates, teachers and students (Forester, 1994, 1999, 2006). Further, it builds on the idea of a reflective planner, by reminding planners of the motivation for their work in the broader context of their actions or inactions on future generations, and re-affirms that change takes time and patient leadership. Critically, collaborative processes begin within an organisation and take time, a sentiment echoed by interviewees in their acknowledgement that a clear internal message of the importance of responding to climate change resonates outwards into the public realm.

Box 4.4 Role of the planner

INTERVIEWEE: I would say, I can only do my bit and we are. I am *building dialogue* that is what I do. And you can only chip away at it. For instance we have 63 councillors. Whereas up until last year we only had 52, but because of demographic change 63. What we've done in the development plan is, we've invited all of those councillors in, over a dozen or more meetings over the past six months. Informal meetings, to go through their issues, their concerns; and explained to them what the development plan is about and what

policy is about and the benefits of policy, and the policy is for the good of the
city, for the common good. All that stuff.... There's an increasingly educated
level of councillor out there ... they're educated ... because they are politicians ... because they want to be the owner of policy and get ahead of it. But,
there is that thing ... what is happening is that the traditional party politics are
breaking down, so you have a whole left of centre thing happening in the city
now. And those are mainly independents and small parties. Whereas the traditional way was ... if you explained to the leader of Fine Gael and Fianna Fail
that we need this policy, because it is good for the city. They would go away
and say, 'I will get the caucus of my party to support that in the[ir] name'.
You wouldn't have to. You are getting a block vote, just by explaining to the
party leader, traditionally. Now you have to explain individually to every
councillor because every councillor is their own party, they are independents.
And that is, I don't know whether that is a good or bad thing....

INTERVIEWER: I can see the good and bad of both... How do you verify what they
are purporting for the community is what the community wants?

INTERVIEWEE: Well, this goes back to the core of what this thing is about. Are you
voting for future generations or not? Are you voting for your children? I don't
think some councillors are. Not only that, one of the things you get again, and
again, is gated communities. Politicians hate gated communities, so do planners.... Politicians can't get into the gates to canvas and meet the people. That
is probably a bad thing in planning. But it means that their door-to-door can-
vassing is people who live in 2-storey houses. And they are the people who
then vote and there isn't any reach. There are vast areas of this city where
people don't engage with local politics at all.... The point I was making, there
are 63 councillors for a population of 500,000, 1 per 8,000, that is all the con-
stituency an elected member has to look after. So when you talk about, when
an elected member comes in and says, 'I have come from an area where there
are 8,000 people. There's been a sex shop just put up in the corner in my
8,000 person area, and down with sex shops. I want that to be put policy
number 1 in your strategic plan. No more sex shops.' Hold on, that is hardly a
strategic policy for the city. The rest go quiet, a vote will go through. Yes,
that's it; it becomes policy. So that is how it gets compartmentalised and bal-
kanised and that is the downside of it.

INTERVIEWER: So how do you, in your role and your legacy with the planners that
are coming up, how would you encourage them to work around these constraints. How do you make sure the 8,000 voices they are representing, are on
the same page as this one councillor?

INTERVIEWEE: Now, what we do have in all our local plans, and all our plans and
planning applications, we have a public consultation process. Say when we go
out on our public display now in October. We will have a series of evenings
and weekend meetings, maybe a dozen with local community groups and
members of the public and anyone can come along and express their view.
That is a portal that doesn't have to go through elected members. We do have
to listen by requirement to other agencies. Our development plan can't be just
a vox pop of opinions. It has to accord with government policy and central
policy, so that keeps pulling it up out of the localism. So, the trick for us, as
planners is you just have to keep, and as I say to the younger planners, 'you
can't go into your shell and say I am not sharing the information with council,

> because they are going to abuse it'.... We just have to keep explaining, why
> we are doing things. That there is a public good, there is a wider interest in
> what we are doing. Hopefully, like we've done with the Docklands, slowly,
> slowly people are saying, 'By god that is a good project. You know. High-
> density living does work! The Grand Canal Theatre and all around that, all
> those uses that support it, the restaurants, the theatre, all that. It is a good
> place'. So, you slowly, slowly.... A colleague of mine in traffic engineering
> said, 'A thing you might think is good, say a new cycle way along the grand
> canal, strategic green cycle way. Which wouldn't be objected to by local resi-
> dents. You know they are objected by local resident groups.' He said, 'it
> would take three development plans to get one of those in'. That is 18 years
> before something is a germ of [an] idea to actually happen. Well, if you are to
> think like that and bawk, and not even bother trying, you'd never have the
> premier one, Rathmines.... The one thing they have to do on that one is
> changing the lights for cycles. You are held up more than the traffic. I notice
> people still go along the roadway, because you are quicker on the road, than
> on the cycle way. But small things, but that doesn't mean you give up on it.
>
> (Interview 3, Dublin)

Leadership for collaborative planning on climate change

> Right now it is about finding, trying to identify what you might call, cham-
> pions of the cause.... People who will take climate change and say, 'This is
> a serious issue, I understand how it is going to affect my community or
> where I work and I am going to make sure I do as much as I can to influence
> matters'. Where you want these people to be is in positions where they can
> influence.
>
> (Interview 13, Dublin)

Leadership by an individual or team has been identified as a key factor in the
ability of cities to be leaders in developing policy to achieve resilience to climate
change. This call for leadership poses a challenge for collaborative planning
theory, which has promoted consensus building as a means of sustaining equitable relationships and building dialogue (Heywood, 2004; Innes *et al.*, 2007;
Agger and Löfgren, 2008; Faehnle and Tyrväinen, 2013). Collaborative planning
is about knowledge gains, and using knowledge to achieve mutual benefits.
Power is not in the dynamic, equity in the process is; as the focus is on networking, exchanging expertise to collaboratively address a policy issue (Heywood,
2004; Agger and Löfgren, 2008; Faehnle and Tyrväinen, 2013). Therefore, collaboration is not achieved through centralised power, but dispersed power or
network power as suggested by Innes and Booher (2004); power is not about
exerting control over the process, but shared responsibility of the process and
ownership. Box 4.4 also highlights this and the necessity of slow, persistent
leadership within an organisation to achieve action for the broader 'public good'
(Interview, Dublin, 2015). As such while critics of collaborative planning argue

that power to hold leadership, will inevitably create conflict in the process, theory calls for leadership in practice to be not about power but coordination and facilitation of action. (Further, conflict is seen as an asset (Innes *et al.*, 2007) as demonstrated by the case study cities, conflict has allowed for them to identify areas in which they are deficit and respond.) However, the case study cities progress this idea of leadership to include empowerment. To illustrate this evolution of the meaning of leadership in the context of collaborative planning it is valuable to consider Dublin's challenges with leadership, namely the absence of a directly elected mayor. Then to consider that in the context of the views of leadership provided by interviewees from all case studies and how it has shaped climate change policy in these cities. In particular, the evolution of the 'role' of leadership and its ownership.

An elected mayor with a mandate

> How do you bring about change, no matter what that change is the challenge? And you know it applies to eco policies, green clean type initiatives as well. You can do very successful pilots but getting something embedded as an organisational policy as a city deliverable. It takes a lot longer period of time, needs advocates and sponsors and at some point somebody needs to be willing to jump off the power button, somebody needs to take the plunge and stand behind the decision. Any of those change, requires somebody to be brave.
>
> (Interview 6, Dublin)

Collaborative planning is about engaging and promoting the participation of stakeholders in the development of policy. However, as interviewees have stated, there is still a need for leadership (and ownership) to guide the process. This recognition in practice that leadership is necessary for collaborative process by urban policy makers is reflected in the literature investigating the relationship between leadership and collaborative planning (Gedikli, 2009; Fahmi *et al.*, 2015). A challenge with collaborative planning, as discussed in Chapter 2, has been 'power' which was argued by Allmendinger (2002) to undermine collaborative processes; the response by Innes and Booher (2002) was network power, a concept of sharing power amongst stakeholders through dialogue. Power, though, is not leadership, and it should not be confused with leadership. Moreover, leaders and leadership in the policy development contexts of Glasgow, Portland and Vancouver are not about *a leader* holding *power* and *delegating* actions. Rather, the institutional structures developed by these cities support the growth of leadership, identifying and fostering the growth of *leaders* who *empower* and *guide* processes to facilitate collaboration in policy development. Consequently, leadership becomes a characteristic of stakeholders in the policy development process and leaders are able to emerge and guide various processes. Critically, leaders are able to take ownership of solutions and problems, and be accountable to other stakeholders, while inspiring ownership and accountability in others. For cities it is about identifying leaders, plural; individuals that have the 'bravery' to move policy forward and to take the risks; and to bring people together. More succinctly, adaptive governance supports collaboration, and collaborative planning is a tool of adaptive governance in these cities.

Considering the context of Dublin, there is recognition by policy makers in Dublin City Council that there is a need for Dublin to take the lead, particularly on climate change policy. Further, there is recognition within Central Government that Dublin and local authorities have this desire and could lead. Yet, for Dublin to take a leadership role in responding to climate change, it needs a directly elected mayor with a mandate, as the capacity to lead within the current institutional structure is limited. There are political reasons why Dublin does not have a mayor. In particular Dublin being the capital city, holding 40 per cent of gross domestic product (GDP) and the highest concentration of people, a mayor could be a significant 'threat' to the power of central government. However, interviewees saw the value of a mayor as lying in the individual being directly elected to the position and being held accountable to their mandate by citizens. As one interviewee highlighted, an elected mayor would have the capacity to respond to climate change and explain the responses to citizens, a point also re-iterated by another interviewee, who acknowledged that 'successful global cities need good mayors' who are able to communicate and instil ownership of problems and solutions (Interview, Dublin, 2015). Overall, there is a broad sentiment that an elected mayor with a mandate would create the conditions necessary for Dublin to lead on climate change, as cities at the 'forefront' of building resilience to climate change have strong mayors. This emphasis on a leader who can be transformational (Fahmi *et al.*, 2015) is important to addressing climate change as Pitt and Bassett (2014) found in their study on clean energy policy, found that policy leaders were from the community. However, while a leader was a key factor in policy success, it was not necessarily a mayor who was the leader.

Policy makers in Vancouver, Glasgow, and Portland acknowledge that policy success was due to leadership that fostered ownership of the problems and solutions. Further it has been found that in attributing responsibility for addressing a specific climate change problem, it drives the development of policy, as individuals can see their impact and internalise their successes (Bickerstaff *et al.*, 2008; Gedikli, 2009; Laurian, 2009; McKay *et al.*, 2011; Pitt and Bassett, 2014). 'Once people are intimately involved in a project' (Interview 3, Vancouver), individuals and community take ownership of the process and buy in to the project and its outcomes. Developing an internal organisational structure that enables civil servants within each local government to give direction to the vision and implement the ideas of their elected councils with their expert knowledge, is critical (this is particularly true of the DLAs which are faced with an impending exodus of staff who have a wealth of knowledge that may be lost once they retire).

The structures created fostered internal leadership and collective ownership that permeated through all city departments. Climate change adaptation for these cities was not left for a single department to address, but included in all work areas and was therefore the responsibility of all. What became the remit for a single department, or team, was the responsibility and leadership of joining and bringing internal stakeholders (and external) together to collaborate to identify and respond to climate change challenges. Critically, by making formal changes that delegated the oversight of climate change responses, a clear message that climate change adaptation is a priority is sent to staff and to citizens of the city. Consequently, ownership of the responses to climate change is fostered.

From Vancouver, Glasgow and Portland it is evident that leadership for developing responses to climate change is not about an individual who is elected with a mandate to address climate change. Rather, leadership lies with an individual or group of individuals who can create the discourse needed to generate action by stakeholders. Therefore while there is a broadly held belief that an elected mayor would create the conditions necessary for Dublin to lead on climate change policy, it is perhaps not a necessity. Further, the current political reality for Dublin is that there is no democratically elected mayor. As such, the question is how Dublin establishes itself as a leader in the absence of a mayor. The excerpt in Box 4.5, while intended for Central Government, discusses the necessity for action to be driven by civil servants in their daily work. The proposed structure, while argued by the interviewee to require a mandate from the Taoiseach, can be localised and therefore provides an option for how Dublin could set itself up for leadership on climate change.

Box 4.5 Collaborating for leadership in climate change policy

INTERVIEWEE: What happens is that people think it is a really good idea to work together, and they may go to the first meeting. If there is no tangible product or outcome, or no target or nothing to be concretely done together and then the level of interest can dissipate and wane and enthusiasm. So you often get the level of representation filtering down the food chain. So you get high level people at the first meeting, and after 3 or 4 meetings there are lower down the food chain people coming, because they can't see what it is that they have to do to contribute and its not becoming part and parcel of their daily work. They go back to the office and their own day job takes over.

INTERVIEWER: What would be the target that would unite? Or the indicator? ... What is the barrier, to getting all of them to sit in a room together?

INTERVIEWEE: Well there is traditionally a silo'd way of working, you know I suppose each department has its own business plan and work plan, it has to fulfil the pieces of work that are going to demonstrate adherence to that. So, I think it's back again to that conceptual framework that has to be put in place and a real commitment to that conceptual framework. And that is demonstrated through either positions or appointments to be the cog, if you want to think of it as a whole of series of cogs that have to interact to mesh together to make the machinery and grind and operate effectively. But, you know, its not just put the cogs in place. Someone has to turn the cogs and ... it's somebody's responsibility to turn the cog and somebody has to get paid to put the cog in place and be the cog and then determine how effective the interaction and interworking and interdepartmental working has been.

INTERVIEWER: Who could be the cog?

INTERVIEWEE: I think of it as having people in the individual department with responsibility with earmarked responsibility. So, it is my job in the Department of Health to be in charge of health and well-being but part of that is to be cooperating and to doing things, concretely with other government departments. And it is somebody's job in the Department of Environment to be actually concretely working with me in health. So you know its not just I go to a meeting, but I have to show in my business plan that there are certain things that have been achieved as a result of this working together on the things we are trying to do together. That is going to give us the greater chance of hitting those targets.

(Interview 15, Dublin)

INTERVIEWEE: You can't put a desire into an individual and you can't make leaders. What you can do is facilitate and identify those who are. They can be at any level, any level in an organisation both in and outside ... I thought the city, in terms of leadership, was much better in the very recent past, I am old enough to kind of see that distance. Like 80s or mid 90s or something like that, things were you know, not great. There was a period not just because of the boom, or maybe because of the boom, where there was a sense of civic leadership and things that were being done in the city, were positive and there was a constant message of positive change. Now, I think I live in the inner city and I would not advise anyone to buy in the inner city. Where as, I would have advised them 10 or 15 years ago. And that's a shocking indictment of the city....

INTERVIEWER: How do you make the city understand?

INTERVIEWEE: The citizen only has so much time.... Engaging with the citizen is not about talking to them. Because they don't want to talk to you, and I don't think they should be talking to you.... The solution is simple actions. So, if I am walking down a street and it's dirty all the time, it should be cleaned. It should you know, I don't need to draw a community group to listen to the city's reasons. There are many simple things a city can do that communicate to the residents of the inner city, while there is a resource challenge and there's an economic challenge. We are with you and therefore we are going to do small actions, that give you hope value. I don't think a lot of that is done. I don't think the city at the moment is communicating much to urban dwellers that we understand the challenges of urban living and we are trying to make it better for you. One of the issues [is] anti-social behaviour, I think Dublin has a horrendous problem with low grade edginess that most people dismiss as 'ah sure its grand and sure they are doing no harm' then they drive out to Malahide and they would never dream of rearing their kids in the inner city and the victims of the low grade edginess are poor people, and so they talk about you know, 'ah sure you know the life story of the heroin addict its awful, of course more tax dollars should be spent on making their lives better.' But you don't open heroin clinics all over the inner city, because 0.03% of the population use them, versus 0.00000% of the population in Blackrock. You are condemning 98% of the population including all the kids in the flats. You are basically communicating to them that this is your future, this is what we think of you, this is what we think is a good service for your area....

(Interview 4, Dublin)

Further, the proposed system of accountability fosters collective ownership of the solutions and problems that has been demonstrated by Glasgow, Vancouver and Portland, but it also serves another purpose. In relation to an earlier argument made, that collaborative planning is a tool *of* adaptive governance; the excerpt demonstrates that collaborative planning is also a tool *for* facilitating a shift towards adaptive governance (Figure 4.1). Box 4.5 demonstrates how a call for collaborative processes can mobilise government to consider the broader context of the impacts of climate change on society and consequently understand and acknowledge that the responses are not the sole responsibility of one department, but the whole of government. Further, as the second excerpt demonstrates, reflecting the views of interviewees from other case study cities, local government has the capacity to send messages in regards to the importance of addressing climate change through their actions.

Dublin could take the lead on climate change policy by addressing its internal organisational structure and following the lead of Glasgow, Vancouver and Portland and create the necessary entity within Dublin City Council to oversee collaboration across departments, elected council and Central Government departments. However, the process of forming a leadership team should be deliberate and considerate, to avoid the potential risks of alienating departments within Dublin City Council. Endeavouring to create a leadership team to respond to climate change within Dublin City Council will be time consuming and an ongoing process, and it is important to identify rather than create leaders, and that the leaders have the capacity to convey a message that inspires collaboration. Collaborative efforts, as has been shown, begin with a shared focus that has meaning for stakeholders. In policy terms it is the alignment of policy, its consistency, that is the starting point.

I'll keep it very high level, it is making sure that policy is saying the same thing. And even advocating, but even if it was a complete climate denial kind of policy that would be a consistency. Which might not be a bad thing.

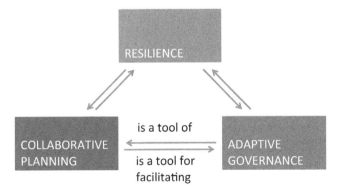

Figure 4.1 Revised relationship between adaptive governance and collaborative planning.

I don't know if that is going to happen. I think its acceptance that your agri-
cultural policy, your rural development policy, your economic policy, and
your older people policy, all these things have a climate change element to
them. And that isn't there at the moment. They are not proofed, they are not
sustainable development proofed, they are not climate change proofed. That
is the big thing, bringing all these things into line, not developing short-term
policies for the sake of it.... That's really it and then it's a grown-up conversation about growth, the sort of cities we want, the sort of transport infrastructure that we want. And then finally it's a grown-up conversation about
energy infrastructure. Renewables, the mix of renewables, what sort of
renewables we are going for and how we are going to link all that up. Wind
energy guidelines are eminent, but I think there is political pressure to not
publish those, because wind farms and transmission lines aren't popular.
Maybe the only way to get all those things lined up is if there is wider public
demand for them. And I don't know how you kind of start that virtuous
circle. Its probably making people more aware of what they are facing.

(Interview 18, Dublin)

As resilience-based policy responses to climate change requires the integration
of knowledge from diverse stakeholders, leadership that empowers and guides
stakeholders is necessity for collaborative policy development. Moreover, as
resilience to climate change is an ongoing process, collaboration needs leadership that sustains stakeholder engagement by empowering stakeholders through
aspirational goals to facilitate ownership. This is a challenge, especially in a time
when attention spans are short, and the demand for instant results is high,
holding and maintaining attention to stay the course needs aspiration.

Power in aspirational vision

Forester (1996) discussed the importance of planners being able to communicate
with stakeholders to achieve success in policy. Interviewees in all cities studied
re-affirmed the need for planners and leaders alike to be able to communicate
effectively the purposes of policies whilst not delivering a message of doom, but
rather of hope and optimism. Further, interviewees in discussing policy leadership acknowledged that some goals laid out in their development plans were
intentionally aspirational, in recognition that there is power in those goals in that
they inspire action. Further, with organisational structures created to monitor and
evaluate progress on climate change targets, and fostered accountability by
various stakeholders, aspirational goals become realistic goals. Consequently, a
virtuous circle of aspirational goal setting emerges that drives progress on policy
objectives. Further, as the following excerpt suggests:

How will you hold each other accountable? Or you have to have such high-
level commitment and leadership that, that you are always fully accountable
out of the desire to get it done. And I think that is even harder when you

have that many people signed on.... Success doesn't necessarily mean that everything gets checked off. In some cases, success means we threw something out there and it pushed the envelope, but it didn't quite land. But you know what, in five years, we are going to come back and we are going to rethink it a little bit and it's going to land!

(Interview 2, Portland)

There is an undeniable value and power in setting aspirational goals and being transparent about the successes and failures of these goals. This enables collaboration to continue and ultimately foster resilience. Leadership and aspirational goals, though, need tools and narratives to convey the objectives and targets of goals and the underlying rationale of taking action on climate change. Technology is one such tool.

Collaborative planning practices and technology

I would say don't be afraid of a different approach in which to encourage and interact with people. Because sometimes you know as contexts change and the way people get information changes. It's time to adapt those skills in which to reach out [to] folks and the importance of relationship building. With community partners and organisations and folks in general, to take this work on... And resourcing it properly, having the right people at the table is important. There have been so many awesome synergies that have happened, based on those interactions.... We can achieve multiple different goals with certain action, like the healthy city strategy was talking about that. How do we connect those dots? And the Greenest City we can connect it to. Looking for opportunities across the way to connect things. 'Cause the answer and solutions to one problem are often the solutions to another.

(Interview 3, Vancouver)

Collaborative planning theory emerged in the 1990s, when technology was not as prevalent as it is today. The emergence of technology as a means of communication through social media is recognised to be changing the way people engage with each other and access information. As such, it is changing the way in which governments engage with citizens, from e-governance platforms to designing 'smart' cities. Social media platforms like Twitter and Facebook permit people to voice their opinions to a wide audience instantaneously, resulting in a breadth of data that can be interpreted and used to inform government. Technology though is not limited to social media, but includes smart phones, applications, infrastructure, energy efficiency and so on: with technology there is a promise of better services, higher quality of life, and smarter cities (Castán Broto *et al.*, 2013; United Nations Human Settlements Programme (UN-Habitat), 2016). However, the benefits of technology in the context of collaborative planning for climate change are contingent upon the capacity of urban policy makers to harness its power, by identifying how technology can complement, strengthen and/or evolve existing planning practices. Critically, it is not about reliance on technology to solve urban problems; urban policy makers cannot ignore the human element of cities.

Research investigating the potential of technology to enhance public participation highlights the capacity of various technological tools to convey information to the public such as GIS, and the challenges with technology (Epstein, 2002; Hanzl, 2007; Sutriadi and Wulandari, 2014). It is evident that the success of technology-based solutions is dependent on the tools chosen to display and disseminate information. For example, using GIS, which requires specialised knowledge, limits who can interact with the information (Hanzl, 2007), whereas mobile technologies can be widely accessible (Sutriadi and Wulandari, 2014). Technology offers new opportunities to engage the public through a range of solutions, however, it is not intended to replace face to face interactions with the public (Epstein, 2002; Hanzl, 2007; Sutriadi and Wulandari, 2014). Epstein and Buhovac (2014) highlight that online forums for discussion can also polarise debates, which is contradictory to the objective of building consensus in collaborative planning debates. Critically, echoing the concerns of interviewees, Epstein and Buhovac (2014) argue that the design of technological tools for planning requires consideration of the risks and benefits of using technology, in particular the digital divide. Therefore, while technology has increased the ease with which information can be accessed, local governments need to embrace technology's potential while 'adjusting the process and allocating resources to non-technological activities that contextualise online political deliberation' (Epstein and Buhovac, 2014, p. 342). Succinctly, in the context of responding to climate change events such as the aftermath of an extreme event, technology cannot take the place of the social cohesion needed in times of crises that enables citizens to help their fellow citizens. (Not everyone has a Twitter account, and if the power is out they may not have a usable phone.)

Demonstrating how technology complements existing processes, the plans that were analysed in this research were all found online on the respective cities' official websites. As an interviewee discussed, the placing of plans and policies online is beneficial to the work of policy makers. However, that benefit is lost if plans are too cumbersome to download and review (Interview, Dublin, 2015); a sentiment echoed by a planner in Portland. As a response, Portland has developed Map App, an online tool available to the public that allows people to see any development applications that have been submitted and where they are located in the city, and submit comments. The objective of this tool is to streamline public comment and enable citizens to see what is happening in their city in terms of development.

It is evident that technology is changing and strengthening the planning process; specifically, with social media tools such as Twitter being used as a platform for engagement. For these cities the use of social media has generated an interest in the work of the city by demographic groups that were previously challenging to engage. This was particularly evident for Dublin in the public consultation process for cycle paths. The City of Vancouver, through an effective social media strategy, engaged people on its Greenest City Action Plan, which has resulted in the city using social media to creatively engage the public on other issues, such as the city bird competition. The reach provided by technology, and the speed with which it can gather data for cities is evident. While the benefits to public consultation are evident in increased engagement, there are challenges with technology; as the excerpt below suggests, there is a risk that technology's speed and proliferation is counter-intuitive to collaborative processes.

> That engagement that you talk about, that sophisticated interaction. It's again, it is totally time consuming. Dubliners are moving away from that. You know that whole thing of spending time with people and we are becoming Americanised in that way. Time has to be rushed through, I've seen it myself, you know the way that emails are. They [technology] have created a sense of urgency to your life even at 9 and 10 o'clock at night.
>
> (Interview 3, Dublin)

Technology, particularly social media, was seen as 'speeding by us', according to several interviewees; as it evolves quickly and while more information is beneficial it can also be detrimental. Emerging research in this arena acknowledges that while it brings more data to local governments, urban policy makers are competing for the attention of stakeholders (Filippi and Balbo, 2011; Poplin, 2012; Papa *et al.*, 2013; United Nations Human Settlements Programme (UN-Habitat), 2016). Therefore, while technology may enable local governments to disperse information about the city to citizens quickly, its effectiveness is uncertain (United Nations Human Settlements Programme (UN-Habitat), 2016). More critically, there was the acknowledgement that social media creates a world of soundbites, where the risk of being 'hoodwinked on 140-characters' is present, due to people already being too busy in their lives and not having the time to investigate issues further (Interview 2, Dublin, 2015). Therefore, acknowledging that collaborative planning is a time consuming process, in that it takes time for policy makers to build trust, relationships and consensus with stakeholders (Healey, 1998a; Forester, 1999; Innes *et al.*, 2007); the challenge then for urban policy makers lies in harnessing technology to drive engagement online and off-line, as communicating the complexity of the social ecological system's vulnerability to climate change cannot be reduced to a virtual platform.

Another challenge with technology is 'who' is engaging; this is as prevalent as it is in formal public consultation processes. While technology is seen as transformative, having the potential to address issues such as poverty, it can also contribute to inequality via the digital divide (Epstein and Buhovac, 2014; United Nations Human Settlements Programme (UN-Habitat), 2016). A concern around technology from interviewees is that it is a select proportion of the population that is savvy about its usefulness and power, and can potentially manipulate technology to their advantage. Thus, there are risks with it being abused, creating a challenge around assessing the value of the information emerging from the process. In response, local governments in cities such as Chicago, Vancouver and London are developing digital inclusion programs to mitigate issues of access to technology, while ensuring that the 'voices' heard through social media are representative (United Nations Human Settlements Programme (UN-Habitat), 2016).

Social media and technology, then, are tools that need to be used, however, there needs to be more consideration given to how to maximise the potential of these tools. Given the proliferation of mobile technologies, such as smart phones, there is an opportunity for urban policy makers to engage with citizens through the development of apps that foster engagement with citizens. For example, transportation and mobility-oriented apps may provide an opportunity for urban policy makers to facilitate the uptake of walking, cycling, car-pooling, and public transportation by providing citizens with relevant information on comparative travel times, and perhaps health information and their contribution to reducing carbon emissions. A key consideration for urban policy makers investigating the public education opportunities through technology, as highlighted by interviewees, is that citizens and stakeholders need to understand their contribution to the solutions and how they can be a force for change. Thus, it is important that cities approach technology deliberately to understand and maximise its potential for improving urban life for all citizens, while minimising risks associated with privacy.

The cities studied in this research are at varying stages of their use of social media and technology. Vancouver has a dedicated social media team that is strategically analysing the engagement (Interview 4, Vancouver, 2015). For example, Vancouver's engagement around the Greenest City Action Plan on Twitter (the City has 141,000 followers) employed hashtags, such as '#talk-greentous' to generate dialogue with the city and between citizens. The result of the online engagement was an influx of ideas from around the world, and demonstrated for urban policy makers, the value of a narrative that stakeholders had 'an affinity' towards to foster dialogue with policy makers (Interview 1, Vancouver, 2015). Further, in using social media the City was able to facilitate and observe dialogue occurring between stakeholders demonstrating that citizens were taking ownership of 'green issues' and developing solutions together. Vancouver is now endeavouring to use social media to spur in-person engagement with citizens, by announcing on various platforms where city staff will be to talk citizens (City of Vancouver, 2016). Through its smarter cities programme, Dublin is identifying ways of using technology to improve the quality of life in the city by introducing smart management systems for traffic and energy (Interview, Dublin 2015). While there is a city council Twitter account (with 106,000 followers), planners in Glasgow face the unique issue of not being permitted to use social media, due to fears that someone may 'tweet about green bananas' (Interview 1, Glasgow, 2015). Initially, this appears to be a benign fear, however, in the context of urban planning legislation and regulations it presents a legal question that local governments should consider: is the information disseminated through social media legally binding? The wording of development plans as discussed with interviewees, particularly in Glasgow and Dublin, can result in legal disputes; therefore, what is said via social media could potentially bind local governments to action, as transparency and accountability are benefits of technology (United Nations Human Settlements Programme (UN-Habitat), 2016).

Ultimately, technology and social media are recognised to be beneficial for urban planning, especially in the context of climate change. Critically, the case study cities demonstrated that while technology enables urban planners to access new information instantaneously about the city and respond with policies that are informed by the data obtained from using technology, it is not a substitute for in-person engagement. The data tells a story of what is happening, but in-person dialogue is needed to understand the impacts of the 'story' on livelihoods and to collaboratively develop responses, and build the narrative that enables urban policy makers to engage with stakeholders.

The narrative for climate change

Narratives are critical for engaging stakeholders in collaborative processes to build resilience to climate change. Specifically, those narratives need to be place-based to ensure that stakeholders engage in long-term collaborative processes. A rationale for narratives being used for collaborative policy development is that theory risks homogenising policy responses and consequently cities themselves (Friedmann, 2005; Van Assche and Lo, 2011; Neal, 2015). Narratives permit the unique identities of cities to be central to policy development, and critically, foster public participation in the development of the city through a collective desire to 'tell the story of the city' and be a part of it (Van Assche and Lo, 2011; Lake and Zitcer, 2012). As such, the fifth research objective sought to identify the narratives employed by urban policy makers to engage stakeholders in dialogue to develop adaptive responses to climate change.

From the case study cities what has emerged is that while narratives are important for collaboration, especially in the context of climate change, the narrative needs to be tangible and understood by all stakeholders, from citizens to government (Box 4.6). The case studies have demonstrated that local governments face challenges in facilitating dialogue around climate change. However, by endeavouring to engage stakeholders, urban policy makers have come to acknowledge the value of identifying a starting point narrative that evolves over time into new narratives to sustain ongoing dialogue and collaboration with stakeholders.

Box 4.6 Engaging in long-term dialogue on climate change

INTERVIEWER: What would get people engaged on climate change?

INTERVIEWEE: They would want to know it is going to happen in the next 10 years. It's the long term. Most of us will be dead by the time it happens. But we are seeing the slow changes now and the extreme events. But, to the people that I know – to actually change their lifestyle, what would it take? To do it voluntarily? It would have to threaten their family.... You can sometimes get through to people, when you ask how they are going to be able to look their grandchildren in the eye, when they say you knew this was happening and you didn't stop it? It is fear mongering! But, it is actually the shame; they are saying it is a moral obligation, its like poverty. How we can stand around with all these poor people dying around the world. Showing them the picture. Climate change is harder to show. You can show them a picture of a drought in North Africa. But people do know that's been going on, all the time. It is nothing new. It is becoming more frequent. But why should Irish farmers be acting? The threat to our weather patterns, if it becomes unpredictable, they won't be able to grow their crops reliably.

(Interview 16, Dublin)

Identifying a narrative that resonates: place-based challenges

How well do citizens understand the impacts of climate change? The responses to this question varied greatly from there being a keen awareness (Vancouver) to an awareness it exists but it is like the big bang theory, something that is acknowledged to have happened but too complex to understand (Dublin). This spectrum of understanding is in some ways reflective of the progress that each city has been able to make in terms of responding to climate change through policy and engaging various stakeholders in the policy development process. With each city being at varying stages, a broad view of the engagement process and evolution of narratives was obtained. This is valuable in that it provides a road map for policy development from which other cities can learn and assess their progress.

For example Glasgow has used the social determinants of health to guide their policy development process in responding to climate change. This decision emerged from a need to understand why the 'Glasgow Effect' persists, which saw urban policy makers looking more closely at the demographics to identify vulnerable communities, specifically those that were benefit reliant (welfare dependent). This led policy makers to initiate an effort to engage with residents of Lambhill and learn their hopes and concerns for their community and the future they desired (Interview 2, Glasgow 2015). The story of individuals, showing the city that they wanted a future with community gardens is illustrative of how communities have the capacity to develop solutions (which may be similar to those suggested by experts) to their problems and they are empowered to do so by being included in a dialogue. The health status of citizens was a short-term focus for Glasgow. In the process of identifying the underlying causes and subsequent engagement with citizens has facilitated further engagement with citizens. Specifically, it has seen a shift in the way Glasgow City Council forms policy from 'planners know best' to planners working with citizens to create a place that is about how 'People Make Glasgow'. This shift was also seen in Portland in a different context around aboriginal engagement and youth engagement. For both cities, identifying the 'in' into the community has enabled them to establish relationships from which to build a network of stakeholders to engage. Further, by establishing these relationships around narratives that are of concern to these stakeholders, both cities are now able to engage in dialogue on multiple issues, namely the impacts of climate change on their livelihoods. Critically to climate change, urban policy makers can empower and guide these stakeholders in a collaborative process that allows them to take ownership of their 'problems and solutions'.

Establishing networks that foster collaboration in the short run is to enable long-term collaboration on policy to address climate change. However, identifying the overarching narrative that can sustain long-term vested interest to continually identify new areas for collaboration is valuable for climate change adaptation now and in the long term in Dublin and other cities. A long-term rhetoric requires knowledge of what will mobilise stakeholders. As discussed, for Glasgow it emerged from their short-term focus that in the long run it is about people, as 'People Make Glasgow' and are the city's greatest asset. In Vancouver it emerged from engaging stakeholders via the aspiration to be the Greenest City that being a healthy city is also important. While in Portland the need for equity to be the guiding framework emerged from its focus on climate change adaptation. For Portland, there was a realisation that a discussion around climate change would not mobilise people to act unless there was a discussion about inequity. This awareness that responding to climate change is not solely about the science and economics of climate change but the social impacts and therefore requires action by all people is not limited to these cities (Barton, 2009; Corburn, 2009; United Nations Human Settlements Programme (UN-Habitat), 2016). The quote here from an interviewee in Dublin acknowledges that action on climate change is everyone's responsibility. Further, it aptly describes an overarching narrative for climate change adaptation, livelihoods, which can foster the ownership needed for collaboration. The excerpt also highlights, and re-affirms, that the role of leadership on climate change action is not the remit of one leader or level of government, but that all stakeholders must take it on; thus, climate leaders can emerge outside government.

> On the social side, then obviously this is something that affects everybody. It is not just for government; it is not for municipal authorities to deal with. This is something that has to be taken on board by everybody, because it is essentially about how we are going to live our lives from here on in and into the future and how our children live their lives in terms of kind of a low carbon society, but also in terms of where people want to live in terms of adapting to climate change and so forth.
>
> (Interview 13, Dublin)

Considering this in the context of the earlier discussion on technology in this chapter, there is potential for local governments to combine education and technology to stimulate engagement around climate change issues. Further, as discussed technology-based solutions represent an opportunity to disseminate knowledge, but the barriers are access and implementation. If informing an increasingly busy and time-constrained public of planning activities is a priority, a probable solution is online interactive classes or citizen planning academies (Mandarano, 2008) led by local governments. This perhaps would allow for local governments to identify community leaders, while stimulating the conditions necessary for ownership of the problems and solutions.

Ownership of the problems and the solutions to climate change

> I believe in big government we can solve all kinds of problems. At the same time, there's an onus, our job is to create the conditions that are conducive to communities being able to solve their own problems.
>
> (Interview 4, Portland)

Acknowledging that people and their livelihoods are or should be at the centre of policy on climate change in terms of developing and implementing, as the above excerpt proposes, how do local governments create the conditions necessary for policy ownership? Especially, if they do not exist for some. Humility, risk taking and a willingness to acknowledge failure in order to learn, play a role in the process of building relationships to engage in dialogue with stakeholders about their hopes and concerns. When policy makers demonstrate accountability, this sends a message to citizens that an issue is important. Succinctly, urban policy makers acknowledge that taking ownership of their actions, past, present and future, and engaging transparently are critical for collaboration. However, the collaborative process is not owned solely by urban policy makers, stakeholders are critical to policy success, consequently their ownership of policy is necessary.

Earlier chapters discussed the institutional structures each of these cities operates within, where it was highlighted that institutional structures influenced and shaped the cities' capacity for policy development, which is reflected in the structures that have been formed to respond to climate change. Vancouver and Glasgow have both created a department that is responsible for climate change adaptation, and whilst their positions within the organisational structures are slightly different, interviewees acknowledged that having a department that is dedicated to climate change has enabled collaboration internally and externally. Internal collaboration across departments for interviewees, especially in Vancouver, was seen to facilitate a sense of ownership of the issue of climate change due to the Sustainability Group overseeing the progress of the Greenest City Action Plan. Glasgow created the Place, Strategy and Environment Team. Interviewees viewed this team to be essential in Glasgow, facilitating collaboration between departments and outside. As discussed, Portland's climate change preparation strategy was intended as an internal document to guide the various city departments. At the time of the interviews, it was being revised and incorporated into a comprehensive plan. However, due to Portland's remit, the city is working with Multnomah County to build relationships in the community to facilitate collaboration which saw the formation of the Equity Working Group.

Of the four cities, Dublin is at the beginning stages of integrating climate change adaptation, evidenced by interviewees highlighting that for the first time the draft development plan has a full chapter dedicated to climate change. Further, Dublin does not yet have a set structure that supports ownership of climate change adaptation, although there is potentially an avenue for this through the Public Realm Strategy. The city's public realm strategy has emerged out of the recognition that there needed to be a more cohesive way of integrating the work of various departments in the city to address the social, economic and physical aspects of the city.

One objective of the Public Realm Strategy, according to an interviewee, is to bring cohesion to the city and make city about place and people. A significant aspect of the Public Realm Strategy team's work involves working with stakeholders outside the city in Central Government, the private sector and communities; similar to Glasgow's Place Structure and Environmental Strategy Team and Vancouver's Sustainability Group. Arguably, it could be the group within Dublin City Council that takes the lead and ownership of collaborative process, as it is evident that having a team own the collaborative process for local government enables leadership to emerge that can empower and guide stakeholders within and outside local government. More importantly the projects implemented by the team involve adapting the city to climate change, such as a sustainable urban drainage system to reduce flood risk, and green infrastructure to mitigate rising temperatures. Therefore, the Public Realm Strategy team could potentially be the group that leads Dublin's work on climate change.

Dublin is the city in this research that has the potential to learn from Glasgow, Vancouver and Portland with regards to creating an internal structure that enables the city to take the lead and ownership of responses to climate change; as was previously discussed by an interviewee, a challenge for climate change adaptation is the lack of clarity around who is leading the initiative. In the earlier section discussing leadership in Dublin, it was recommended by an interviewee that a clear reporting structure be created and that collaboration with other departments be a job performance measure and in this way silos could be overcome. Further, Dublin demonstrates that collaboration can be a tool for facilitating a shift to adaptive governance approaches to address the impacts of climate change and build resilience. Collaborative planning is not solely a tool *of* adaptive governance but is also a tool *for* adaptive governance. In addition to creating clear reporting structures within the city, having a department that is responsible for coordinating collaboration on policy benefits the public, in that anyone can contact the department to ask questions and be directed accordingly. Therefore, a clear structure has external benefits in that it fosters public engagement, and signals to citizens that they are important to the process, according to interviewees.

Citizens: assets and agents for collaborative policy

> The citizen, the visitor, the lay person will see the city as it is, through their eyes. The city council and decision makers and bureaucrats don't see things. They see storylines that they have from being at meetings. So historians or conservation people will look at something and be imagining the past. Somebody else will look at a derelict site from here and be thinking that is the process of planning, or there's a story there, or it could be in planning ten years ago its getting planning again, or [name] is going to be developing that. They don't see what the citizen sees, which is that is a hole in the ground for the last ten years. So, you need a therapist, or a psychologist more than scientists to explain why these things are not developed. And I think a huge explanation is that they don't live there. So if you don't live in an area where it is physically challenging it doesn't annoy you, so the derelict sites themselves, become maps. They don't become experiences so none of the city makers would even walk by them, because they are maybe... when you get to a certain grade in the city council you don't leave the building. And if you get to a certain grade or a certain social income, you are not in those areas very often. So the daily, depressing-ness of walking by the building is not part of your mental map ... what I think explains all of the peculiar things that don't work in Dublin, it still comes down to the fact that the city decision makers don't live in the city, from apartments to why the traffic lights don't coordinate.
>
> (Interview 4, Dublin)

The view of citizens as assets in the development and implementation of climate change adaptation policy was highlighted by interviewees in all cities. While the interview extract above is a critique of the decision-making process in Dublin City Council, it highlights the importance of engaging citizens in what Healey has discussed in addressing conflict, the meanings and understandings of what the city is by stakeholders (Healey, 1998a). In Box 4.3 where interviewees were asked to provide their lessons for other cities, each interviewee echoed the importance of citizens being involved in the process. Directly in line with the above excerpt was the knowledge that policies around climate change will not succeed if citizens are not included from the outset.

As discussed, Glasgow, Vancouver and Portland are further along in the development of responses to climate change, and their stories of practice have demonstrated how each have found narratives to engage citizens in climate change beginning with a short-term focus that helped identify the overarching focus. Therefore, with an understanding that in order to engage stakeholders in a collaborative process, there needs to be a shared focus that has meaning for all stakeholders; interviewees in Dublin were asked what would be a short-term focus for engagement:

> Ten years ago I use to appeal to people to save the planet and now I say to people, I can save you money. It's a direct let me show you how to save money. Put insulation into the attic. The next time you change your car go for a low emission model. Walk to work, health, the walking thing is one of

those magic buttons of saving you money, good for the planet and good for you. And it's a very simple message to communicate, but there's so many organisations that are working and trying to make this happen and we can use the city to do that. Because transport is a huge emitter and little shifts we can make in transport policy.

(Interview 11, Dublin)

Is your commuting time going to be reduced because you have a proper public transport system that happens to run on a more sustainable fuel? Requires less energy? Is your house going to be more comfortable because it is better insulated? People are signing up to home improvement grants, not because of climate change. Its because they can reduce their costs and make their lives more comfortable.

(Interview 12, Dublin)

The excerpts above, while focused on citizens and saving them money, show the economic argument has short-term value for stakeholders within Dublin City Council and Central Government. Interviewees stated that having been in a period of austerity has been a strain on Dublin City Council. There has been no hiring, and budgets have been severely cut since 2008 (Interviews, Dublin). The economic argument of saving money is potentially a valuable focal point for collaboration on policy. Critically, several interviewees acknowledged that identifying ways to connect policy responses would save the city money and address multiple issues. Moreover, it is important to understand where work joins up with other work areas as Box 4.5 illustrates, to realise the cost savings to the city. Dublin has had success with Dublin Bikes, and the Docklands SDZ that have created opportunities for joined-up work. Whilst these projects were not without controversy, they serve as building blocks for policy makers to reflect on for future policies. Building on these successes will not be without challenges, however, as the literature on collaborative planning discusses, local governments need to find avenues to communicate and balance the short-term costs with the long-term benefits (Faehnle and Tyrväinen, 2013). As discussed earlier, technology and public education are avenues through which urban policy makers can engage with citizens around issues such as climate change, however, it is critical to identify narratives and focuses that are of value to citizens.

Knowing from research, and the stories of practice from policy makers that responses to climate change requires action by all, interviewees in Dublin were asked what would speak to Dubliners and engage them over the long term. Emerging from the interviews was that while in the short run the economic savings could be used to imbue a response to climate change today, in the long term the appeal for taking action would lie in emotive narratives (Lake and Zitcer, 2012; Neal, 2015). Specifically, calls to action that, revolve around children and home, as they are concepts that are understood by people in Ireland (Box 4.7). Critically, they are narratives that individual stakeholders can take ownership of, and therefore responsibility for and leadership on.

Box 4.7 Owning the solutions

INTERVIEWEE: You got to own, it only works when people own it themselves ... we got to get the people to own a narrative that is a part of what we do.

INTERVIEWER: What is stopping people from owning the narrative? In your experience as a councillor with the public consultation process?

INTERVIEWEE: You get protest people, you don't get the people who benefit. You put in a cycle lane or a bus lane. The people on the road, the shopkeepers who lose traffic 'cause the parking is not outside, they will protest about it. The people who benefit in terms of quicker journey time, they are not going to make a comment, unless they are involved in a cycling campaign network or a bus campaign, they are too busy, unless you are directly affected you don't comment. So you are right in terms of the political system maybe it heeds the squeaky wheel gets the most oil, I say most.... We need public pressure. To get our political system to be able to do the hard choice. Because you are taking on vested interests. You are changing [a] system in its entirety, you are changing the entire transport system, you are changing the food system, you are changing [the] energy system, and you are changing the industrial system in one generation. That is what we have to do. That is not a small challenge. There are people who will lose out, and those who will win, the people who lose out are the squeaky wheel. The shopkeepers on the side of the bus lane who are going to be objecting every step of the way.... If you just rely on someone from Europe tells us to do it.... That doesn't really work; you have to own it yourself. Europe helps, tremendously in terms of having a collaborative approach, making sure you don't have competitive disadvantages, as different countries take different approaches. Building up expertise, a small country like Ireland doesn't have all the expertise you have to share and collaborate to be able to do it. But Europe as a watchdog, or big bully. It's not going to work, because ultimately you can't trump political will.

(Interview 20, Dublin)

INTERVIEWER: How do you get policy makers to see the broad picture, how do you get them to see that they are connected?

INTERVIEWEE: If you can introduce some joined-up work, my own view.... It takes leadership, it takes a mandate, and if you want to call it crudely, it takes incentivisation. The mandate for that level of co-operation really has to come from the Taoiseach or the prime minister. Ideally if you want to get that joined-up working, you have to [have] them reporting in some fashion back into the Taoiseach's department, leadership can be exhibited by him in terms of giving a mandate to a group to operate on that basis and then what you have to really consider is how you can encourage. If it is stick and carrot methods to get that cooperation.... So, if you want to call the directors of public health, the leaders of the local education authorities, the leaders of the health authority, the leaders of the local environment authority have to sit around the table and they are allocated from central location a certain pot of money and then they have to collectively agree how they are going to spend that, so that forces them to come to the table and they don't get to discharge those funds, until they actually agree a plan for the city or for the county or the region.... The other way is you have it, 'It is my job to actually cooperate with you', if I work in the Department of Health part of my portfolio or part of my benchmarking is against the degree of contact I have had with other government departments. How I have been able to interact with them. What I can show at the end of the year. How many engagements we have had. What work we have done cooperatively. What goals and targets we've addressed collaboratively. Then your performance bench marked against those criteria. So its not just there should be a working group on, an interdepartmental group on the environment.... But there are actually indicators of successful addressing of the issues that you are doing on a joined-up cooperative, worked out plan and basis.

(Interview 13, Dublin)

Throughout the interviews with stakeholders in Dublin it emerged that a significant challenge for Dublin City Council is the relationship its residents have with the city. The excerpt above is one illustration of this difficult relationship, but it is a demonstration of the challenge Dublin faces ahead if it wants to take a lead in responding to climate change. A key argument for cities taking the lead on climate change is their proximity to citizens and their everyday lives, where small changes in behaviour will contribute to climate change adaptation, from walking and cycling as opposed to driving to work, to recycling and water conservation (Barton, 2009; Galvão *et al.*, 2009). An underlying assumption is that people care about their living environments and that high-quality living is not only provided by the city but something they participate in (Van Assche and Lo, 2011). For the cities of Glasgow, Vancouver and Portland, there is a sense of ownership of the city, and people take action to make it a place that is liveable. However, while the excerpts (Box 4.8) present and suggest some of the reasons for the existing disconnect between citizens and the city of Dublin by the interviewees, there are civil society movements that are striving to reshape this relationship. Interestingly, these movements i.e. Lovin' Dublin are based online (100,000 followers on Twitter), and were acknowledged by interviewees; yet due to the uncertainty around harnessing technology seem to be overlooked by Dublin City Council as viable pathways to engage citizens

More than the challenges of instilling ownership of the city in citizens, the excerpt in Box 4.8 demonstrates how inspiring ownership of the city in citizens is about policy makers taking ownership. Specifically, that policy makers need to recognise that collaboration is going to take time and several attempts before action is taken, which is demonstrated in Box 4.3 and Box 4.4 earlier in this chapter, as well as Box 4.8. However, as has been stated by interviewees in addressing the impacts of climate change on the social ecological system, taking the time to develop deliberate and considered responses yields policy actions that are owned by all. Connecting the lessons from policy makers in Glasgow, Vancouver and Portland with their experiences of fostering a sense of ownership of the city in citizens, the lesson for Dublin is to create opportunities for communities and citizens to be empowered to create solutions, rather than being

---

Box 4.8 Whose city is it?

It is only recently that Dubliners, I mean recently, say since the 60s that Dubliners have started to think of the city as their city. Up until the 60s, there were vast tracts of Dublin here in the Georgian Quarter just demolished, and because the city and urbanism was associated with the British colonialism and the wealthy protestant middle class, and it was their city.... It is only in the last 20 years that Dubliners are really, maybe the 80s, up until the 1980s.... There were areas across there, surface car parks, the city had been hollowed out. By disrespect and an anti-urban sort of thought process and that's because they didn't think it was their city. Rural people didn't think it was their city. But so the last 30 years since the 1980s there has been a dramatic turn around as the country matures, 'No this is our city; it is not the product of the British Colonial system'. I think there was a start from very small things; things do start from small things. It was demonstrated that the plastering, these very sophisticated plaster mouldings in these Georgian houses, was done by Irish craftsman, they weren't English craftsman, they were Irish craftsman. It was oh I see! It was that slow awareness.

(Interview 3, Dublin)

If you take the problem of litter, you know there's a huge effort put in, an enormous economic cost to pick up litter. And we've 400 or 500 people morning, noon and night picking up litter. And I say to myself, 'Look you know how did the litter get on the ground? You know we are every day from five am until one at night tackling this symptom of a different problem.' Which is that Irish people or Dublin people are extraordinarily either careless.... We have to find a better way than just picking up the litter. Like it is something that I find that the standard, despite our efforts, and it is not a reflection of staff. You come into the city at half seven and the place will be spotless.... Something has to change. I would be in early in the morning and going around, see our guys pick up all the litter. And yet there's a time of day when it's just appalling, our whole management of litter. And its not just the physical picking up of the litter, we have to start addressing the behaviour of Dublin people towards their own city. That's one thing we do, that behavioural issue, we are very poor in addressing that.

(Interview 1, Dublin)

---

forced into solutions. As one interviewee indicated, though counterintuitive to the job of a planner, a means of achieving this was 'not to plan' but to create opportunities for people to be part of the solutions; which supports the recurring advice that communities that own the solutions to their problems are best able to respond to the challenges they face in other words they are resilient.

Dublin City Council is working on identifying how it can affect behavioural change in residents, so that they own the city and become part of the solutions and responses to climate change in the city. Interviewees were asked, what the avenues are for Dublin City Council to build ownership of the city and more broadly the responses to climate change. For interviewees, education was viewed as key policy tool (Box 4.9). Education is a key factor in that it is an opportunity to build a lifelong value of taking care of one's environment. Glasgow, Vancouver and Portland have all three utilised education to foster a sense of ownership in future generations of not just the city, but the development of policy responses to challenges facing the city. These cities recognise the role of education in engaging citizens in a dialogue about what they see the future of the city to be, and how they play a role in that future. Critically, as knowledge is 'power', opportunities to educate people on issues such as climate change counters fear and enables policy makers to engage in a deliberate and considerate process for policy development, that gives 'hope value' to people that they can be part of the solution. This is just one avenue for Dublin to build relationships with citizens and develop their sense of ownership, and aligns with an overarching theme of the Climate Change Action Plans. Education as each of the cities in this research has demonstrated is an important aspect of responding to climate change. Similar to technology it is a policy tool that needs further consideration with regards to maximising its potential for engagement and action. Moreover, education is an underutilised policy tool that has benefits for building awareness and understanding of climate change. The challenge is not just integrating climate change into education systems, but into broader public education, which can be facilitated with narratives; and as discussed, technology has a potential role in the delivery of public education around climate change challenges and responses.

Box 4.9 Ownership through education

One area that we are looking at, at the moment, is trying to develop educational material that will go into the schools. There are three areas we are trying to identify. One would be the primary school level, and what would be appropriate there in terms of working with Department of Education and then bringing in the relevant agencies to help with that, the likes of the EPA. And trying to make it more meaningful for that particular age group. Maybe the fourth or fifth class side of things, there might be a better understanding of concepts. And then secondary school and how you might increase the level of detail and how you might work with that. And then finally on the third level, we would do, or be interacting with a lot of research out there on climate, which kind of brings in interaction with all the universities. But also to try and actually make sure that climate issues as much as possible are on the syllabus of kind the college courses. Where possible. See if we can go and give guest lectures on climate in different universities.... At the moment we have a regular slot in DCU and UCC and places like to just do that. But it often depends on the people running the courses and what they want on the content.

(Interview 14, Dublin)

Lessons

This chapter has sought to present the lessons in collaborative planning learned by Glasgow, Vancouver, Portland, and Dublin. It is evident that each of these cities is at varying stages of responding to climate change. Yet, common themes have emerged that provide insights for cities in developing climate change adaptation policy through a collaborative process. Through the stories of practice from interviewees in each city, it is evident that the collaborative approaches used in developing climate change responses in cities require leadership and ownership of the process by all stakeholders. As has been presented in this and previous chapters, institutional structures that support leadership and ownership of policy send clear messages of the importance of responding to climate change, such that collaborative action is sustained first within local government and then beyond the city with stakeholders from citizens to higher levels of government. Further, institutional structures that are adaptive support collaboration, and collaborative planning emerges as a tool of adaptive governance. Simultaneously, in the absence of adaptive institutional structures, collaboration with diverse stakeholders is possible, thus collaborative planning emerges as a tool for facilitating adaptive governance.

Within local government, planners and urban policy makers through the stories of practice from interviewees acknowledge that their role is changing. While in line with the ideals of the planner's role according to the works of Forester and Healey, planners seem to be adding to their roles the importance of self-awareness. There is a growing recognition across all cities by planners that in order to engage with stakeholders, especially citizens, they need to understand not only the living conditions and histories of these individuals, but also how they view planners and urban policy makers. Acknowledging this and being open with communities, that they (interviewees) do not have all the answers, enables the building of trust and relationships with stakeholders. This underpins leadership for developing policy around climate change.

A challenge that emerged with leadership is the concept of leadership, specifically in Dublin where the view of interviewees was that an elected mayor would shift the power dynamics and enable Dublin City Council to take a lead on climate change policy. As discussed, leadership is not about solely about an individual having power in the form of a mandate, but the capacity to influence and guide the process. Thus, leadership could be a team of experts leading the process. For Glasgow, Vancouver and Portland it was discussed by interviewees, that their goals and targets for climate change policy are aspirational, but have become realistic under the leadership of teams that are made up of diverse stakeholders who recognise the importance of addressing climate change, and are able to communicate the need to address it collaboratively.

Lastly, narratives for climate change used by the cities to engage stakeholders in the policy dialogue around climate change adaptation and resilience. Interviewees acknowledged that responding to climate change is an ongoing process, and therefore engagement needs to be constant. However, the key challenge with climate change for all cities is the understanding of what climate change means for individuals. As such, each city sought to build dialogue from a focal point that resonated with citizens. Consequently, Glasgow's responses began with addressing the health status of citizens, Vancouver's began with being the greenest city, while Portland focused on equity. From these initial challenges, the cities have turned them into opportunities to engage with citizens and build a narrative around climate change that is understood, and is explicitly about climate change adaptation, but also about how citizens can improve their lives. Thus, citizens are becoming agents and assets of the policy responses to climate change in cities, because they own and understand the issues.

The lessons of practice from local governments responding to climate change has demonstrated the value of collaborative planning as practice. In endeavouring to collaborate with stakeholders, practitioners have shown that leadership is a necessary tool for collaboration, especially in the context of climate change with its diverse impacts requiring integrated responses. Further, in order to collaborate, ownership of the process by all stakeholders is needed. This is achieved through narratives that emerge from understanding the hopes and concerns of stakeholders, such that stakeholders can collaboratively develop responses that facilitate resilience. Collaborative planning in turn has shown that climate change resilience calls for policy responses that begin with addressing the livelihoods of stakeholders, through the narratives identified by them. From these narratives, urban policy makers can continue to identify new narratives to sustain and evolve the policy dialogue with stakeholders.

References

Agger, A. and Löfgren, K. (2008) 'Democratic Assessment of Collaborative Planning Processes', *Planning Theory*, 7(2), pp. 145–164. doi: 10.1177/1473095208090432.

Allmendinger, P. (2002) *Planning in Postmodern Times*. Taylor & Francis (RTPI Library Series). Available at: https://books.google.ie/books?id=nt2AAgAAQBAJ.

Van Assche, K. and Lo, M. C. (2011) 'Planning, preservation and place branding: A tale of sharing assets and narratives', *Place Branding and Public Diplomacy*, 7(2), pp. 116–126. doi: 10.1057/pb.2011.11.

Barton, H. (2009) 'Land use planning and health and well-being', *Land Use Policy*. Pergamon, 26, pp. S115–S123. doi: 10.1016/J.LANDUSEPOL.2009.09.008.

Bickerstaff, K., Simmons, P. and Pidgeon, N. (2008) 'Constructing Responsibilities for Risk: Negotiating Citizen – State Relationships', *Environment and Planning A: Economy and Space*, 40(6), pp. 1312–1330. doi: 10.1068/a39150.

Castán Broto, V., Oballa, B. and Junior, P. (2013) 'Governing climate change for a just city: challenges and lessons from Maputo, Mozambique', *Local Environment*, 18(January 2015), pp. 678–704. doi: 10.1080/13549839.2013.801573.

Corburn, J. (2009) 'Cities, Climate Change and Urban Heat Island Mitigation: Localising Global Environmental Science', *Urban Studies*, 46(2), pp. 413–427. doi: 10.1177/0042098008099361.

Epstein, M. J. and Buhovac, A. R. (2014) *Making Sustainability Work: Best Practices in Managing and Measuring Corporate Social, Environmental, and Economic Impacts*. Berrett-Koehler Publishers (BusinessPro collection). Available at: https://books.google.ie/books?id=RfvxAAAAQBAJ.

Epstein, P. R. (2002) 'Climate Change and Infectious Disease: Stormy Weather Ahead?', *Epidemiology*, 13(4). Available at: https://journals.lww.com/epidem/Fulltext/2002/070 00/Climate_Change_and_Infectious_Disease__Stormy.1.aspx.

Faehnle, M. and Tyrväinen, L. (2013) 'A framework for evaluating and designing collaborative planning', *Land Use Policy*. Pergamon, 34, pp. 332–341. doi: 10.1016/J. LANDUSEPOL.2013.04.006.

Fahmi, F. Z., Prawira, M., Hudalah, D., and Firman, T. (2015) 'Leadership and collaborative planning: The case of Surakarta, Indonesia', *Planning Theory*. SAGE Publications, 15(3), pp. 294–315. doi: 10.1177/1473095215584655.

Filippi, F. De and Balbo, R. (2011) '(POP-071) [S78] Planning for real: ICT as a tool in urban regeneration', *The Built & Human Environment Review*, 4(1), pp. 67–73. Available at: http://usir.salford.ac.uk/18534/1/44-120-1-PB.pdf.

Forester, J. (1994) 'Bridging Interests and Community: Advocacy Planning and the Challenges of Deliberative Democracy', *Journal of the American Planning Association*. Routledge, 60(2), pp. 153–158. doi: 10.1080/01944369408975567.

Forester, J. (1999) 'Reflections on the future understanding of planning practice', *International Planning Studies*. Routledge, 4(2), pp. 175–193. doi: 10.1080/1356347990 8721734.

Forester, J. (2006) 'Exploring urban practice in a democratising society: opportunities, techniques and challenges', *Development Southern Africa*. Routledge, 23(5), pp. 569–586. doi: 10.1080/03768350601021814.

Forester, J. (2012) 'Learning to Improve Practice: Lessons from Practice Stories and Practitioners' Own Discourse Analyses (or Why Only the Loons Show Up)', *Planning Theory & Practice*. Routledge, 13(1), pp. 11–26. doi: 10.1080/14649357.2012. 649905.

Friedmann, J. (2005) 'Globalization and the emerging culture of planning', *Progress in Planning*. Pergamon, 64(3), pp. 183–234. doi: 10.1016/J.PROGRESS.2005.05.001.

Galvão, L. A. C., Edwards, S., Corvalan, C., Fortune, K. and Akerman, M. (2009) 'Climate change and social determinants of health: two interlinked agendas', *Global Health Promotion*, 16(1_suppl), pp. 81–84. doi: 10.1177/1757975909103761.

Gedikli, B. (2009) 'The Role of Leadership in the Success of Participatory Planning Processes: Experience From Turkey', *European Urban and Regional Studies*. SAGE Publications Ltd, 16(2), pp. 115–130. doi: 10.1177/0969776408101684.

Hanzl, M. (2007) 'Information technology as a tool for public participation in urban planning: a review of experiments and potentials', *Design Studies*. Elsevier, 28(3), pp. 289–307. doi: 10.1016/J.DESTUD.2007.02.003.

Healey, P. (1997) *Collaborative Planning: Shaping Places in Fragmented Societies*. UBC Press (Planning, environment, cities). Available at: https://books.google.ie/books?id= psW_hMb3AH8C.

Healey, P. (1998a) 'Building Institutional Capacity through Collaborative Approaches to Urban Planning', *Environment and Planning A: Economy and Space*. SAGE Publications Ltd, 30(9), pp. 1531–1546. doi: 10.1068/a301531.

Healey, P. (1998b) 'Collaborative planning in a stakeholder society', *Town Planning Review*, 69(1), p. 1. doi: 10.3828/tpr.69.1.h651u2327m86326p.

Heywood, P. (2004) 'Collaborative community planning', *Australian Planner*. Routledge, 41(3), pp. 30–34. doi: 10.1080/07293682.2004.9982367.

Innes, J. E., Connick, S. and Booher, D. (2007) 'Informality as a Planning Strategy', *Journal of the American Planning Association*. Routledge, 73(2), pp. 195–210. doi: 10. 1080/01944360708976153.

Lake, R. W. and Zitcer, A. W. (2012) 'Who Says? Authority, Voice, and Authorship in Narratives of Planning Research', *Journal of Planning Education and Research*. SAGE Publications Inc, 32(4), pp. 389–399. doi: 10.1177/0739456X12455666.

Laurian, L. (2009) 'Trust in planning: Theoretical and practical considerations for participatory and deliberative planning', *Planning Theory and Practice*, 10(3), pp. 369–391. doi: 10.1080/14649350903229810.

Mandarano, L. A. (2008) 'Evaluating Collaborative Environmental Planning Outputs and Outcomes: Restoring and Protecting Habitat and the New York–New Jersey Harbor Estuary Program', *Journal of Planning Education and Research*. SAGE Publications Inc, 27(4), pp. 456–468. doi: 10.1177/0739456X08315888.

McKay, S., Murray, M. and Hui, L. P. (2011) 'Pitfalls in Strategic Planning: Lessons for Legitimacy', *Space and Polity*. Routledge, 15(2), pp. 107–124. doi: 10.1080/13562576.2011.625222.

Neal, Z. (2015) 'Making Big Communities Small: Using Network Science to Understand the Ecological and Behavioral Requirements for Community Social Capital', *American Journal of Community Psychology*, 55(3), pp. 369–380. doi: 10.1007/s10464-015-9720-4.

O'Brien, K, Sygna, L., Leichenko, R., Adger, W.N., Barnett, J., Mitchell, T., Schipper, L., Tanner, T., Vogel, C., and Mortreux, C,. (2008) 'Disaster Risk Reduction, Climate Change Adaptation and Human Security Report prepared for the Royal Norwegian Ministry of Foreign Affairs', *Global Environmental Change and Human Security Project*. www.unisdr.org/files/7946_GECHSReport3081.pdf

Papa, R., Gargiulo, C. and Galderisi, A. (2013) 'Towards an Urban Planners' Perspective on Smart City', *Journal of Land Use, Mobility and Environment*, 6(1), pp. 6–17. doi: 10.6092/1970-9870/1536.

Pitt, D. and Bassett, E. (2014) 'Innovation and the Role of Collaborative Planning in Local Clean Energy Policy', *Environmental Policy and Governance*, 24(6), pp. 377–390. doi: 10.1002/eet.1653.

Poplin, A. (2012) 'Playful public participation in urban planning: A case study for online serious games', *Computers, Environment and Urban Systems*. Pergamon, 36(3), pp. 195–206. doi: 10.1016/J.COMPENVURBSYS.2011.10.003.

Shipley, R. and Utz, S. (2012) 'Making it Count: A Review of the Value and Techniques for Public Consultation', *Journal of Planning Literature*, 27(1), pp. 22–42. doi: 10.1177/0885412211413133.

Sutriadi, R. and Wulandari, A. (2014) 'Towards a Communicative City: Enhancing Urban Planning Coordination by the Support of Information and Communication Technology. Case Study Bandung Metropolitan Area, Indonesia', *Procedia – Social and Behavioral Sciences*. Elsevier B.V., 135, pp. 76–81. doi: 10.1016/j.sbspro.2014.07.328.

United Nations Human Settlements Programme (UN-Habitat) (2016) *World Cities Report 2016 – Urbanization and Development: Emerging Futures*, *International Journal*. doi: 10.1016/S0264-2751(03)00010-6.

5 Dublin

Responses to climate change

> Dublin has been here since 874 or whatever it is and it has been through all those hundred of years of change.... It is a resilient city ... we had to make it that way. In the 1980s, in the city centre within the canals was under 50,000 people, now its up to 200,000. We've increased. It started off by investment in apartments, tax incentives for apartment schemes for the private sector to fill up those surface car parks I talked about there. So there was a response to that. There was a shame in the hollowing out of a city.... In the 80s, we didn't realise we made this city, the resilient thing to do. Then in the 90s ...rather than let those docks become huge brownfield zones, through the Docklands Authority in the first instances ... with the strategic development zone have brought I would say about 30,000–40,000 jobs in there ... and thousands of new population. That's an example of resilience. Against all the odds, we've introduced a bike scheme. We've introduced a Luas [Dublin light rail system] scheme in the city, that's a tram system. And we're extending the tram system from here out to Grangegorman. And there's a new DIT campus out there for 20,000 kids.... All of these things demonstrate that the city can do things. It is resilient. It's determined to keep itself a consolidating city.
>
> (Interview 3, Dublin)

The excerpt above was provided by an interviewee as an illustration of Dublin's resilience, and demonstrates economic resilience and political resilience. It is, however a limited illustration of resilience, in that it does not demonstrate social ecological resilience and how it is achieved through collaboration with diverse stakeholders to create a 'net of policies'. Continuing from the previous chapters, this chapter presents examples of how Dublin to date has engaged in collaborative processes. As such, the analysis of Dublin builds on the international case studies, endeavouring to add to the theoretical and practical understandings of collaboration through an investigation of policy development in Dublin, while also setting the stage for the ongoing process of developing climate change action plans, where these lessons in collaboration can be applied in practice.

Important to understanding the starting point for climate change policy development is an awareness of climate change; as such, interviewees were asked to indicate the awareness of Dubliners with regards to the impacts of climate change. The responses to this question from interviewees ranged widely, and Box 5.1 presents these responses. The public's understanding of the issues of climate change was best described as similar to 'understandings of the big bang theory'. There is a basic knowledge that it is happening, but how it impacts livelihoods is not fully understood due to the language used around climate change. The language used by the general public is different: people understand flooding, transportation and energy issues but the connection to climate change is not made. Therefore, there has been policy success in responding to climate change indirectly through addressing flooding, energy and transportation, rather than addressing flood resilience, energy efficiency, de-carbonisation and supporting modal shift.

There were three policy responses that were viewed as addressing climate change: the Dublin Bikes Scheme, flood mitigation and the Docklands Strategic Development Zone. The Dublin Bikes Scheme represented a policy that councillors, planners, and citizens were able to effectively engage in and collaborate on; a long-term process for not only the Dublin Bikes Scheme directly, but for improved cycling routes within the city. Success has been beyond what was anticipated. As a positive consequence the city is now facing the challenge of responding to a greater than anticipated demand. The engagement around the bike share scheme is a demonstration of Dublin's potential to lead and influence national policy response. The success of the Dublin Bikes lies with key stakeholders championing and giving a voice to a local grass roots movement (Interview, Dublin, 2015). While interviewees acknowledge that creating the modal shift in transportation is about addressing climate change, the dialogue around cycling was about creating safer routes and making the city more attractive for cyclists. By responding to the requests emerging in the dialogue and implementing a successful bike share scheme, Dublin City Council has empowered community groups and influenced national policy, as Central Government in response developed the Cycle-to-Work scheme, which has promoted cycling as a viable mode of daily transport across the country (Box 5.2). This process of policy development highlighted the capacity within Dublin City Council to shape policy from a different position and through new avenues. The process also identified new groups that are keen to engage with the council and showed new modes and tools for engagement.

A key climate change issue facing Dublin is flooding. There is a keen awareness of flooding being a challenge for people living in Dublin. Dublin City Council has developed extensive flood mitigation and adaptation plans that were developed through collaboration with various stakeholders from the Office of Public Works to residents' associations with the aim of adapting Dublin to flooding. Dublin City Council works closely with neighbouring local authorities and the Office of Public Works (OPW), to prepare Dublin for future flooding events. From the interviews, it is evident that responding to flood risk requires

Box 5.1 Climate awareness

I think there's limited understanding of environmental awareness, ideas around sustainable development, ideas around planning, and development, and climate change ... I don't think its climate scepticism; I think it's something like the big bang theory. Something that you know probably makes sense, but it is very hard to break down. So there's engagement on it.... The Development Plan is a perfectly logical place to have that discussion about, 'we are making these changes to deal with climate change'. But nationally, I think it is something that we've not done a very good job of problematising, describing how we are going to address it.

(Interview 6, Dublin)

Very poor level of awareness. It's a circular problem because if there's poor political awareness and poor media coverage that in turn creates poor public awareness. Unless there is public awareness or concern, that undermines political concern and media coverage. We have this very much triangular relationship between the three, which is self-feeding.... Simple things like doing a word search on Irish media sources for climate, you can't really do climate. If you do climate you will get financial climate. Not climate change. One of the problems we have with word searching, if you do ecosystem you get business ecosystem – it has become trendy to talk about the business ecosystem.

(Interview 17, Dublin)

Climate change, its too heavy and people fall asleep and it is a difficult subject to get people engaged in. I would imagine you are talking to lots of people saying we are doing wonderful things and maybe technology itself in 5, 10, 15 years, technology will solve all of this and then we can all can continue 50-mile commuting distance. You know, I would hope that, that didn't happen, not that climate change wouldn't be resolved by technology. There is an opportunity with climate change, but technology can only do so much and the opportunity is to consolidate the centre of the city to make it more desirable to live for all sorts of social and economic benefits. The fact that they currently align themselves with climate change is great, but I would have a heavy heart if somebody discovered in the morning we could press the switch and climate change was solved and we could then give up on, the wider challenges of consolidating the cities. You know, the last 20 years, most western cities have just gotten more desirable to live in. Dublin is the same, but there's a big 'but'. You know, Paris, Vienna, New York Copenhagen, Tel Aviv, the wealthy live in the centre of their cities.... The wealthy don't live in the centre of our city. And it's very interesting, why it's very interesting is the contribution it could make if that was a focus of policy in terms of consolidating the city for climate change, for commuting.

(Interview 4, Dublin)

People talk about a lot of things related to climate change and they don't know it. Things like flood risk, they don't call it flood risk, and it is flooding. Clontarf floods, Sandymount floods, the Quays can flood.... People know all about flooding and what it means to them in practical terms, their houses are flooded.

(Interview 8, Dublin)

Box 5.2 Championing cyclists

Public consultation, we are absolutely hung up on public consultation. I am never really sure what the point is, because some things are just inevitable. We've found in the past that you go out to the public to propose social housing. It will be dominated by people who don't want social housing.... But we found recently ... we noticed with the North Quays cycle route, obviously there's a whole lot of new cyclists who are generally young and engaged in terms of social media, and that was overwhelming dominated by people who wouldn't normally participate in public consultation, and as it happened very much in favour.

(Interview 1, Dublin)

The Dublin Bike Campaign, there is an awareness of cycling as a good way of travelling around the city. Dublin is a fairly flat city, and its very compact, even if you live 3, 4 or 5 km out it is a good city to cycle around. Whether or not people link that to climate change, I am not sure. They link that car congestion is very high and you can get from places like Ranelagh, and Sutton, you can get into the city more quickly on your bike than [by] car.

(Interview 3, Dublin)

While we were in government we brought in the cycle to work scheme; it has been extraordinarily successful. There are now bike shops in every small town in Ireland and people can write off the tax costs of the bike and it gives them a feelgood factor. It's revitalised the cycle sales and service industry in Ireland. That is a nice short-term thing that exploded, a brilliant success. And that was not giving anybody any message about climate change. It is 'here's a way of saving you money on your bike'.

(Interview 10, Dublin)

---

consideration of numerous issues and finding balanced responses that address stakeholders' concerns (Box 5.3). As in the case of cycling, the dialogue around flood policy was not directly about climate change, but about reducing risk, and protecting individuals and their livelihoods.

The third example is the Docklands Strategic Development Zone (SDZ), which is seen as a 'golden goose' (Interview, Dublin). It is a modern area of the city that has become home to the city's information technology (IT) industry and simultaneously a diverse population. For interviewees, the Docklands SDZ is an area of the city where they were able to experiment with development policy and innovate. This experimentation, though, may be the result of how an SDZ can permit development, in that an SDZ is exempt from public consultation once an area has been designated (Planning and Development Act 2000). This does not mean that public opinion was not considered; rather, in the process of developing this area, Dublin City Council was interested in the challenges facing the area and addressing them (Box 5.4). As with the cycling consultation, the Docklands increased the city's awareness of the changes needed in public

Box 5.3 Engaging the public in flood adaptation dialogue

INTERVIEWER: How do you educate the public? How do you educate them about flooding, if only 20 responded to this development plan? How do you get people to start talking about this?

INTERVIEWEE: We have public consultation days for the flood maps. We had over 100 people in the civics, the last time, for the flood extents. We are meeting all the residents' associations. I suspect a lot of them are fairly happy with what we are doing, already.... Sometimes we go out to planning for these, all we get is the environmental people. So, I talk to the locals some of them have been very severely flooded and people have nearly died at times. Particularly, elderly people have come close a few times. I meet the residents' associations and they sort of say is there anything we can do to help. I say send submissions in, because if all we get are the people objecting to it, and there is nobody on the other side saying we want it. The people here on [name] Avenue, which is just downstream of Ballsbridge, they got a petition together and they got over 4000 names.... It helped a lot because when the planners saw it they could see ... they felt they had to listen more to the people who were flooded. There has to be a balance, obviously between amenity and view but, if no one had commented, if all the people said we are happy with that we won't bother commenting.... You have to talk to all the people, not just the people you are doing works with, the people close ... I like talking to individual people 'cause often you have the councillor and then maybe the council you know or the area committee. So, you are two or three removed. Whereas if you talk to the person directly, you learn a lot more and most people are very appreciative of what we do. Areas like Clontarf where you have four or five hundred houses at risk of flooding in a 200-year tidal event, you have thousands that drive by. A few years ago, a colleague of mine had planned to put an embankment along here and just the week before it started there were major objections, the people who were flooded still wanted it to go ahead, but they were outnumbered 20 or 30 to 1 by the people who drive by or live up on the hill, who didn't want their visual amenity obstructed.... There was one big meeting there on flood walls in Clontarf and all the people who are objecting to the embankments and walls were standing up one after another. And then one person who had been flooded stood up and said that he wanted the embankment and over half the people in audience clapped him. But they were all afraid to stand up themselves and have their say because there were all these other people who were totally against it, they thought they were on their own so ... I like talking to the people who are flooded to try and give them a bit more confidence to stand up.

(Interview 9, Dublin)

Box 5.4 The Docklands – Strategic Development Zone

For a while we have been promoting the whole mixed-use philosophy of getting employment places, retail, residential, cultural and recreational to be as close as possible to each other. As opposed to say Americanistic zoning.… Because if you get them close together, you minimise the need to get in your car, you can use public transport. You can use a bike and you can walk more often. Its astonishing to hear, I think there's something over half of the workers in the Docklands Strategic Development Zone walk to work, which is a big change. That mixed use philosophy is important to use, but you get for instance, motions from elected members and some elected members saying to take out a mixed use, the occasional office or the occasional shop or from residential areas, they want a mono-zone, which is a concern.… Then the other big thing that the development plan has is the green infrastructure, that broadening out of the green space, that's not just parks, public open space. And that the, spaces are multi function[al], if you know that you absorb water, absorb CO_2, they are recreation, they are good for health, they are good for biodiversity, for all different things and squirrels and all the rest of it and badgers. That multifunctional thing is important and that's promoted in our new development plan as well.

(Interview 3, Dublin)

Your jewel in the crown in the Docklands, that is attracting all your foreign direct investment (FDI). That is keeping the economy going, the Googles and the Facebooks. If you go down and talk to them, and ask them what they want, they want their workers to come and enjoy a really nice, green environment. The Google Building is gold rated in the LEED system. And they are proud of that, they were trying for platinum, but they didn't quite make it. They got a very high rating. The same with Citibank, the same with large firms located down in the Docklands. And we've talked to a lot of them for one reason or another. What is striking, they have a policy, value of environmentally healthy places to work, unlike their corresponding Irish members. So you go down, right well, these people will come here and invest the money to keep the economy going, want this. Even when you say that, it is a very hard message to get across. Why should we spend another million on keeping the place clean, when we don't have to?

(Interview 21, Dublin)

---

consultation, and the areas in which the city is deficit in terms of engagement, i.e. 'the transient population'. Through the SDZ, the city has come to terms with the changing demographics of Dublin and how that connects to broader policy issues, such as attracting foreign direct investment (FDI), which correlates with the provision of high quality living environments (Box 5.4). The acknowledgement of the importance of high-quality living environments and 'green' policies to attracting FDI has also recently been reiterated at an event hosted by the Irish Planning Institute, where a councillor from the City of Vancouver highlighted that the draw for companies to locate in Vancouver in spite of their core business being located elsewhere was the city's green policies. Dublin City Council recognises this, and several interviewees discussed the corporate social responsibility objectives of multinationals, such as Google, for the environment. Critically though, for interviewees the SDZ is a demonstration of using mixed use zoning to foster the movement towards a low-carbon climate resilient society, as buildings in the SDZ are also to be ready for a district energy system based on the waste-to-energy plant that was completed in 2017.

Collaborative planning in Dublin

Public consultation, as has been discussed, is a cornerstone of the Irish planning system, which is recognised to be a transparent process. However, as with the other cities discussed in this book, there are challenges with public consultation and its contribution to collaborative policy making, namely, who is engaging, and the accessibility of the process. Further, in Dublin as mentioned, the distance between the Irish citizen and a minister in central government is only a few layers. The proximity to political decision makers is both a benefit and challenge to the policy making process (Interviews, Dublin, 2015). This section will discuss how this shapes the collaborative planning process, particularly engagement and consensus building, by considering the processes involved in the formulation policies discussed in the previous section. Finally, the discussion will consider the challenges that Dublin faces to build on the success of policies and make Dublin a climate-resilient city.

Relationship building: addressing conflicting demands

A challenge for Dublin City Council in building relationships with citizens and higher levels of government is a misunderstanding of the role of local government. This has stemmed from the increasing centralisation of services that were once the remit of local authorities in Ireland. Coupled with the ability of citizens to bring issues directly to politicians at higher levels of government, it is difficult for Dublin City Council to engage with citizens. In the previous chapter, each of the cities recognised that engagement in collaborative planning was an ongoing process that needed to be sustained, this is in line with Healey, and Forester. Further, engagement with citizens is a characteristic of local government that reinforces accountability of civil servants and politicians (Brand and Gaffikin, 2007). From interviewees in Dublin, building relationships with citizens is challenging, partially due to its relationships with various departments in Central Government, which from the interviewees appears to be strained.

The work of Innes (2004), and Forester (2012), has emphasised the role of building relationships between stakeholders that will allow for the exchange of ideas and knowledge and give a voice to stakeholders. In the process of building relationships, stakeholders need to acknowledge histories, beliefs and values that may be barriers to meaningful relationships and collaboration. However, the recent history of the relationship between Central Government and Dublin City Council has been marked by loss of responsibility. The sentiments around the loss of this capacity demonstrate that the relationship between Dublin City Council and Central Government is strained. Further, that perhaps it is of a 'parent-child' nature, as opposed to a relationship of 'equals' that fosters collaboration. One interviewee reiterated that the relationship between the city and Central Government has been referred to as 'like a master/slave' (Interview, Dublin, 2016). For Dublin, these barriers are seen in the responses of interviewees to direction from Central Government; there is an underlying tone of frustration that is a source of conflict, as demonstrated by the excerpts below:

> Irish Water can do what they like. They don't need permission from us. They are supposed to come to us. ESB [Electricity Supply Board] can declare an emergency and open up anywhere. They could dig up O'Connell Street or Grafton Street. Gas, electricity and water can all make the case for emergency, especially in proximity to a hospital. We have tried to mitigate that, by sending them through a process, but while we are the doorkeeper we don't have the keys.
>
> (Interview 6, Dublin)

> The areas in which we can innovate are increasingly limited. One of the things they gave us was the responsibility for economic development. But we don't have the policy instruments for economic development. We are producing these community plans, economic community plans. We don't control any of the policy. Simply, I don't know, nobody quite knows, giving somebody nominal responsibility for economic development when they don't control the instruments for economic policy.... There are a lot of things we can do to encourage economic development.... For example, we produce the Dublin Economic Monitor every quarter on the Dublin economy.... Our recently published City Centre Plan is a very good example of a local authority giving real leadership in an area, a public policy area. Notwithstanding, we think there is a good support, you talk to motorists or you listen to radio, you wouldn't get that impression. But we've driven up the modal share, very significantly, over the last 10 years ... notwithstanding significant opposition....
>
> (Interview 1, Dublin)

Interviewees expressed the opinion that Central Government has a tendency to favour other stakeholders, such as developers, by creating more onerous procedures for the council to follow in order to develop a project, such as Part 8,[1] which arguably contributes to the 'image' of Dublin City Council being an ineffective body by a public that may not be aware of these procedures (which were discussed in the section on the planning context in Ireland). Considering the excerpts presented earlier, there is a suggestion that there is a conflict between Central Government and Dublin City Council over Dublin as a city. Conflict, though, as Healey's work indicates, is not necessarily a negative, more a point from which to create new understandings. The potential for conflict, and conflict itself, force the reality that for people the city has different meanings and expressions, and that the planner is not the sole proprietor of the city, but rather their role is to formulate a cohesive city from the array of imagined cities by citizens (Healey, 2002). Therefore, the city is a collective effort.

Considering the perspectives of interviewees within Dublin City Council and those outside, it is evident there are differing views of Dublin City Council's capacity for shaping the city and contributing to national policy as it pertains to climate change. The perspective of those interviewees outside Dublin City Council is that Dublin has been given the capacity to shape the city, in spite of the constraints stemming from legislation as demonstrated in the following excerpts:

> What the role of local authorities is within climate policy.... Their role is changing quite a bit. They would have had to deal with water in the past, now Irish Water does. That is one area of work that has moved away from them. Roads and transport is another area that has moved away from them into a centralised approach.... Their role has evolved to some degree and has probably taken on a more economic, social, environmental role let's say, in terms of what they do now. Or what they are going to be doing into the future. A key part for them is to try to think about what role they will have in terms of, kind of, what initiatives at a local level. What can be done at the local level to feed into the national efforts to do a national mitigation plan to bring down our emissions? It's not just what the government decides to do, but how it gets implemented on the ground. Obviously, there are several local authorities, communities, that are doing their own thing, and trying to make a difference at a local level. It is trying to tap into that and expand that out to other local authorities. And see if local authorities can work together and share experiences.
>
> (Interview 14, Dublin)

> Remember the scale, it is a very small country.... The chains of command, for me to progress policy, say from the national level to a local authority in Cork, in the south of the country. You are talking about 3 or 4 layers of people. It is that compressed. I advise a minister, a minister has certain functions in relation to planning, you know. I'll deal with the chief executive of the local authority, who is organising planning through a chief planner and that's it. So, it's a very direct, so there aren't many layers. A lot of it in Ireland works through people. Rather than very complex systems and processes.
>
> (Interview 13, Dublin)

The above excerpts also again highlight the closeness or proximity of citizens to government and suggest that the lack of complexity in Ireland's system lends itself to collaboration. However, the excerpts in Box 5.5 and Box 5.6 suggest that there is a recognition that perhaps central government has 'put handcuffs'

Box 5.5 Evolving role of local government II

INTERVIEWEE: The role of local government is changing and they are getting more autonomy in certain areas. Some tasks have been taken away from them, but they have been given an economic development role. So, they have to develop an economic development plan for their local authority... They don't do anywhere near as much as they used to do, for example waste management is all private sector now. Water and the roads are more or less gone. So the hard core, the hard edge, to local authorities in terms of engineers has probably now been taken over by the more environment community kind of sections. And you often see that in how local authorities are organised.... The thing for me, and this has been said to me by a couple of chief executives on the climate side, they feel now they need to take the lead. There is this kind of changing role. When things are changing it is a very good opportunity for a particular sector to say, 'Ok, are we going to sit back and wait for the next way? Or continue to do what we always did? Or do we say, maybe we should be proactive here and take the lead?' Which in areas like this to me they clearly can make a lot of difference. There are a lot of cities that are in partnership with other cities around the world who are doing work. Dublin is obviously kind of very different to other cities. All cities are different, but there are things they can learn and do things about. I think resources are an issue for them. I think it is the same for everybody. I think there is when you see people at that high level talking about being leaders and saying maybe we should get out there and do what we think is the right thing to do ... Dublin City would have certain constraints that they are working to. But I also think there is also plenty of areas where they can do, or look to work in and kind of lead work on, in terms of climate. I think our role, 'cause in terms of what we've said, we said, 'look we want to work with you on this, we don't want to tell you what to do. We will do what we can to work with you on it. And more importantly, we will get all the relevant sectors to work more closely with you.' Because often, local authorities would be working in isolation, and wouldn't necessarily have the collaboration of other government departments like energy, transport, agriculture in a lot of cases in the rural local authorities. And that's kind of really important in terms of the process that we have set up that we do make sure that they all interact. Because, if the local authorities feel that they are part of what you might call the sectoral planning side of things, whether that be transport or energy, then they can probably kind of find a place to fit their role into, rather than trying to do something completely on their own....

INTERVIEWER: What are the areas that Dublin can innovate in?

INTERVIEWER: I don't know. That's kind of an interesting question, when we went out on our seminars, I suppose the downside of what we do is at a national level, we haven't got the time to get down to the issues at the local level. We've tried to look at case studies in certain counties, just to give you an example of what they might do on the adaptation side. And we are looking at developing more robust case studies, to be used by all local authorities to look at in terms of an answer to that kind of question, if this local authority is looking at what can other local authorities look at. I am not sure, to be honest in terms of Dublin. I suppose kind of living, more or less on the borders of Dublin City and Dun Laoghaire–Rathdown, I am shaped by my own environment and the issues around there. I think transport is something that Dublin City struggles with very badly. And I think most people would agree with that.

(Interview 14, Dublin)

Box 5.6 Evolving role of local government II

INTERVIEWEE: Local authorities have power to engage with [the] public in whatever way. Say in doing a local area plan, if you look at the legislation and what it says about doing a local area plan. Which is the one that is most relevant to the community. Because it is the area where we are living. The legislation is very broad, a local authority can under take such consultation, interaction with community groups as it sees fit, and you are given a blank sheet.... A lot of planners tend to confine themselves to the framework for public engagement that is set out in terms of the development plan process, the higher level process and they use that as a proxy for ok, we are going to a local area plan, by putting up a notice in the paper, put it up in the library. The legislation actually says you can do what you want. Something that a lot of planners seem to forget.

INTERVIEWER: How do you remind them?

INTERVIEWEE: Its something that we intend to address when the minister publishes guidelines on different topics, and we have one set of guidelines on doing development plans, and local area plans. And local area plans' guidelines are very strong towards engagement with social media or atypical techniques. The development plan guidelines are very old. We reflect that approach, so yes, we can remind them through that process.

(Interview 13, Dublin)

---

on Dublin: when interviewees were probed for ideas on how Dublin could innovate, there was a subtle recognition that perhaps the capacities for policy development are lacking. From the perspective of the researcher considering the experiences of interviewees, while Ireland is a small country, Central Government is still too far removed to respond to Dublin's urban challenges, and this became increasingly evident in developing the climate change action plans.

The question then emerges of how Dublin can move past these barriers and give itself a voice to engage with Central Government, and simultaneously build this relationship? An interviewee suggested Dublin needs to represent itself as a leader, and to take action to shape its relationship with Central Government and citizens, as the following excerpt shows:

I think Dublin City Council misses the trick in terms of presenting itself as a thought leader, presenting itself as custodian of the city. As a leader of the city. Not only in the things it has direct control over, but also in the things it doesn't. So, if Dublin City Council says, 'Hey you, Dublin Bus, electrify your fleet. Dublin Port do this or do that. Central Government, give us the means by which we can make the investments that we need. Allow us to raise city bonds. National Government change the spatial strategy so that we can create flood plains.' Different ways of thinking about it ... I think Dublin needs to lead and not just take policy from above, respond to business requests from below, and also citizen requests. It also needs to kind of give a vision of the city and the development plan is where you do that.

(Interview 19, Dublin)

This excerpt also brings attention to a challenge not just for Dublin, but for cities in general, and that is leadership of the collaborative process. Someone has to own the process and nurture it, and bring people in to engage in new ways.

Engagement and consensus building with diverse stakeholders

Public consultation is mandatory under the statutory planning guidelines that Dublin City Council is required to follow, and while these are perceived to be restrictive, they do foster collaboration. However, interviewees have stated the public consultation process laid out in the legislation, while transparent, is a barrier to itself. As the following excerpts demonstrate, the public consultation process has not evolved to capture the changes in how people communicate:

We have local economic and community plans now that are coming into play, and there is a requirement for those under local government reform.... It formalises how we communicate with community groups ... irrespective of what legislation might have been brought in. The world has changed quite a lot, through simple things like people having smart phones, there's a lot of democratic output from people just having smart phones, people responding on Twitter. That feeds kind of the media ... things come through a lot quicker. Big opinions.... The corporate framework has to be responsive to that.

(Interview 5, Dublin)

If you are doing a development plan, you will probably be lucky to get 1% of the population engaged with you, whether it be by submissions, or attending meetings.... The development plan needs to be shorter; documents around the development plan need to be punchier. Clare County Council, and South Dublin County Council would be two examples of local authorities that have stripped back the issues papers; they have stripped back the process. They've done videos; they've done small brochures. They've tried to make it as straightforward as possible. So that is one way of doing it, strip it back to the bare bones. And have the final document that is meeting legislative requirements but very straightforward. The other part would then be technology. Development plans are moving online. But there is no point to having a development plan process online.... A lot of local authorities will tell you they are moving online and that's a good thing, but if it's a chapter and it's a PDF, and they have to download 20 to get the whole thing.... So its using technology properly. The final thing, I think there's a lot of scope in visualisation and stuff like that. You have companies like Realism where conceivably you might be able to model what sea level rise would mean for Dublin, against existing buildings. And then ideally watch what the planning input could mean, or if we did A, B or C this is the impact, for example. I think there is scope there to try and show people the effects of climate change. But also to show people the effects of certain policies. You could do that for density policies. This is what Dublin would look like if we use certain density. Like that map on the wall, this is what Dublin would look like if we had certain policies, if you restrict growth to transport routes. I think that is probably the opportunity to engage people in the development plan, and engage people on climate change. It is to visually show the effect and not in graphs, but actually modelling it against buildings they are familiar with.

(Interview 6, Dublin)

When we did our consultation on the Strategic Development Zone, we were aware that all we were hearing from were the long established traditional residents. And they actually used phrases like 'one of our problems here is the transient population' and we thought, 'transient'? I asked is there a way to consult the transient population. So there's a transient population, as derogatively told. But its very hard to access the transient population.... We had a little group do vox pops in the open, with your board and have a little kiosk and come here to talk about the development SDZ, intercept people as they are walking along the street and have a conversation with them.

(Interview 3, Dublin)

Public consultation and participation has changed quite a lot over the years.... Preparation of the Docklands, they do other things, like set up a little temporary shop on the street and look for people's opinions, something that is a bit more informal, that gives people the opportunity to speak their minds.

(Interview 5, Dublin)

Emerging from the interviews was a recognition that the public consultation in its current formal form is in need of reform. Acknowledging that reform of planning at the level of Central Government will take time, there is evidence of Dublin City Council using informal opportunities to engage citizens and other stakeholders in policy responses to climate change. As such, interviewees in Dublin were asked to provide examples from practice for overcoming the challenges to engaging public, building relationships and consensus, empowering communities with a sense of ownership, and creating leadership. The stories of practice discussed by interviewees were reflective of the guidelines provided by Healey and Forester for planners.

Earlier, it was noted that a challenge has been engagement and building consensus amongst stakeholders as often those engaged with the public consultation process represent specific groups. The example of flood response highlighted the challenge in bringing diverse voices to the dialogue. Further, the example demonstrated how urban policy makers in Dublin are collaborating with stakeholders informally by speaking directly with individuals and encouraging their participation in the formal public consultation process. Policy pertaining to flood mitigation is also an area where there appears to be collaboration across levels of government, specifically with the departments responsible for flood mitigation within each level of government (i.e. the Office of Public Works, Department of Environment). As flooding is one of Dublin's key climate change risks, the city has endeavoured to address this issue with a wide range of stakeholders. The collaboration on policy development has been thorough and has led to integrated solutions as demonstrated by the excerpt in Box 5.3 (although it should be noted that the solutions are not without controversy, as Box 5.5 also highlights). The interview excerpt in Box 5.3 is an example of how a policy maker has given Dublin a voice by asking citizens who have been impacted by floods to respond to government policy consultations, to enable and empower Dublin City Council to implement policies that protect them. It is also a demonstration of policy makers giving citizens a voice, by understanding their history and concerns around flood risk, and incorporating their 'voice' into policy.

What works about the bikes? I don't know. We also have a cycling organisation that really cares. You've got the Dublin Cycling Campaign, you've got Cycling.ie and they're a bunch of nerds who campaign on the issues, and I am member of those organisations. They are [a] bunch of nerds who have managed to build up – I remember going to cycling campaigns meetings and there might have been five or six people, now you might get 50 or 60 at their meetings and it reflects the growth of cycling. It was one of my ambitions when I proposed Dublin bikes was that, I felt it was very hard to get people on board with me to campaign for better cycling facilities. And I thought if I bring in the Dublin Bikes, if I get more people cycling they'll say, 'Hold on a minute these cycling conditions are crap, we want better cycling conditions'. I wanted them to use the Dublin bikes, to bring in cyclists who would demand more. And that's kind of what happened, it's worked out that way.

(Interview 10, Dublin)

The development of policies in support of cycling in Dublin is another area where Healey's principles can be seen. However, the story of practice provided by an interviewee around a proposed cycle path discussed an interesting and emerging theme in collaboration; an evolving theme of self-awareness by planners and urban policy makers of their identity and its impact on engagement (Box 5.7). This was also an emerging theme discussed by interviewees in Glasgow, Vancouver and Portland. Further, the example highlighted a challenge for Dublin City Council in developing projects with public benefit, the Part 8 process, and how the city worked around this issue. Acknowledging that the Part 8 process is subject to public consultation, and that if there are objections to a project, the length of the process will increase. As such, in advance of submitting a proposal, Dublin City Council engaged an outside stakeholder to work with the community where the cycle path would be developed. The process revealed the challenges and the 'hopes and concerns' that would be raised by the community to Dublin City Council. Notably, as discussed there is often disconnect between what policy makers view as 'good' for a community and what the community itself views as 'good'. Box 5.7 discusses the public consultation process undertaken by a consulting firm on behalf of Dublin City Council on the proposed cycle path. Healey's guidelines, particularly numbers 7 through 10, can be seen in practice, as the consultants and Dublin City Council worked with stakeholders to develop a project that achieved the community's goals of a safer area and the city's goal of adding to the cycling infrastructure. Lastly, the interviewee noted that while for Dublin City Council there were climate change goals behind this project, for the community addressing climate change was not the objective. Rather, the discourse focused on the concerns of the community – anti-social behaviour. Ultimately, the collaborative process resulted in a solution that embodied the objectives of the stakeholders involved. It is also an example that demonstrates that discourses around climate change issues are indirectly about climate change and directly about issues that are of concern to stakeholders.

Another area in which Dublin City Council has engaged in ongoing collaboration is in the area of energy. Energy is a key challenge facing Dublin and Ireland, as reducing dependence on fossil fuels is key for Ireland meeting its climate change obligations. The City of Dublin Energy Management Authority (Codema), while technically an independent body that is supported by Dublin City Council and funded through the European Union, has been working in the space of energy for over ten years to build awareness across the city, from citizens to civil servants:

> Our approach is more bottom up … we were set up as a bottom type of operation, so we employ all the tactics of a bottom-up approach, which would be networking with peers, information giving, in terms of unbiased scientific information, trying to empower groups, citizen groups, administrative groups.
>
> (Interview 21, Dublin)

Codema is a demonstration of the ability of an organisation to lead on an issue and create a network that supports collaboration with a range of stakeholders, from citizens through to international governments. While the success of its home energy kit (Box 5.8) has yet to be shown, Codema's work is an example of

---

Box 5.7 Engaging and collaborating with the public for cycle paths

We were asked to engage with a community or an area, along one stretch of it [Royal Canal Greenway]. This had particular challenges, it was only really about 800 m long along the stretch, that we engaged people around. There was a derelict site behind these people, the site that was going to be converted to a cycle lane along the canal, and because [of] the back-lane nature of the site … there had been a lot of dumping and a lot of anti-social activity … problems with unemployment, drug addiction, and crime. So they want to put in this new facility there, and I suppose the point you know one would think, its apple pie, what is not to like? You are cleaning up the site and what have you. I think with community you can't always assume that. Something that on the surface that seems positive and you are creating a nice new park, cycle way, walking route. But what are the issues? Our work was trying to identify the hopes and concerns of the local community … the positives they'd see in it and the potential negatives in it and try to identify what those are. Work through them with the community and feed back some potential solutions to the community and then again to get their response and that would then inform a final document that would be used; then taken by the designers or who ever as sort of design guidelines. So, in the case of a local authority funded project, in order to get planning they go through what is called a Part 8 process, where the local authority applies for planning permission to itself and that requires a certain amount of public consultation but often it is seen that this isn't enough and so what… we were doing was beyond that sort of statutory requirement for Part 8 consultation, we were doing pre-consultation, identifying the issues before you even get to that stage, before the preliminary design stage.… It was DCC who commissioned us to do this. They were the ones acknowledging that additional consultation was required. We engaged from door to door, dropping leaflets in, having public events, trying to get people engaged. Going into schools, getting an artist involved working with schoolchildren. Doing trips along the canal for schoolchildren and then culminating in an event that we held alongside the canal.… And turned it into a proper collaborative planning occasion … over 200 people come along.… Whereas you might get a dozen people coming into one of the open sessions in the local library or community hall. This one attracted 200 people. So what has that got to do with climate change? Climate change was not discussed during that whole process. The context of the overall scheme was that it's a greenway, promotes walking and cycling, which are more sustainable transport which by default are less carbon polluting or not at all.… But in terms of community, that wasn't really discussed. What the community concern was anti-social behaviour. Having connections in from certain cul de sacs, dead end streets that would be opened up, there was real concern about that. How would it be maintained? What would the security be like? Would it just attract more anti-social behaviour? Would there be joy riders going up and down those scramblers and rob the cars? Which is currently the situation.

(Interview 12, Dublin)

Box 5.8 The Home Energy Kit

INTERVIEWEE: We are working through the council's library system at the moment to reach the public rather than going out to parishes, which is difficult for a small office. You need a whole team of 50 people covering the city. While we can work through the library system, which is a source of information for communities, so that they will pass on the information to their local communities. And we would support them by running events in the libraries. We also have this toolkit that we are developing at the moment. People will be able to rent it out in the library, like a book and take it home, and with the equipment do home energy diagnosis. The kit, an idea from Australia, again being in touch with what is going on. They have been using it in Australia for a couple of years now. So we looked at that and adapted their one to the Irish situation. And it was done with European funding from European projects, Interreg.... So we are leading this project [with] about a four million euro budget and with partners from Northern and Western European countries: UK, Ireland, France, Germany, part of the Netherlands, Belgium and Luxembourg, with similar climate.

INTERVIEWER: Has it been successful?

INTERVIEWEE: I think it has, this is a good product here.

INTERVIEWER: Is there any incentive to put it into schools?

INTERVIEWEE: Yes, under the project we got 20 of these made. We are teasing out any wrinkles and then it can go wherever it is appropriate. We've done lots of inquiries; there is all kinds of minutiae to tease out, as we go down the road. At the moment, we are struggling to convince people that the thermometer isn't a health hazard, with the legal department. Will someone sue them because it has a laser pointer in it? These are a myriad of obstacles that you come across everyday and what we do, we just have to knock them down one-by-one. But because it is no different from a laser pointer in a conference room, because it has a warning on it, 'don't look straight into it'; the legal people are saying, 'Well, you know worse can happen, suppose they kill something with it?' They are going to be liable. We are dealing with bureaucracy in a big way.

INTERVIEWER: How much does bureaucracy affect your work?

INTERVIEWEE: Quite a bit.

INTERVIEWER: How do you respond or work with it?

INTERVIEWEE: The bureaucracy is there for a reason; we got to recognise that. Our way is to understand where it is coming from and find areas of common interests. We might have an interest in say, for example, climate change and our interests would be in reducing the carbon footprint of the city. When we go to City Council, their interests are in primarily keeping the city going and reducing the budgets. So then we would say there are areas of common interests. Obviously if they can reduce their energy bill, so they can save money and we can save CO_2, and we are both happy.

(Interview 21, Dublin)

successful relationship building and collaboration within a constrained environment. Further, the process of Codema's work is an example of time being taken to develop 'deliberate and considerate' projects that educate while addressing the needs of stakeholders such as 'saving money on energy bills'.

Building on success to strengthen collaboration on climate action

Considering the policy examples of how Dublin City Council can build on its current successes, and strengthen its work with stakeholders to address climate change, is the next step. There were three themes that emerged: leadership, technology, and the narrative of home. In discussing the challenges of developing the city's public realm strategy, the barriers to leadership, the complex policy environment that has been discussed throughout this chapter within which Dublin City Council operates, are key. Box 5.9 highlights the importance of leadership, as reflected in the other cities, which is able to respond and facilitate relationship building amongst stakeholders, such that there is ownership over projects and policies.

Box 5.9 Ownership of the city's challenges and solutions: the public realm strategy

The public realm strategy is currently under review. And we have undertaken a master study of the city core, the commercial core, Dame Street, to Parnell Square and the environments out along the quays. That was to gather data to validate our assessment of the situation to gather some soft analysis in terms of hot spots at night, as in very heavily trafficked places rather, than bad. Spaces for rough sleeping, for pan handling, for street performance, for night-time versus daytime and lighting ambience, noise. All of those pieces, proliferation of bus stops and the queuing space and how much space is required for the infrastructure at a location. And we've developed a calculator to find what Dublin needs in terms of the volume of people on Dame Street. That fed into the analysis of what the street furniture, what the clearance space is for movement, what ... seating the café culture piece needs. What then you need for the pedestrian to move comfortably, and comfortably is a very important part in that statement. Because it is about tourists being able to move at their pace, and commuters move at their pace and there not being frustration and antagonistic forces... we've worked those up as it relates to Dublin.... So you might [have] really big wide pathways across the quays and you have 20 pedestrians on it at the moment.... But its not going to happen.... We are trying to ... ensure that whatever space the pedestrian has currently remains pedestrian space, and in the city core it's amplified and increased. Yes, absolutely the city needs a good public transportation system, and a linked-up transportation system. And those plans are in place. To be delivered, if not already. But everybody when they get off their transportation is a pedestrian, whether it's a bike, plane, car, bus, train. You are a pedestrian. So in that city core, nearly every single tourist who comes to Dublin, goes past Trinity, not because it's Trinity, but because it's the hub to get to everywhere else.... When you put that in the context of increased tourism, the fact that there is a tourist trail through there, that it is the access point for Grafton Street and it is where the buses drop off and it's the exit point for a major city university, and it's a meeting point. It is all this other stuff and now there's going to be a Luas stop just around from there. So you have to look at what the space has to do and for how many people and then you decide what the modal split of the space should be. Rather than being set by the train needs this, and bus needs this and that, what is left? And then you have to look at the air quality when you have all those things going through there. And that it has sufficient monitoring. I mean some air quality is improved by its location, because geographically it has up winds or it has wind tunnels or whatever it might be. So it's never a problem. But in a city core, you need to have enough trees. Dublin doesn't have a proper tree canopy for a capital city. It is way below the European and international averages. We are integrating that back into projects as they are being delivered, as well as a greening strategy ... the theory of that is fine. When you go to put them in, the tree has as much underground as over ground and there is no space left in the city. What is the mitigation here? It is to accept that not all trees can grow to maturity in a city context and they need to be replaced. It is to accept that you plant smaller trees with branch clearance for buses and whatever you need to do. And that in small spaces, whether they are private or public you put in green infrastructure of some sort. And if that's linear beds, if its raised beds. One of my issues with Dublin is there's nothing planted into the earth between those twos. One is very high maintenance and the other is very space hungry. We need an in-between. Thomas Street has just put in 20 planters with seating. Any piece of street furniture that is going in the future has to have dual function; it needs to provide more than one service. There isn't space for all this multiple of infrastructure, like bins, lamps, bollards.

(Interview 6, Dublin)

As mentioned previously, leadership is a theme that has emerged consistently across all case studies. For Dublin, the challenge with leadership according to interviewees lies in the absence of a directly elected mayor, with a mandate to action policy. Thirteen interviewees felt that an elected mayor would create the needed political capacity to take action on climate change and make Dublin a leading city in climate change responses not just for Ireland but, globally.

We have a sh** planning and administrative system because we don't have local power, we don't have ... a directly elected mayor of Dublin. We had the legislation through all stages, coming to the very end. And the new government comes in and gets rid of it. And I think what we are bad at is planning and we are bad at long-term thinking and partly because there is a lack of political responsibility at the city level. And there's a lack of coordination in agencies. Successful global cities need good mayors. Because ultimately, to make strong decisions which you need to coordinate housing and transport and bureaucrats can never do it. Or if they do it, they tend to get it wrong – because you need to be brave. You need to sometimes do things that are difficult. And it is very hard for a bureaucrat to make a brave decision because they don't have the mandate to do it. Whereas if someone is elected, they do; and they are also better at explaining it and better at communicating it. Because that is what you do, you go door-to-door; you meet people and explain it in a simple way. You are not stuck in an office. And it is that lack of political leadership is our biggest problem, well one of them anyway. Its not impossible it might change.

(Interview 20, Dublin)

However, there was recognition that policy leadership could also originate elsewhere within the institutional structure.

Ireland is a very centralised country and subject to the national interests which are valid of course, but the national interests are not always identical with the environmental interests for a start, or the local interests of citizens, or the city.... Local authorities have less power than in other parts of the world. We must start from there, and I think still that the bottom up approach is the way to do it. I think in some ways agencies have fared better in Ireland than in some other countries, which are hierarchical for example, Austria or Spain. You must look to the strength of the agency type of operation, the bottom-up approach. You must first of all think that there are various types of organisational structure, but the two we are mainly dealing with, hierarchy is one. The European Commission, the governments, the nation state, the local authorities, where it comes down from the top. We are quite different; we are kind of a network, with nodes. So how do we see the two types of organisational structures engage? I think to engage you have a network that is kind of here, and you have to get not just at the top, but you have to have lines into different operations, and the different levels and the different departments. That is a much more multi-faceted task. It is not replacing the hierarchy. It is there. They don't quite fit together, never have and never will, but they can work together to a large extent. You have to recognise different structures and find strategies to work together. What we do here is we have this, the innovation, from the European projects, these are kind of the day-to-day action that the city must do to kind of keep going and then we have to bring in the new ideas. We have to look at the technology adaptation life cycle and then have a strategy to bring that in.

(Interview 21, Dublin)

This recognition that leadership can emerge from within, when there is acknowledgement of the institutional challenges that one is operating in and finding an alternative path to collaboration that works within an existing structure, mirrors the perspective of other cities that it is valuable to work with challenges and create opportunities to move forward. Further, the city has demonstrated its capacity for harnessing leadership from within its organisation through the policies discussed. There is awareness by the city, that as an organisation Dublin City Council needs to look beyond the formal processes of engagement and use new 'tools' for engagement.

> We use a range of different techniques.... The last two development plans we had online submissions. We also have a kind of Twitter, which is the conversation.... We would have [a] series of public meetings. Both here and around different parts of the city to discuss the development plan and the contents of it with, you know, community groups, and we also have sectoral meetings, we bring tourism interests, employment interests, conservation interests, and have sessions with them to explain the development plan. And encourage debate and encourage submission. The more the merrier. The statutory notices in the paper, statutory displays are somewhat superseded by social media. We are grappling with the social media and how to exploit it as a means of communication, as a means of engaging. Because we got more submissions online last time around, and we got more comments in on Twitter than we did in physical writing.
>
> (Interview 2, Dublin)

Technology, particularly social media, presents an opportunity for broadening the reach of public consultation and creates opportunities for collaboration. This has not gone unnoticed by Dublin City Council: the public consultation process for the Dublin Bike Scheme and cycle routes demonstrated the power that technology, specifically social media, has for bringing out demographic groups that previously did not engage with the city. There is an increasing awareness of the power of social media in engaging citizens, and harnessing that capacity is crucial for the city. Capitalising on Dublin's large base of multinational information technology (IT) companies who have corporate social responsibility targets, the city has partnered with IBM's Smarter City program. Building on the work of Codema, IBM together with the city produced a document recommending the use of solar photovoltaics on civic buildings (Interview, Dublin). The city, according to interviewees, is attempting to transform itself into a smart city, and to build on the work by IBM and establish partnerships with other IT companies such as Intel. The smarter city program aims to integrate technology into the workflows of all city employees (Presentation on Smarter Cities, 2016). However, technology also presents a challenge. As one interviewee suggested, creating the platform for using technology to improve citizen experience and engagement is ineffective if the back end and support are not able to respond because they are ill equipped (Box 5.10).

A third theme that emerged was the narrative of home, as a dialogue for policy around climate change. Recalling boxes Box 5.3 and Box 5.7 regarding policies on flooding and cycling, it is evident that stakeholders are responsive to an issue when it impacts upon their livelihoods or home. For interviewees who were asked about how to engage citizens on climate change policy, it was reiterated that people needed to understand how climate change impacts them personally in order for them to take action (Box 5.1 and Box 5.11). This call for 'home' to be the focus of dialogue on climate change as discussed in Box 5.11 is

Box 5.10 Harnessing social media for public consultation

The willingness to trial.... Trialling has a huge place in social engagement, in building, sustainability and vested interests. Buy-in, social credit all of that. The social media end accelerates past us still, because we still haven't really got an idea or a dynamic of how to harness the social media to work for us. It's always accusatory or commentary, and not feeding into something that actually produces.

(Interview 6, Dublin)

The organisations that want to curtail the scope of development seem to be very successful in getting the message across using social media, hence we have policies in the plan that are limiting and very conservative with regard to density and height policies. And that whole issue, there's contradictions there because the same people would be very much advocates of climate change, and often there's a kind of you know a contradiction between say, they don't want tall buildings, they don't want dense development in urban areas, at the same time... they want us to adhere to you know, good climate change policies. But its difficult to do when you have contradiction in your policies.... On non-statutory stuff, on the development plan, I think there is scope for us to expand out on the social media, and how to utilise social media, in having that public engagement ... I do know that they're becoming more and more important as a means by which people communicate. I do know that the downside of it all, is people live in soundbites, everything is distilled down to 140 characters, and therefore there isn't the scope, there isn't the tolerance, there isn't the patience, for having, you know, the informed debate or discussion; it's how you crystallise soundbites, so as to win over the public argument. But then you are into media manipulation, then you are into propaganda, then you are into bringing in your PR spin doctors. I am not too sure whether that is a desirable thing. You know it would be kind of hoodwinking. Like, you are an intelligent person, do you want to be hoodwinked on 140 characters? No. You will do a bit of more depth, but you are student of public policy, so you take the time out. What shocks me is that there are people, are very well-paid media commentators, who write in for newspapers and they seem to able to write, they don't have difficulty in writing about things and being factually incorrect. Nobody seems to worry about facts any more. There is a challenge out there for how we manipulate social media, how we can actually get the message across and engage in the public debate and how [we] could use our resources. Because none of us here are in any way reluctant to or nervous about engaging in the public, it is just, how you use that resource. There's nothing worse than going out to talk about a development in the month of October to a suburban location and ten people turn up. You know, that's not what its about. We have to kind of, how best we can get the message across, but not propaganda. Give people the opportunity of answering the hard questions, or asking hard questions and getting good answers for them.

(Interview 2, Dublin)

Box 5.11 Home as the climate change narrative

Because home is a deeply emotive issue, and if you talk about the importance of home it can allow you to talk about climate change. And we also talk about you don't kind of hit somebody on the head and throw science at them. You say, 'Look I need your help' which is a very emotive plea. So that is kind of how we are trying to come at climate through these climate gatherings, we've been trying to come up with a communication system for how you affect behaviour change or implement changes in policy.

(Interview 11, Dublin)

The ability to win over the hearts and mind of people is the most important thing.... We have lost the attention of the people, we have made them feel guilty, we have scared them about it. We haven't given them credible pathways to deal with it. We've concentrated on the individual and their actions rather than the source of the problem. We've been telling people what to do rather than listening to them.... We need to stop preaching to people and start listening to people. We need to ask people for help rather than telling people what to do. We need to admit uncertainties, we don't know all, even the modelling there's uncertainties in that. There is no doubt about the science in my mind.... We need to hasten slowly, which is kind of counterintuitive because there is a sense of urgency for those interested in climate, the scale of the challenges are huge, we got to rush, we have to really panic. There was a metaphor used; the Shannon Air Sea Helicopter Rescue Service is based on the west coast of Ireland and if they get a phone call, it's really an emergency, they have to get out quick because a boat is going down and they have to save people. The first thing they do when they get the phone call and when they put the phone down, is they put on the kettle and they have a cup of tea because they force themselves to slow down. Hang on, what is [the] best approach for us to take? You don't panic response ... it's similar to our response to climate, we need to be calm and we need to be considered and we need to pause for a moment, what do we do... if we are going to stop people from going from A to B, you have to have an alternative C. You can't just say, 'Stop going there'. You have to have a better alternative. And that better alternative is a new economy. It's a better digital economy. Last, but not least, we talked about a lot of home narratives; we kind of came to the conclusion ... I suppose it was influenced by the English philosopher Robert Sutton he argued that, he would come from a conservative tradition, the Greek word 'Oikos', the management of the home, the love of the home. That is where we have to place some of our narratives. And it's kind of from a bigger perspective, I think again, the Irish philosopher, John Moriarty, would argue, 'if we've left this earth and, which we did, to the moon, and haven't the ability to come back to the earth, from what we have seen from afar, then we will have missed this evolution leap that we need to make'. And I think it comes to language when we talk about climate. My sense is you bring it back home, you don't just speak about the planet, you speak about practical, local ways of improving your quality of life and how we look after our home and pass, and its touching sort of core emotional instincts that we have to protect our home and to provide for a home for our children.... The solutions to climate change is the communication of it or the narrative, the broader narrative that we share, because I could talk all

> day about electric vehicles versus hydrogen fuel cells, or one form of insulation versus another form of insulation, wave power, versus wind power, versus nuclear. Its been caught in that debate for so long, but without the foundation of understanding how this effects your identity your sense of self, your sense of purpose, your sense of future, your sense of belonging.
>
> (Interview 20, Dublin)

also reflective of collaborative planning practice in that it is shifting the dynamics of policy making from planners being experts to planners being facilitators (Forester, 1994; Healey 1998). Further, in line with the experiences of the cities, there is an understanding that policy success for climate adaptation lies with the people whom policy directly affects. As such, underlying this narrative proposed by interviewees in Dublin of 'home', and the narratives used by Glasgow, Vancouver and Portland is a common theme of ownership.

Planning for climate change

Dublin is a unique city, in that unlike Glasgow, Vancouver and Portland it is a capital city and the largest city within its country. It is this uniqueness which creates challenges for Dublin City Council in responding to climate change. This chapter has sought to present how Dublin City Council's position within the institutional structure of Ireland shapes its capacity for policy development and to engage with stakeholders to collaboratively develop policy.

It is evident that Dublin faces constraints from statutory guidelines set by Central Government, and challenges with engaging stakeholders on broad development issues. The formal statutory guidelines, coupled with a decreasing policy remit, appear to be the greatest challenges for Dublin City Council, as without the policy tools to respond to nationally set targets, Dublin City Council is unable to achieve the objectives for responding to climate change formally. Moreover, the underlying pressure of being the capital city places the spotlight of policy leadership on a local government that is subject to the same legislative guidelines as small local governments, but that has the largest proportion of the nation's GDP. As such, Dublin City Council has had to find ways of working with and around the legislation and with diverse stakeholders to respond to climate change.

This chapter presented three policy areas that were highlighted by interviewees as successes for Dublin City Council: flood risk management, cycling and energy. The city has demonstrated its capacity to influence and support collaborative responses to climate change through Dublin Bikes and cycling improvements around the city, flood response, and energy awareness (Codema). Simultaneously, in working to develop these policies and working with stakeholders in Central Government and in the communities, Dublin City Council has developed an understanding of how it needs to build policy and to respond to climate change. Significantly it has done so in the absence of leadership in the form of directly elected mayor. As such, Dublin City Council together with the neighbouring Dublin Local Authorities (DLAs) of Dún Laoghaire–Rathdown, Fingal County Council, and South Dublin County Council can lead in climate action by leveraging its existing success and by maximising the potential of available tools from public engagement to technology and innovation. Central to this will be sustaining dialogue beyond the development of their Climate Change Action Plans to their implementation and subsequent iterations.

Note

1 Part 8 is the planning and development procedure that local authorities in Ireland undertake when applying to develop projects (Planning and Development Act 2000)

References

Brand, R. and Gaffikin, F. (2007) 'Collaborative Planning in an Uncollaborative World', *Planning Theory*. SAGE Publications, 6(3), pp. 282–313. doi: 10.1177/14730952070 82036.

Forester, J. (2012) 'Learning to Improve Practice: Lessons from Practice Stories and Practitioners' Own Discourse Analyses (or Why Only the Loons Show Up)', *Planning Theory & Practice*. Routledge, 13(1), pp. 11–26. doi: 10.1080/14649357.2012.649905.

Healey, P. (2002) 'On Creating the "City" as a Collective Resource', *Urban Studies*, 39(10), pp. 1777–1792. doi: 10.1080/0042098022000002957.

Innes, J. E. (2004) 'Consensus Building: Clarifications for the Critics', *Planning Theory*. SAGE Publications, 3(1), pp. 5–20. doi: 10.1177/1473095204042315.

6   Dublin

From theory to practice and back

Introduction

> What do resilient Dubliners look like? ... They ideally don't use, they are reducing their resource, they are sustainably transporting themselves and they're kind of being a bit mindful of the impact of their resource use.... This points to so many different policy areas. It is not just planning ... if you were to interview someone from the community end of things, [someone] involved in community projects, green business, or at the engineering end of things there's a different response.... People feel that they have, if you like, a sufficient understanding of how the system works to get involved at a personal level, at a community level, to help influence policy in the right direction.
>
> (Interview 4, Dublin)

This chapter delves into the process that is currently under way to develop climate change action plans for the four local authorities that make up County Dublin (Dublin City Council, Fingal County Council, South Dublin County Council and Dún Laoghaire–Rathdown County Council) and how the processes undertaken by Vancouver, Glasgow and Portland are informing Dublin's Local Authorities. It is evident that taking action on climate change for Dublin is a policy window. It is an opportunity to call for change in governance, yet it's a challenge because of the city's history (political, cultural and recent). The county is trying to leap forward through the Smart Dublin initiative, which has the potential to yield benefits economically, socially and environmentally. However, as will be discussed this is not without challenges.

This chapter is written in the first person, as I believe this is perhaps the best way to communicate the application of theory into practice. Writing in this manner permits reflection on how my research has shaped this project, specifically the internalisation of the lessons from urban policy makers in Vancouver, Glasgow, Portland and Dublin. Further, it is challenging to detach myself from a process that I have invested in. I am keenly aware of my accountability to the DLAs and the responsibility of developing and writing the plans to address climate change adaptation and mitigation for the DLAs. This book in many ways is more than a discussion highlighting the challenges of policy making in the urban context; it is also a policy tool, a call for change in the way policy is developed and the way governments communicate.

When I was hired to take on the role of climate change researcher for this project, it was and is undoubtedly a dream for someone who completed a PhD investigating the policy development process of cities responding to climate change. As an individual who has trained in public policy, it is an incredible opportunity to be in the space between research and practice, bridging the two. Therefore, I hope that I am able to communicate the learnings of the project, which will be through my eyes, now in the role of policy maker. The chapter will begin with a background to the plan, a description of the process and finally, reflections on the process connecting theory and practice.

Background – strategy towards climate action

Codema, Dublin's Energy Management Agency, produced *A Strategy Towards Climate Change Action Plans for the Dublin Local Authorities* as the starting point for the Climate Change Action Plans that have been in the process of development since April 2017 (Codema, 2017). Codema was established in 1997 as an energy agency responsible for advising the Dublin Local Authorities on energy use. Since then, Codema has worked with the DLAs to implement a range of projects that have resulted in the installation of renewable energy systems, to achieving energy efficiency gains in council owned and operated buildings. Responsibility for climate change adaptation is new: while a natural and logical complement to their current role; it is a novel area for the organisation.

However, as has been discussed and will be addressed, climate change is about more than energy, it is about resources, the environment, transport and overall quality of life in the Dublin Region. In recent years it has come to the fore as the result of the increasing frequency of storm events and extreme weather being experienced in Ireland. What is evident is that responses by the DLAs need to be integrated and collaborative in nature. The solutions to climate change's risks cannot be the sole responsibility of engineers, planners, architects, ecologists, or economists. It is a collective responsibility that demands, in the words of the Irish Government, 'joined-up thinking'.

Therefore, in developing the Climate Change Action Plans, consideration was given to the findings of the research, particularly the lessons from Vancouver, Glasgow and Portland. The first was applied in deciding the focus of the plans. As a starting point for the process, it was determined that the plans for the local authorities would be limited to the direct remit of local authorities in Ireland. The rationale for this was two-fold: first, to guarantee that the plan would be actionable and second, to clarify the role of local authorities in Ireland with the objective of building the case for resources to be allocated to local authorities to implement their plans.

Policy context

Responding to climate change is a key priority of the Dublin Region's local authorities, as flooding, rising seas, extreme weather and rising temperatures impact on the region's economic and social growth. Developed in response to international, European and national calls to action, the Climate Change Action Plans set out the actions that the Dublin Local Authorities will be taking to adapt to and mitigate climate change within the legislative remits of local government in Ireland.

The Irish Government's *National Mitigation Plan* and *National Adaptation Framework*, which emerged from the *Climate Action and Low Carbon Development Act 2015*, have tasked key national government departments with the development of statutory sectoral adaptation plans, and local authorities with responsibility for developing adaptation strategies that will inform development planning and other statutory plans, and engage communities (Government of Ireland, 2015; Department of Communications, Climate Action & Environment, 2017; Department of Communications, Climate Action and Environment, 2018).

Recognising the capacity of local governments to lead on climate action, the DLAs have signed the voluntary EU Covenant of Mayors for Climate and Energy, which commits them to reducing their carbon emissions by 40% by 2030, from 2006 levels, and to building resilience to climate change through integrated and collaborative responses.

With this in mind, the DLAs have embarked on a process to develop their Climate Change Action Plans. Following the ICLEI Five Milestone process and using the *EPA Local Authority Adaptation Strategy Development Guideline*, the DLAs, in association with Codema, assessed the risks posed by key climate change impacts and the CO_2 emissions from their operations, to determine the adaptation and mitigation actions to be undertaken to 2030 (Gray, 2016).

By 2030, the DLAs will have implemented actions to adapt the region to climate change, such that the risks of flooding, sea level rise, extreme weather, and rising temperatures are reduced. Furthermore, by 2030, CO_2 emissions from the DLAs' operations will be less than the 40% Covenant of Mayors target.

Responding to climate change is an opportunity to strengthen the Dublin Region's economic and social competitiveness, and environmental record. Key to this is undertaking a holistic and integrated approach to building climate resilience. Acknowledging this, the plan was developed by bringing together DLA staff to identify Dublin's vulnerabilities and actions to respond to climate change.

Five-step process

In developing these action plans for the DLAs, the Local Governments for Sustainability (ICLEI) Five Milestones were adapted to meet the needs of the DLAs. It should be noted that the current process incorporates Milestones 1 to 3 to produce the plan, while Milestones 4 and 5 concern the plan's implementation and monitoring, and subsequent iterations.

Milestone 1 – initiate

Codema produced *A Strategy Towards Climate Change Action Plans for the Dublin Local Authorities*, which identified seven thematic areas related to the remits of the local authorities to begin collecting data and actions, and how the plan would be developed. It was through this process that the case was made to develop the climate change action plans that I was hired to develop.

Milestone 2 – research

DLA staff were engaged via one-to-one meetings and a series of workshops to identify actions currently underway and potential future actions. The workshops provided an opportunity to bring together staff from the four local authorities to discuss the challenges and opportunities in addressing climate change, and their ideas for how to climate-proof their operations and service delivery. Vitally, the workshops provided an opportunity for staff to collaborate with each other. Simultaneously, an adaptation assessment was undertaken to identify the current climate change-related risk facing the region and to establish the DLAs' mitigation baselines, which show the current level of GHG emissions for each of the DLAs.

Milestone 3 – plan

The outputs of Milestone 2 were integrated to develop the vision, objectives, goals, targets, actions and indicators that comprise the DLAs' individual Climate Change Action Plans. The development and selection of the actions for these plans were guided by the vulnerabilities created by climate change facing the Dublin Region identified during the workshop and from staff input. They were further honed through additional feedback from experts, and from meetings and workshops with staff. The result to date is a plan that is guided by two overarching themes that enable the DLAs to respond to national requirements and contribute to Ireland's transition to a low carbon society:

1   Climate Leaders and Innovation – to lead by example by climate proofing their operations and service delivery
2   Connected Citizens – to influence behaviour by providing information and learnings from experience

These two themes serve as the basis for the actions which fall into five interconnected areas – Energy and Buildings, Transport, Flood Resilience, Nature-Based Solutions and Resource Management. Success of the actions in the plans is dependent on collaboration across departments, and on leadership that supports ownership of these actions. Further, these two themes intentionally mirror the dual role of local government to lead in the development of solutions that make the city resilient to climate change, and to create a system that supports behaviour change.

Milestone 4 – implementation & milestone 5 – monitor & iterate

Milestone 4 and Milestone 5 concern the plan's implementation and monitoring, and subsequent iterations. Responsibility for this lies with the DLAs. The next step is for the DLAs to set up their regional climate change office, as per the recent directive from National Government. The role of this new office will determine how the plans are implemented, monitored and updated. A critical challenge in the implementation and monitoring of the plans is data. While staff were able to identify and discuss the vulnerabilities stemming from climate change and the actions to address them, the need for localised, reliable, and valid data was emphasised for developing action indicators. Currently, the DLAs are reliant on various central government departments for data on air quality (Environmental Protection Agency), transportation (National Transport Agency), energy (Sustainable Energy Authority of Ireland), and flood risk (Office of Public Works). This challenge of accessibility and availability of data impacts on policy decisions, and the ability of the DLAs to monitor their progress on their climate change actions. These Climate Change Action Plans are the starting point for present and future action on climate change, and an opportunity to create a resilient Dublin Region. The plans will also strengthen the capacity of the DLAs to encourage citizens to contribute to the region's resilience, and Ireland's transition to a low carbon society. I will discuss my views on the challenges ahead for the DLAs in implementing and monitoring their plans, after a reflection on the process to date.

Reflections on theory and practice

Developing these plans was not without challenges, tribulations, concerns or fear. Having worked with Dublin City Council's Smart Dublin team prior to taking the role with Codema, and being familiar through my research with the challenges facing DCC, I had the opportunity to build relationships with a few staff. However, I was unfamiliar with the other three local authorities of the Dublin Region and their unique challenges. Fortunately, I had the benefit of the knowledge of theory and practice gained from those that I interviewed. Therefore, listening and learning were central to the development of the climate change action plans and critically overcoming the barriers that arose.

There are several aspects of this process that are unique and interrelated, that I will attempt to reflect on in this section, in an effort to link theory and practice. The first is myself, non-Irish, an interloper in some ways but in others not, with the responsibility of developing a plan for a city and region that I have temporarily made my home. It is through this aspect that I have become keenly aware of the importance of policy makers being self-cognisant of their identities from the viewpoint of the individuals they are interacting with and how their views and perceptions of situations shape their ideas of how policy should be. Second, how theory and the stories of practice shaped the approach taken to developing the climate change action plans.

From objective researcher to embedded policy maker

The opportunity to write this book provided the catalyst for reflecting on a process that I have been immersed in for the last year and actively applying the lessons and insights gained from my research. In the absence of this project I would not have given consideration to my own immersion in the process or reflected on my position. At the outset of developing the CCAPs, I viewed myself initially as an advisor, an expert of sorts, with regards to the development of climate change adaptation policy in cities. Specifically, an individual with knowledge of how cities globally have been responding to climate change; how these cities have address the challenges formally and informally based on inter-views with 35 urban policy makers in four different cities. Therefore, my job would be to facilitate the identification and formation of the actions defined by local authority staff to develop a cohesive CCAP for each local authority based on my existing knowledge and new knowledge that I gained during the process.

On the surface this was the process, however, there is a difference in being a researcher and a practitioner. As a researcher, my interactions with policy makers is shaped by my position as an observer and a fact finder; I am removed from the daily challenges of policy making. My outsider status, as an academic, permitted a freedom of expression by the policy makers that I was interviewing. There was limited recourse for a policy maker in telling me their experience and stories of practice. Furthermore, my research was merely a snapshot in time that reflected the interviewee's challenge at the moment, which was analysed in the context of all other interviews and critically within the context of a theoretical framework that my research argued to be valid and the ideal method from which to produce policy; in this case collaborative planning and adaptive governance. Finally, another element of being a researcher is the fact that I would leave and be unlikely to interact with the interviewees again. In this instance I returned.

As a policy maker, or rather a facilitator of collaborative policy making, my interactions with DLA staff changed. As a researcher, my questions were not confined and were open ended. There was a freedom to ask questions and receive answers that contributed to theoretical understandings of planning and policy making. Moreover, my analysis of the responses was clinical and void of an attachment to the daily challenges and need to fully understand the constraints that the policy makers face beyond the dictates of a theoretical framework. I could freely apply my perspective on how things should be and put forth recom-mendations with nominal regard to the realities of how things work in practice. This would not be the case in this process of developing the CCAPs, especially as there was a need to put forth recommendations for implementation with an understanding of the institutional context.

The case studies discussed in this book show that, for cities to lead on climate action, an adaptive governance approach is needed, an approach which can emerge from the collaborative process. Therefore, the focus of the process undertaken in developing the plan was to ensure that it was at its core collabora-tive. Given the highly centralised nature of governance in Ireland as discussed in my research findings, fostering a collaborative environment presents a challenge. Furthermore, my knowledge of the workings of the local authorities stemmed from single-contact interviews, and I did not have a full sense of the silos or the impacts of the hiring freeze. As the individual tasked with developing the CCAPs, I would have to gain a deeper understanding of the inner workings of the local authorities and build relationships with staff: in short, build capacity by building bridges within the local authorities and across through multiple inter-actions (e.g. meetings, emails, workshops and phone calls) to nurture the collab-orative capacity I knew existed in the DLAs.

I had to develop a deeper knowledge of the policy landscape in Ireland and the stakeholders, to produce a plan that would be workable, and that would critically foster an integrated and collaborative approach to adaptation (as detailed in the EU Covenant of Mayors signed by all four DLAs). This required an in-depth under-standing of the barriers facing staff in their day-to-day work beyond a general overview of the institutional landscape in which the DLAs work. The shift in understanding the institutional and policy context is illustrated by the figure below which when contrasted with Figure 3.4 becomes evident. Figure 6.1 illustrates the institutional and policy context in relation to climate change policy in Ireland. The figure is as simple as possible; the reality of the policy environment in Ireland is that it is far more complex, an aspect that became increasingly evident after meeting with over 100 staff and working through revisions of the actions in the plan. (Everyday I learned something new). Furthermore, the policies in the boxes to the right of the diagram are the high-level policies that are related to the climate change action plans. In the action plans themselves there is an appendix listing over 80 additional statutory instruments, legislation, regulations, and directives that are related to climate change actions, that policy makers in the local authori-ties must consider in their work,. Ultimately, for me, what has become evident is that the legislative and financial systems in Ireland need to be reformed to enable climate action. Not just for the purposes of enabling local authorities to take the lead on climate action, but for Ireland to be attractive to the emerging businesses and investors that are concerned about climate change, something that the City of Vancouver recognises, and that other cities are moving to address.

In policy speak, the development of the climate change action plans comes at a policy window. While the global call for cities to respond is one aspect, the media attention is another, and the demand by large multinationals for policies that support their investment in environmental endeavours, many in the IT sector and located in Dublin, is a further aspect. There is no justification for ignoring the increasing number of climate related events that are creating vulnerabilities for Dublin, economically, socially and environmentally. This policy window has lent itself to this process, as staff recognise the opportunity in front of them to bring attention to the work that they have been doing on a limited budget and the work they want to do. My role then became focused on finding opportunities beyond the workshops run by the Codema team in developing this plan, to iden-tifying synergies in work and other cities that the councils can look to and high-lighting ways of communicating challenges faced by the local authorities.

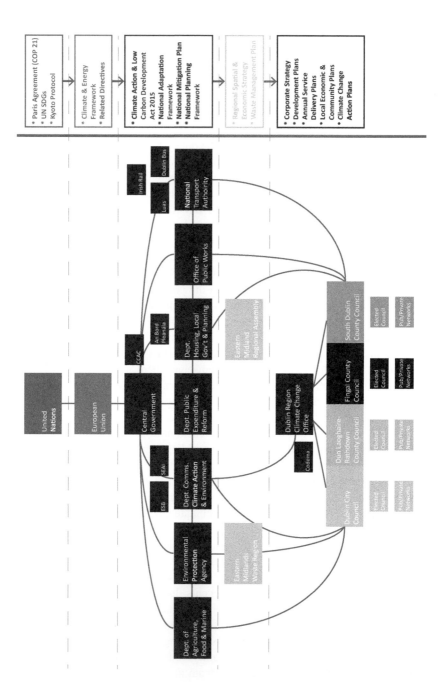

Figure 6.1 Institutional and policy context.

Applying theory and lessons from practice

Recognising the challenge of working within the constraints, it became clearer that limiting the actions in the plans to the remit of local authorities in Ireland (Figure 6.2) was the best course of action. Further, it confirmed findings in my research and my own experience that there is a limited awareness of what local authorities in Ireland have the capacity to do and what central government is responsible for. As such, a clear goal of the plans has been to effectively communicate the remit of the local authorities in Ireland, and highlight their desire to do more, and to lead in climate action. Critically, the realities of their ability to deliver on central government's expectation that Irish local authorities support communities in building climate resilience, which given the nature of public financing in the Irish State is a significant barrier. At present the Department of Public Expenditure and Reform disburses funds to other departments, which

Housing services

Environmental services & waste management

Land-use planning & development, public realm

Roads & traffic management, including the promotion of sustainable transport

Flood protection, river basin management, surface water management & coastal protection

Parks & recreation services

Local economic & community development

Figure 6.2 Remit of Dublin Local Authorities.

then allocate funds based on reviewing requests from local authorities. The Irish Government has committed 2.5 million euro over five years to a regional climate change office for the Dublin Metropolitan Region Climate Change Office, a drop in the ocean of what is truly needed.

Especially when considered in the light of the lessons from Portland, Glasgow and Vancouver clearly highlighting the importance of funding communities in their endeavours, it becomes evident that doing something with nothing will not be possible. There are, as eloquently demonstrated by Portland and Glasgow, histories, cultures and perspectives that require a considered and deliberate approach to begin a process of building dialogue that will form the basis of a relationship that will enable local government to do more with less. However, perhaps it is possible that if effectively invested in building relationships that will pay dividends, it may be enough.

In the case of the Dublin Local Authorities there is also a relationship that needs to be reconstructed between them (and internally) and other levels of government. During the process of meeting with staff, it became evident that there is an incredible wealth of information and expertise within the councils that is not always viewed as a resource or valued by higher levels of government. Going forward, this will need to be addressed, and it will be challenging. There will need to be an acknowledgement that whilst the civil service has a 'reputation', there are many civil servants who, as was succinctly stated by an interviewee in Vancouver, 'don't choose to work for local government because of the pay cheque'.

As such, the development of the plans has been done with this in mind and therefore focused on the work the councils are doing to climate proof their operations and service delivery and their subsequent use of leadership to influence citizens and businesses alike. Fostering ownership of the plan has been vital to this development. Similarly to a researcher, I had to be detached and external to the project, as Codema, and therefore I, were consultants to the local authorities, which by default in certain ways allowed for fostering ownership. Continually clarifying my role in the process was a feature of my interactions with DLA staff, and the vast majority of conversations were caveated with 'This is your plan, we want to bring attention to what the local authorities can do and are doing'. Another aspect that perhaps permitted me to be outside of the process was my otherness.

In Portland, Vancouver and Glasgow it was highlighted that there is a need for policy makers to consider who they are as a person in terms of race, gender and economic status. First, as mentioned, I am not Irish, I am Canadian. Second, I am biracial and as some have noted look racially ambiguous. In many ways this has been to my benefit, as there is an element of curiosity around who I am, and why I came to Ireland, which in some ways gave me the freedom to ask questions about Irish culture, politics, history and identity, and deepen my understanding of what the barriers and challenges are for local authorities in Ireland. Most importantly, it has provided a way to start building relationships and trust with staff. Sharing stories, laughter, and experiences and discussing the different approaches to climate change (and other policies), has hopefully created a connection and foundation for the next phase of this work, which is implementation and really the start of the marathon. Admittedly, there were instances where this was not always the case and building trust was a challenge; in those instances I had to rely heavily on listening to the individuals I was speaking with and ask questions.

Despite this caveat of being detached, I recognised how I began to take ownership of the process through acting as caretaker, and documenting it for future iterations. I became invested in the process as I built a rapport with staff, and sought out ways to identify opportunities for collaboration across departments and with outside organisations. In many ways, I felt a sense of duty to the staff, and that I had an obligation to support their success by being a champion of their work. For context, local authorities in Ireland have since 2008 been placed under a moratorium, and were not able to hire new staff; indeed, many staff have been let go. This has placed a strain on the local authorities trying to do more with less, and coupled with the limited remits, morale has been low and fear pervasive. It has only been in the last two years that they have begun to hire again, and have the opportunity to restart old projects and initiate new ones.

Turning a challenge into an opportunity

A criticism I received of my early research findings was the perception that my analysis posited Vancouver, Glasgow, and Portland as being good and Dublin as being bad; this was an early foray into the challenges of explaining the barriers to local governance in the Irish context. Discussing my research with people, especially those who have grown up in Dublin, it was insightful to realise the confusion between what national government and local government (and regional government) are responsible for in a country of five million people. While misunderstanding of what local government does is not unique to Ireland, the assumption that local government has similar powers to a city like New York or Vancouver prevailed over the reality, which is that local authorities in Ireland have a limited remit compared to these cities. Of the cities studied, Portland's remit is similar to the Dublin Local Authorities, and consequently the approach taken by Portland informed our approach. Specifically, Portland's initial climate change preparation strategy was done to address the local government's own operations and service delivery and served as the starting point for the integration of climate action into the Portland Plan and the Climate Action Plan that the city partnered with the county to develop.

While Dublin is similar to Portland, it is the institutional setting as mentioned earlier that adds a layer of complexity to policy making at the local level. Ireland is a centralised state that is dabbling in multi-level governance but needs to apply an adaptive governance approach in order to progress, and for the Dublin region to be globally competitive. However, as I found in my research, an adaptive governance approach is not a necessity for collaboration, but collaboration can facilitate the adoption of adaptive governance. This is still the case; however, Dublin will need to 'leap frog' over the natural progression from mono-centric govern-ance to multi-level governance to adaptive governance and go from a mono-centric system to an adaptive system of governance. However, this rather paradoxically will take time and needs to be a considered and deliberate process, that begins with the local authorities.

Key in developing the plans is the need to build bridges within the councils, across departments, then across the four councils, and recognising that while the organisational structures adopted by Vancouver, Portland and Glasgow may potentially be options for the Dublin Local Authorities, those structures would not thrive without an internal culture of communication and working across departments.

As such, bringing the four local authorities together was key in developing this plan, for a number of reasons:

- This process is not just about planners, it is about all staff in local govern-ment and their contribution
- Providing an opportunity to talk to counterparts within and across the DLAs
- Building trust
- Building relationships
- Starting a dialogue about what each person/department is doing already and can do
- Highlighting barriers and challenges that will affect implementation, moni-toring and reporting
- Fostering ownership, accountability and leadership

It is too early to say whether the workshops were successful in achieving and fostering collaboration. Moreover, as Codema and I are consultants to the DLAs, the real challenge of building capacity by building bridges is the onus of the local authorities: we have merely started the process. Therefore, I can only spec-ulate as to the future of collaboration across the DLAs. I am optimistic, and hopeful. There are several staff who have taken it upon themselves to initiate workshops with fellow staff. Furthermore, as drafts have been developed, addi-tional staff have emerged and have actively voiced their opinions on the plan and the work ahead. A rather non-traditional indicator of potential success is that there is a recognition that this plan may fail, something that I am relieved is acknowledged as a possibility. My concern with this is that if it fails, nothing will be attempted again, as there is a tendency for local authorities to 'go into their shells' when something goes wrong, something which emerged in my research. Yet my optimism stems from the recognition that it is not 2008, and the local authorities are hiring and are taking the opportunity to make changes.

I would also argue for another non-traditional indicator of success, that I was constantly reminded of by my colleagues during periods of frustration. First and foremost, staff engaging, whether positively or negatively, showed that there was interest. When the frequency increased it could be taken as an indication that responding to climate change is important. Alternatively, my sense is that

---

Box 6.1 Lessons for facilitators

- Value the expert knowledge of staff – they are assets, their experience cannot be lost.
- Be ready to learn, ask staff to explain their job and teach you about their work.
- Be patient; listen and understand, ask probing questions.
- Be a caretaker of the process, document it.
- Be aware of the challenges, negotiate the barriers and find pathways to common ground.
- Facilitate opportunities for connecting staff to resources to strengthen their capacity.

---

there is recognition amongst staff that this is an opportunity to change the way the local authorities work, and to take a lead. The challenge will be in securing and sustaining the collaborative work. Looking ahead, there will be a need to face the past and how things have been done and whose ideas have been given preference. This will be an uncomfortable period, but necessary. Everyone will have their vision of utopia and their way of achieving it, which will more than likely be different from someone else's. Reality is that the collective vision of utopia is far from the individual's vision, but difference makes life.

The road to 2030 and beyond

> The thing about working in planning is you could argue that a lot of my effort is going into a development plan that doesn't even kick in until the year 2017, and that will probably only influence buildings that are going up in 2019. So this is where you have to start taking a much longer view … Irish Water is setting implementation up 'til the year 2040, and these are really interesting timescales, 2040, 2050, because the kind of decisions we are making now will have a huge influence over infrastructure or decisions that are made in 10, 20 or 30 years. If you wanted people to change their cars, you have a 10-year window.... If you want to change the amount of energy we use to supply water in Dublin, that is a 40-year project.... All those long timescales are hugely important.
>
> (Interview 11, Dublin)

The DLAs' climate change actions are time bound: by 2030 they will have to achieve their 2030 emissions reduction targets and Dublin will have be resilient to climate change. However, achieving climate resilience is an ongoing process, it is not demarcated by an end date. Furthermore, responding to climate change is about how we live today and how future generations will live tomorrow. Therefore, while this plan is to 2030, consideration already needs to be given to what happens beyond 2030. As such, implementation of the plans needs to be done with this in mind. These plans are not merely a project to 2030 but an opportunity to gradually shift from a reactionary process to one that is proactive and collaborative. The road ahead is not without challenges.

Implementation: global lessons for local success

> I think one of the questions that came up 'Is this a legal document?' This isn't. There is no recourse, if we don't do anything in there and it doesn't really matter. Other than the world collapses. There's nothing that binds us other than goodwill, other than communities wanting to be part of the discussion.
>
> (Interview 4, Portland)

As has been discussed, my role in this has been to research, to collect data, to develop and to write the climate change action plans, which are still being developed and will likely not go to public consultation until late 2018. Implementation is the onus of the local authorities. Presently there is no statutory obligation for implementing this plan; what binds the DLAs is their status as signatories of the EU Covenant of Mayors, and their acknowledgement of their capacity. As has been discussed in the other case studies (and in the literature around the subject), responding to climate change by local governments emerges from their recognition of their capacity to do so, largely in the absence of a top-down mandate from their national governments. There are apparently plans to change this. At present, the Irish Government views the role of local authorities as providing communities with support to implement climate action; which is not an easy feat and more critically in the case of Ireland fails to fully realise the capacity of local governments to respond. This is not necessarily unique to Ireland, as it was only in March 2018 that the IPCC held the first Cities and Climate Change Science Conference in Edmonton, bringing local governments into the fold and recognising their critical role in climate action, a significant move forward.

However, knowing from my experiences lobbying for solar PV as a valuable addition to Ireland's energy mix and security, it is the wait-and-see approach of Central Government that will possibly impair the efforts of the DLAs to implement their plans and trial innovative approaches to addressing climate change that diverge from the box-standard approaches that have been rubber-stamped by Central Government. Politicians in central government are inherently risk averse and despite evidence of success in other countries with implementing renewable energy technologies, or congestion charges to encourage people to use public transport, they are willing to wait or buy time, despite a recognition that action is needed on climate change. As such, I have concerns that while at the international and EU levels, cities and local governments are recognised to have capacity it will be too late before national government in Ireland realises the same.

As previously mentioned, a key message to be communicated by the climate change action plans is the role of local authorities in Ireland. Another is the

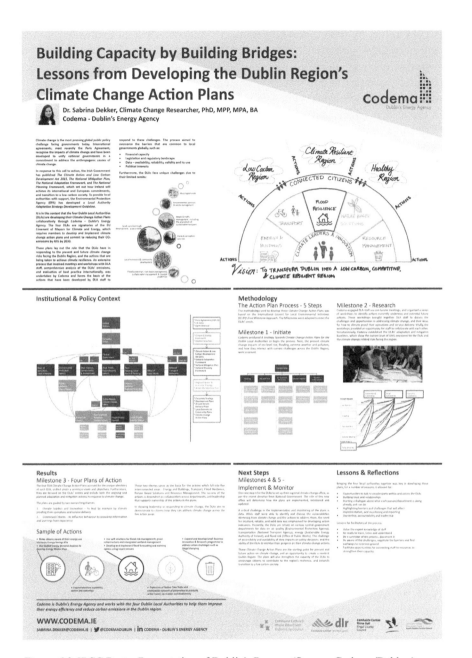

Figure 6.3 IPCC Poster Presentation of Dublin's Process (Source: Codema/Dekker).

expert knowledge that exists in local government in Ireland that is muted, I would argue, by the Central Government's helicopter parent tendencies, hovering over local authorities. It is one thing to hear of something and another to witness it. I was aware of the parent–child relationship that persists between Central Government and local government in Ireland, and during the process of developing these plans I witnessed it several times, but one incident stands out – a discussion around public lighting between a Central Government representative and a local authority representative. Having had the opportunity to research what is needed for WiFi-enabled public lighting, I had a basic knowledge of the challenges of converting public lighting, from the physical to political. As such I recognised what the individual from the local authority was asking of the representative who had just given a presentation on converting lights to LEDs – catch up. The local authority that the individual works for has already installed LEDs, and is actively looking at smart street lighting. Further, the individual had a wealth of knowledge of the challenges to changing public lighting such as pole replacement and how local authorities are charged for the energy used by public lighting. The individual was supported by counterparts in other local authorities but ignored otherwise, as Central Government's desire to keep a level playing field for all local authorities takes precedence, and is therefore focused on the need for LEDs to be in place before giving consideration to the other issues. There are other instances of local authority knowledge being ignored, and I am concerned that if this tendency persists it will be to the detriment of Ireland's ability to meet its climate change targets.

Institutional structures supporting climate leadership

Glasgow, Portland, and Vancouver have established structures that enable the cities to lead on addressing climate change through collaboration. The purpose of creating these structures was to establish internally that responding to climate change is a priority for all departments within the city authority by developing a reporting structure to monitor and evaluate policy progress. While there are leaders, their role is not one of directing and informing. Rather leaders, in the context of these structures, are to guide processes and encourage the emergence of leadership in policy actions by all involved. More succinctly, leadership is focused on fostering a sense of ownership over the problems and solutions. This contrasts with the ideal of a leader who informs and directs action; rather, this view of leadership complements and builds on collaborative planning principles by calling for more than one off participation by stakeholders.

Another benefit of creating these institutional structures is that the message that resilience to climate change is an important policy objective extends into the public sphere. For urban policy makers, having leadership teams not only fostered accountability and transparency within local government, but outside as well. These teams were also responsible for responding and engaging with the public, and as such they were key in building the relationships with stakeholders outside of local government that are essential for responding to climate change.

Critically, these teams allowed for stakeholders to not only participate in policy development but to take on an active role in the implementation of policy, thus supporting the emergence of ownership of problems and solutions by stakeholders in addressing climate change in the urban context.

In the case of Dublin, where leadership in the traditional sense is a challenge, the policy examples of collaboration in response to singular urban challenges, such as cycling and flooding, demonstrate that there is leadership. It is leadership by staff who have knowledge and expertise that should not be ignored. Critically, these successful collaborative responses have built a case for adaptive responses and the value of engaging citizens on issues that hold value for them. The challenge ahead for Dublin, as discussed, is identifying a leader or leaders who are brave and able to identify a vision and cohesive narrative for the city and its citizens to respond to climate change and build resilience. With the recent government announcement of the creation of regional climate change offices across the country, there is an opportunity to bring to the fore the expert knowledge that exists in the local authorities and implement a coordinated and collaborative response to climate change. This, however, depends on the form that the office takes. At present, it will be one office covering the DLAs. Arguably this is a similar approach to Portland's; however, it will be four local authorities with the same limitations, and as such, it would still be advisable for each local authority to establish a team responsible for overseeing their plans, similar to Vancouver's model.

To optimise the success of this Climate Change Action Plan, a Climate Team within each local authority (working in close association with the Regional Climate Change Office) will report directly to the elected members of the council Environmental Strategic Policy Committee (SPC), and to the Chief Executive's Office, through the Director of Services for Environment and Transportation. This will help to track regular progress and updating of this Climate Change Action Plan. This reflects best practice of cities globally, which have acknowledged that progress on climate change adaptation and mitigation calls for cross-departmental action and coordination with all stakeholders.

The mandate of each Climate Team will be to:

- Climate-proof existing and future corporate strategies, development plans, and local economic development plans
- Incorporate climate change into its procurement policies
- Set up a monitoring and reporting structure, including quarterly schedule of meetings to evaluate progress
- Develop new actions and targets
- Coordinate work on actions
- Follow up with respective departments on progress
- Develop a new action plan every five years
- Be a point of contact for the public to learn about climate action in the Dublin Region

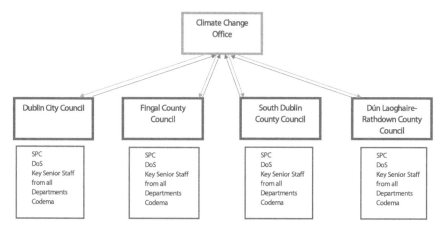

Figure 6.4 Proposed Structure of Dublin Climate Teams (Source: Codema/Dekker).

Public engagement: narratives for ownership of policy responses

While institutional structures are important in responding to climate change collaboratively, they are supported and strengthened by narratives to unify actions
and stakeholders. Collaborative approaches to achieving resilience call for place-
specific narratives that account for the unique characteristics of cities. The
process of identifying the narratives that will foster engagement, though, was not
without challenges. Each of these cities demonstrated challenges with public
engagement – trust and relationship building. From this process of identifying a
narrative to engage stakeholders, urban policy makers in the case study cities
acknowledged that beyond being open to listening to and learning the lived
experiences of stakeholders, they needed to be self-cognisant of their own lived
experiences. In building their understanding of their personal experiences, planners were able to acknowledge the barriers to engagement, and approach collaboration with openness and a willingness to take risks and accept failure;
recognising that successful collaboration would not be defined by 'successful'
policy outcomes but relationships built with stakeholders that would permit dialogue to continue. In each of the case study cities urban policy makers discussed
the importance not only of being sensitive to the histories of the stakeholders
they were trying to engage, but of acknowledging that by the nature of their
position they represent those histories. Thus, interviewees emphasised a need to
be cognisant of who they are, of their beliefs and values, and of how their lived
experiences shape their perceptions of the challenges facing cities and citizens.
In developing this awareness, policy makers have been able to identify narratives that have created the opportunities for engaging stakeholders.

Therefore, emerging from the case studies were narratives that notably did
not address climate change directly. Policy makers acknowledged that climate
change for most stakeholders is not a priority. However, the narratives that

emerged in the process of engagement do hold value for stakeholders and have allowed for policy makers to begin building the relationships and trust needed for ongoing engagement. Critically, as policy makers recognise that responding to climate change involves addressing all aspects of the urban environment to build resilience, they are using narratives of equity and well-being to engage in a deliberate and considered policy development process. Further, by being deliberate and considered, policy makers are taking time to work with stakeholders to empower them and acknowledge their capacity to develop the solutions to their challenges. As such, narratives are valuable policy tools that foster a sense of ownership over the problems and solutions by stakeholders and policy makers alike.

As has been stated, the process underway is focused on the staff of the Dublin local authorities. Public engagement is yet to happen. In developing the plans, it was made clear that their implementation would include the engagement of stakeholders beyond the immediate council, and would be distinct from the current process. One of the overarching themes that binds the actions in the plans is Connected Citizens, the focus of which is on informing and working with citizens to build awareness of climate change and the actions that they can take to mitigate and prepare for climate change. Admittedly, there has been criticism for not engaging citizens in the development of the plans. Again, this was done purposely to build awareness of the remits of local authorities in Ireland. More importantly, given the recent history of public service in Ireland, narrowing the focus of the plans to the operations and services delivery of the DLAs was critical.

Even within this reduced scope, narratives were still applicable. As I mentioned when meeting with staff, it was important to remind them that this is 'your plan, your opportunity to highlight the work that you are doing'. This was one narrative, the focus on their ownership of the actions in the plan as it is their current work, the projects and programmes they want to succeed and those that they would like to do in the future. Stemming from this was the emphasis on how the plan is an opportunity to consolidate work and build capacity by building bridges between the various departments. I would argue that this emphasis on the opportunity to foster collaboration within the councils is having a greater impact on the willingness of staff to contribute to the plan. In the feedback on the initial draft provided to the councils in December 2017 was a demand for more workshops that involve interdisciplinary teams. In response, more meetings and working groups with staff have been organised, an unintended consequence of this process. I hope that this is a sustained direction towards change and that this desire for collaboration led by the staff leads to the institutional change necessary for not only climate change policy, but policy in general, as my voice alone is not enough to say that.

> Technology and data: tools for collaborative planning smart cities can be sustainable. But they are certainly the flavour of the month internationally, everybody is talking about smart cities and measuring this, and measuring

that. Getting the economy going through smart cities. Whereas I would say five years ago, we were talking a lot more about sustainable cities. Indicators of sustainability. I see a moving of the goalpost[s]. I find that worrying. I am also deeply suspicious of smart cities. I see it as a way in the door for [name] and [name] to sell us stuff that we probably don't need.

(Interview 11, Dublin)

A final aspect that needs to be addressed is the role of data and technology in responding to climate change utilising a collaborative planning approach. From meeting the staff and researching the impacts of climate change in the Dublin Region, it became very evident that a critical challenge in the implementation and monitoring of this plan is data. While staff were able to identify and discuss the vulnerabilities stemming from climate change and the actions to address them, the need for localised, reliable and valid data was emphasised for developing action indicators. Presently, the DLAs are reliant on various central government departments (not just the Central Statistics Office) for data on air quality (Environmental Protection Agency), transportation (National Transport Authority), energy (Sustainable Energy Authority of Ireland) and flood risk (Office of Public Works). Each of these sources has its own way of presenting its data and analysis; which can be frustrating. During a workshop I spent almost 20 minutes hunting for a flood map that not three months earlier I found with relative ease in ten minutes. This challenge of accessibility and availability of localised data impacts on policy decisions, and the ability of the DLAs to monitor progress on their climate change actions. Simultaneously, there is an untapped wealth of data that is available but for a range of reasons is under-utilised or not used effectively to inform policy decisions. Across the four DLAs there is a regional initiative to use a smart cities platform to improve data availability in order to produce data-driven policy decisions.

The use of technology in terms of addressing urban challenges such as transport, flooding, and emergency response, is valuable. The possibilities that innovative technologies provide, from connectivity and real time response to automation, promises of an easy future where technology solves everything, are alluring. However, it should not be treated as a panacea (Grossi and Pianezzi, 2017), but rather used with caution, as is evident in the increasing call for open data and big data analytics. The potential of big data is undeniable, yet experts will still advise that it is not a substitute on which to become dependent (Perera-Gomez and Lokanathan, 2017). In Europe, General Data Protection Rules (GDPR) are coming into effect in May 2018; furthermore, the recent calls for social media giants to be more transparent about how personal data is used highlights that big data is not without challenges. Moreover, while the sources of data are in some senses limitless: mobile phone data, satellite data, online data, sensors and credit card data, its value lies in being able to use it to tell a coherent story and this requires traditional methods of surveys and statistics. It is important that policy makers ask themselves what they are trying to use the data for and how it will inform policy decisions, and to do so collaboratively. This is important as, for the same reason big data is meant to be a complement to traditional methods, the data sets (and sensors used to collect data) can be used in more ways than one. For example, traffic sensors can inform policy makers about the number of vehicles on various routes, so coupled with flood risk maps policy makers can potentially use this information to divert vehicles to different routes should a major rainfall event cause flooding on a major route. In addition, traffic volume data can be coupled with air quality monitoring data in real time to verify air quality readings at various times of the day.

Data and sensors to assess the physical conditions of the urban environment is not the only use of technology. As mentioned previously, collaborative planning theory emerged in the 1990s when technology did not proliferate throughout daily life in the way it does today. Urban policy makers in all cities acknowledged the value and role of technology in engaging stakeholders in the policy development process. The key benefits of technology lie in its ability to reach groups and individuals who had not previously engaged with policy before, and to create a debate around issues. Technology tools such as geographic information systems (GIS) and other mapping tools allow planners and citizens alike to quickly 'see' what is happening in different areas of their city. Moreover, social media, as demonstrated by Vancouver's social media use, allows individuals to contribute to policy and provide ideas and data that can be used by policy makers. Furthermore, technology permits the creation of a global dialogue on urban policy challenges, allowing for the exchange of ideas and practices around the world.

However, there is recognition that technology presents the same challenges as 'traditional' methods of public consultation and engagement, such as who is engaging and how they are engaging. A challenge that persists is the 'savvy' of stakeholders who may be the 'loudest' voices on issues, but not necessarily representative of the broader community. Drawing parallels to print media, where journalists can shape the discourse through reporting that emphasises particular aspects of an issue, social media presents the same challenge and the risks of 'hoodwinking' are ever present. Thus the information that finds its way into the wider public through social media channels may not be an accurate representation of the issues and the proposed solutions.

Consequently, the challenge ahead for urban policy makers is to identify ways in which technology can be employed to maximise the benefits of collaboration and information dissemination. It is evident that technology is not a substitute for 'traditional' methods of public consultation, such as public meetings, focus groups, vox pops, and charrettes. Rather, technology could be used as a medium to 'attract' stakeholders and draw their attention to opportunities to work with local government. For example, using social media to announce locations where local government staff will be to meet with citizens, and hashtags to stimulate and track dialogue around issues of interest to the city. Another example is the use of live Twitter chats to stimulate dialogue with urban policy makers. Technology can also be used to build awareness of and promote interest in aspects of the urban environment that are often overlooked by citizens but are impacted by climate change. An example of this was Vancouver's use of Twitter to promote awareness of bird species indigenous to Vancouver through its City Bird competition. Technology represents an opportunity to engage and educate the public with regards to the plans and policies that are being developed in an ongoing manner, and therefore cannot 'speed-by' local government. Thus, local governments need to harness its capacity for engagement of stakeholders in collaborative policy development.

Concluding thought

Cities and urban policy makers have been tasked with a unique problem, but one that is well within their capacity to address. The challenge of engaging people in a dialogue around climate change to develop and implement responses that adapt the city and adapt the behaviour of citizens to achieve resilience is difficult. While the increasing frequency and intensity of extreme weather events has drawn attention to climate change, it is only a small aspect of responding. In reality, it is the slow-burn impacts of climate change caused by day-to-day activities that present the policy challenge. The challenge for urban policy makers is in engaging stakeholders in a dialogue, when their concerns are elsewhere. However, I hope, as these cities have demonstrated, that through their will it is possible for urban policy makers to engage people by identifying narratives that foster ownership and leadership in order to sustain the engagement of citizens in the climate change policy dialogue. Cities can lead climate action.

References

Codema, D. E. A. (2017) *Strategy Towards Climate Change Action Plans for the Dublin Local Authorities*. Available at: www.codema.ie/images/uploads/docs/A_Strategy_Towards_Climate_Change_Action_Plans.pdf.

Department of Communications, Climate Action & Environment (2017) *National Mitigation Plan*. Available at: www.dccae.gov.ie/documents/NationalMitigationPlan2017.pdf.

Department of Communications Climate Action and Environment (2018) *National Adaptation Framework*. Available at: www.dccae.gov.ie/documents/NationalAdaptation Framework.pdf.

Forester, J. (1994) 'Bridging Interests and Community: Advocacy Planning and the Challenges of Deliberative Democracy', *Journal of the American Planning Association*, 60(2), pp. 153–158.

Healey, P. (1998) 'Collaborative planning in a stakeholder society', *The Town Planning Review*, 69(1), pp. 1–21.

Government of Ireland (2015) *Climate Action and Low Carbon Development Act 2015*.

Gray, S. (2016) *Local Authority Adaptation Strategy Development Guideline*.

Grossi, G. and Pianezzi, D. (2017) 'Smart cities: Utopia or neoliberal ideology?', *Cities*, 69, pp. 79–85. doi: https://doi.org/10.1016/j.cities.2017.07.012.

Perera-Gomez, T. and Lokanathan, S. (2017) 'Leveraging Big Data Sources to Support the Measurement of the Sustainable Development Goals'. Available at: file://nask. man.ac.uk/home$/PhD/Literature/Articles/BigData/Others/BackgroundReading/SBBG_2017_Gomez_MeasuringSDGs.pdf.

Index

Page numbers in **bold** denote tables, those in *italics* denote figures.

For Product Safety Concerns and Information please contact our EU representative GPSR@taylorandfrancis.com Taylor & Francis Verlag GmbH, Kaufingerstraße 24, 80331 München, Germany

T - #0116 - 160425 - C0 - 234/156/11 - PB - 9780367518868 - Gloss Lamination